ST MELLION

THE BOND LEGACY

By **Michael Taylor** and **Paddy Flavin**

ISBN: 978-1-9995863-0-0

First published in 2018

This book is dedicated to the memory of

Martin and Hermon Bond.

DISCLAIMER

Every effort has been made to ensure that the information contained within this book is accurate at the time of publication.

Michael Taylor and Paddy Flavin are not responsible for the accuracy of the anecdotes and recollections they gathered during the research process prior to writing this book.

The photographs included in the book remain the property of the Bond Family who kindly loaned the images for inclusion.

Every effort has been made to credit the original source of all images included.

We cannot accept any responsibility for any errors or omissions within this book however caused.

No responsibility for loss or damage, as a result of the material contained in this publication, can be accepted by Michael Taylor and Paddy Flavin, the authors.

The opinions and views expressed within this book not represent the views of any third party service or organisation.

ACKNOWLEDGEMENTS

This book has been written from the transcripts of interviews with a great many people without whose assistance the task would have proven impossible. We would like to thank the following for their help and contributions: -

Martin Bond and his family Angela, Jon, Chris and Alison

Hermon Bond and his family Rachel, Alan, Graham and Clare

David Webb

Roger Bush

Martin Watson

John Shrewsbury

Peter Alliss

Richard Brown

Peter Hunter

Len Owen

Peter Riley

David Moon

Mark Lovell

Di Pile

Penny Baxter

Sue McLaughlin

Thelma McEvoy

Stephen Lewis

Stephen Towers

Jeff Chapman

Mitchell Platts

Derrick Pillage

Jack Spiers

Jack Harcombe

David Brown

Alan Hartridge

Ray Reardon

John Rowe

Jim Elkins

David Glover

Stephen Moss

Alan Leather

We apologise if we have inadvertently omitted anyone from the long list of people who have provided information. Everyone's contribution, however small, is greatly appreciated.

The role that St Mellion's PGA professionals have played over the years needs also to be recognised. For many, these unsung heroes were the daily face of the club and, as such, were often the first point of contact whether it be for praise or complaint. They all always remained Professional.

We acknowledge the work of John Yeo, Tony and Bobby Moore, David Moon, Andrew Moreton, Darren Gass, John Garner and all of the assistants who have learnt their craft at St Mellion - every one of you contributed to the success of the club over the last 42 years.

PREFACE – By the authors Michael Taylor and Paddy Flavin.

The motivation for writing this story of how two Cornish farmers built an internationally-acclaimed golf resort deep in the West of England was born out of admiration. Admiration for their foresight, courage, tenacity, business acumen and, above all, for being decent human beings who retained their sense of humour throughout.

This is not a book about statistics, who scored what and when, that information is readily available elsewhere. Rather the book is about people and how the creation of St Mellion Golf Club affected the lives of all associated with it.

The Bond brothers, Martin and Hermon, have left a legacy. Most see that legacy in a very positive light. Very few don't like what they see.

Throughout our research what has struck us is that even those who opposed aspects of the creation and growth of St Mellion, either as lay people or professional planners, were willing to give credit where credit was due.

The Bonds had the vision and relentless determination to create something quite unique. The overall impression we get is that what the brothers achieved has been good for Cornwall, the wider Westcountry and the game of golf in particular.

The Bonds got Jack Nicklaus to design his first golf course in the United Kingdom at St Mellion. It hosted the Benson & Hedges International Open for six consecutive years from 1990 to 1995 – something they and the Golden Bear were extremely proud of.

It's widely acknowledged that the area would be poorer, had the land been left to grazing farm animals and the plough. If that had been allowed to happen, the seed Martin and Hermon Bond sowed in the early 1970s would never have sprouted. It would never have blossomed and flourished into something far and away beyond their original concept.

Had it not been for that embryo, that kernel of an idea and the germination of that seed to its fragile first green shoots and beyond, the solid and strong foundations for success would not have been in place for the current owners Crown Golf to build on to produce its flagship resort.

Some may accuse us and many of the contributors to this book of looking at the Bond era through rose-tinted glasses. I think we, as the authors, are inclined, even honoured, to accept that criticism because, after all, it was a fairy-tale and the Bonds did make dreams come true.

So, we are proud to unashamedly tell the story of St Mellion, 30 years on from the official opening of the Nicklaus course and 42 years since the original course was opened, as a tribute to the legacy created by Martin and Hermon Bond for the enjoyment of subsequent generations.

About Paddy Flavin: I first met the Brothers through a mutual friend, Brian Hawkins of Ready Mixed Concrete, as he hosted some of the earliest corporate golf days run at the club. From those early meetings it became apparent that we shared mutual interests in golf and property development, so we would periodically meet to exchange ideas and often complaints about the strictures of the planning system. Whilst it was not until some years later that we would work together, it became apparent to me in those first few years how visionary they truly were. They had ambitions that were way ahead of anything other operators of proprietary clubs had at the time.

Not only did they possess vision, but they knew intuitively how to harvest relationships as successfully as they farmed the land.

They had an innate knack of planting the seeds of joint ventures, allowing the idea to take root and then allowing the plans to develop in a healthy fashion. People invested in Hermon and Martin because they trusted them.

I have been privileged to have played a very small part in the growth of St Mellion over a great many years and that gave me an insight into just how much of themselves the Bonds gave to turning their dreams into reality. I came up with the idea of writing this book some nine years ago but life has a habit of getting in the way of one's plans. I enlisted the help of my co-author Michael and I am eternally grateful to him for pushing me to finally complete it.

So much of the story reflects events that had their roots in plans made years ago and as such the reader will find that the tale does not follow a strict chronological timeline.

In telling the tale we have tried to remain faithful to the actual language used by the various contributors, therefore the reader may sometimes feel you are not reading the English language, but just pretend you are auditioning for the next Poldark series and you will soon slip into a lovely Cornish dialect.

Finally, when editing the book it has become apparent that many of those interviewed, not including family, bought into the idea that the Brothers were one dimensional i.e. Hermon was the loud joker and Martin was the quiet reflective one. Their relationship and respective skill sets went way beyond such an over simplification of roles, it was much more complex and subtle than that, but I will let you decide. Enjoy the read. .....

About Michael Taylor: I first met the Bonds in November 1976 when, as a reporter for the Westcountry's regional newspaper, The Western Morning News, I went to interview Martin and Hermon in the still-to-be-completed clubhouse at St Mellion Golf and Country Club. In that first article I wrote this: "Something is happening on a hillside in South East Cornwall which will revolutionise the sporting life of the Westcountry. On the slopes overlooking the snug little hamlet of St Mellion a sportsman's paradise is being created which is destined to attract the gods of the golf world and perhaps the cream of other sports." I followed their intriguing story for well over 20 years. In December 1998 I joined BBC Radio Cornwall as a news reporter, covering North and East Cornwall until I retired in 2013.

When I was approached by Paddy about co-writing this book I was delighted to get involved. Paddy genuinely wanted to put on record the achievements of Martin and Hermon and recognise the legacy they have left. As you read these pages I hope you will agree that we've achieved our goal.

FOREWORD BY PETER ALLISS. THE DOYEN – AND THE VOICE – OF THE WORLD OF GOLF

The first time I met Martin and Hermon Bond I asked them: "What kind of farming do you do?"

Martin said: "Potatoes, we grow potatoes."

I replied: "Don't you have any pigs or cattle?"

Hermon answered: "Oh no, we got rid of all them. We like potatoes because they grow while we'm asleep. Cattle, you have to get up in the middle of the night for them. But, tatties grow while you're asleep. We like tatties."

That was Martin and Hermon! They could be "funny men" but they displayed great foresight and bravery in embarking on their project at St Mellion in those early days.

They appointed J Hamilton Stutt, son of J R Stutt, the golf course contractors and landscape gardeners, originally based in Glasgow, to design the original course. I knew the Stutt family because of their association with the Parkstone Golf Club where I went as joint professional with my brother, Alec, in 1957.

Hamilton Stutt carried on the tradition of his father but had branched out into the world of Golf Course Architecture and, although the original course was a pretty simplistic affair, it was, in many ways, ahead of its time.

A golf course with hotel accommodation as a concept was not entirely new but none existed south of Bristol. However, not even the brothers could foresee the impact that would be achieved by their decision to appoint Jack Nicklaus to design and build their second course.

The golfing world was buzzing with the thought of Nicklaus 'doing' a golf course in England and, it must be said, it was not the easiest of sites, as Jack remarked to me afterwards. He had tens of thousands of tons of earth moved, just to create a golf site and even so the terrain was very difficult to work.

When you played the course, on a number of occasions you finished a hole and wondered where on earth the next tee was, only for someone to point a finger to the heavens and say, "It's up there!" So, to say the course was dramatic but tiring, would not be an exaggeration!

The fame of the new Jack Nicklaus course spread and it wasn't too long before tournament sponsors were considering taking golf down to the West Country, which had been starved of high class tournaments for a number of years.

The Benson & Hedges was the main benefactor and what splendid affairs they produced, well attended and mostly played in decent weather, but very much an assault course for the players - and pity those poor caddies who had to go around lugging great tournament bags weighing up to 80 pounds.

The course continued to develop and, although there was plenty of criticism, generally speaking it was well received, with some dramatic holes. Tournaments in Great Britain were rather 'drying up' and other venues were being found, but St Mellion appeared to thrive and develop its own personality.

I was there on a number of occasions working for the BBC and marvelled at many of the brilliant pictures the television cameramen managed to produce.

I also remember my wife Jacki and I being flown down in the Wimpey helicopter to perform the opening ceremony of the new, modern sales offices and reception areas for the timeshare ownership village. It was in the old farm barn which had previously been used as the greenkeepers' centre and it had been tastefully converted to retain the outside appearance of the old building.

We were welcomed by George Payne, the managing director of the newly-formed Wimpey Leisure Ltd, and 2,000 balloons were launched into the sky, something which would not happen now because of environmental concerns.

Mr Payne presented us with a framed print of Allan Robertson for which the original lithograph dates back to 1857. Allan is described in "Golf, A Royal and Ancient Game – Second Edition 1893" as "the greatest golf player that ever lived of whom alone in the annals of the pastime it can be said that he never was beaten".

One of the highlights for me was the 1994 Benson & Hedges. The last day was wonderful. For Seve Ballesteros to come back to form and win and for Nick Faldo to play so well made great entertainment, not only for the spectators on the course but also for our television audience.

Martin and Hermon and their families worked miracles at St Mellion and this was in no small part due to their own dynamic personalities.

I was privileged to stay on site at St Mellion during many visits and enjoyed the hospitality of the Bond family. So, I have many, very happy memories of St Mellion.

I am sure you will enjoy this book, because I think it captures the true spirit and resilience of Martin and Hermon Bond. They have left, as the title suggests, an impressive legacy. Two Cornish farmers whose contribution to the game of golf has been immense and immeasurable.

Chapter 1

THE BONDS CROSS THE POND TO CATCH A BEAR

The glowing aura of the Golden Bear of Golf radiated all around. It filled the room. Jack Nicklaus smiled as he walked through his splendid wooden lodge beside the 18th hole at Muirfield Village Golf Club, in Dublin, Columbus, Ohio.

It was Thursday, the 27th of May, 1982. Another hot, heavy, humid day. And the weather forecasters had predicted the worst. A tornado warning had been issued and the first day's play in the prestigious Memorial Tournament had been halted.

The King of Golf was about to meet, for the first time, two brothers from some remote part of the United Kingdom called Cornwall.

Cornwall is the Land of King Arthur and Camelot, the home of pasties, cream teas and saffron cake, a land, according to legend, of Pixies, traditionally helpful folk who were also jokers and jesters.

So, Jack Nicklaus might easily have perceived Cornish farming brothers Martin and Hermon Bond as country yokels from Pixie Land. But, just as he was about to shake their hands there was an almighty clap of thunder. Even Nicklaus, who was used to violent electric storms, ducked and crouched. Martin and Hermon Bond didn't flinch.

As Jack Nicklaus stood up straight again to his 5ft 11ins stature, he was still probably thinking, based on what he had heard about the brothers: "Who are these two guys? Do they really expect me to build my first golf course in the United Kingdom in Cornwall?"

The Royal and Ancient at St Andrews and Gleneagles were pretty far-flung. But Cornwall, at the other end of the UK, jutting out into the Atlantic Ocean, next stop New York, that's remote! If Nicklaus had a map of the UK and a pin to pinpoint a location for a course, the last place on it he'd have stuck the pin would have been Cornwall.

Of course, Nicklaus knew the Bonds were serious. They'd proved the point by sending him an advance of £50,000 by way of a telegraphic transfer. It was a big gesture, a lot of money in those days, to show him they meant business and this was no pie-in-the-sky dream.

Hermon and Martin said: "We think it gave him confidence in that we were serious. We wanted to show him that we were committed. We were excited about undertaking such an enormous task with the world's best golfer as our course designer, even though it was a daunting prospect."

The brothers' lawyer Edward Andreae-Jones, AJ as he was known, said sending £50,000 to Jack Nicklaus was an extraordinary thing to do.

"But that was the kind of people they were and the kind of risks they were prepared to take to get Jack Nicklaus. I didn't expect anything else of them. They would go for the best," said AJ.

However, there was, for Hermon, a massive issue over the telegraphic transfer. It incurred a bank charge of £37.50. That niggled him tremendously. He was quite happy about the £50,000, but he thought the charge for the transaction was exorbitant.

Martin kept telling him, time and time again: "Hermon, whatever you do when we meet Jack, don't start complaining about the £37.50 bank charge and asking him for your money back."

As it was, Hermon was on his best behaviour, despite his own, personal medical problems. He was in horrendous pain because of his legendary bad back, which had plagued him for decades. It was caused by tending to the pigs in the low pig houses. The roofs were low to keep the heat in for the baby pigs. Hermon was 6ft 3ins tall! Also, he couldn't resist the competitions there used to be over who could lift the heaviest sack of potatoes. In those days there was no instruction or advice on how to lift weights properly.

His wife Rachel recalled that Hermon's back pain was so excruciating after they arrived in the USA to meet Nicklaus that on the night before the historic meeting he was not fast asleep on the soft, spongy large bed in their luxury hotel room. He had to lie on the hard floor, trying to find some relief from his agony. He didn't sleep well. In fact, he hardly slept at all.

"One morning we were up very early because Hermon didn't have a very good night. The mattress was too soft, so he tried to sleep on the floor, but that wasn't much better," Rachel said.

So it was something of a miracle that Hermon stood up tall, four inches taller than Nicklaus, and kept his counsel when they shook hands. Perhaps Hermon, the joker and jester, most of the time, had decided it was the right time to be serious and he accepted the massive significance of the moment.

Nicklaus didn't mention the £50,000 and Hermon kept quiet about the £37.50.

The great golfer looked shorter in the flesh than he appeared on the televisions in the corner of a room in the brothers' farmhouses back in Cornwall. His small, blue, piercing eyes were firmly focused on the Bonds. And, low and behold, he realised they didn't have straw coming out of their ears! The three men talked.

Top members of Nicklaus's design team had already been to the far South West of England to assess the potential. But face-to-face contact and first impressions were just as vital, perhaps even more important. If things didn't jell, the project might have been permanently bunkered. So, the deposit or "down payment" of £50,000 didn't necessarily automatically clinch the deal. That initial personal contact was crucial.

The three men hit it off, after getting over the shock of the intervention from the skies. The initial bolt was followed by unrelenting thunder and lightning and very heavy rain.

Martin Bond remembered the moment vividly: "Jack was hosting the tournament and entertaining several guests. Just as we were going to be introduced to him, there was the loudest clap of thunder I've ever heard. It came out of the blue. It was like God had come down from Heaven and was in the room! It was unbelievable."

At precisely the same instance, Rachel had a flashback to her visit with Hermon to the Ryder Cup at Walton Health in September 1981. The event had been scheduled for The Belfry, but it wasn't ready on time so it was switched to the Surrey course.

Rachel: "Jack Nicklaus and Tom Watson were standing on a tee. I don't know why there weren't any people around them, I think it was to do with the late switch of venue from The Belfry.

"I wanted to have a look at them because they were such legends. I wanted to go a bit closer because I thought that's going to be the last time I shall ever see them in the flesh, because I'll never be going to America.

"So, we walked up. We didn't speak to them or anything. We

just watched. I thought that was going to be my first and last time to be so close to players of this stature. But, it's wonderful to think it didn't turn out that way!"

Less than nine months later, here was Rachel meeting the Golden Bear: "You could hardly take it all in because it was somewhat surreal, to think we were there, with him. He was very friendly and approachable. You didn't think 'Oh my, this is Jack Nicklaus', you just think of him as anybody else. He wouldn't stand on any airs and graces or anything. He was genuine and he must have thought Hermon and Martin were 'alright', otherwise, he wouldn't have bothered."

Hermon and Rachel's younger son Graham was also there, 18 years old at the time. He remembered the thunderclap! And for him, Nicklaus was God. His presence filled the room. There was an aura about him. Also there was Martin's wife Angela. It was the beginning of a long-lasting friendship between the Bonds and the great golfer and his family.

Hermon and Rachel's elder boy Alan, a veteran professional caddy on the PGA Tour, wasn't at that first meeting. Alan already knew Nicklaus because he worked as a caddy at Muirfield in the early days of his career. He met his parents, brother and uncle later in their trip to the States.

Alan summed up, pardon the pun, the bond between Nicklaus and the Bonds: "They had all warmed to each other. I think Nicklaus was impressed by the honesty and straight-forwardness of my dad and uncle. Mutual respect, which obviously grew over the period of time it took to build the course. I think Jack was refreshed to have someone just to talk to, look him in the eye and just tell him what they want, what they don't want and also listen to his ideas."

But it had been an immense, uphill struggle to initially get Jack Nicklaus to give the Bonds any kind of serious consideration.

According to their bank manager at the time Trevor Furse, the first ever letter to Nicklaus from the Bonds ended up in the rubbish bin.

“My understanding is that Nicklaus’s aide came into his office and announced: ‘We’ve got a letter from England from two guys, pig farmers, who want to build a golf course.’ Nicklaus said: ‘Bin it.’ The Bonds wrote again and Nicklaus was equally dismissive. But he realised that he was likely to be bombarded by similar letters if he didn’t make some sort of response.

“His response was: ‘Tell them we don’t talk to anybody until we’ve got money on the table. We shall need an advance payment of $10,000 before we’re prepared even to talk’.”

Trevor Furse added: “Martin phoned me to ask how they could get money out to Nicklaus as quickly as possible. I told him the best way was by telegraphic transfer which meant it was spendable money as soon as it got to his bank account.

“I told Martin to find out what Nicklaus’s bank account details were and I’d do the rest. The money was much more than Nicklaus wanted. His aide rushed into his office and said: ‘Hey Jack, we’ve got money through from the two English pig farmers’. Nicklaus replied: ‘Perhaps it’s time for us to start treating these guys a bit more seriously’.”

Len Owen was the special events manager for Benson & Hedges. He said Jack Nicklaus confided in him that he turned down the chance to create the course in Cornwall several times because members of his senior staff weren’t happy with what they’d found when they made their initial investigations.

“They came back to Jack and said: ‘They’ve got a golf course, but it’s on the top of a hill. It’s quite a nice course, but all they’re offering us is the sides of the hills’.”

Len's opinion was that the Bonds couldn't put in a course worthy of Nicklaus - and that was Jack's view as well.

"To do it right was going to be hugely expensive. And it was far more than Hermon and Martin set out to budget to do it," added Len. However, Len said no one should ever under-estimate the brothers.

Also, many believe Nicklaus's decision to opt for St Mellion wasn't all about money. He was inspired by the Bond dream and wanted to help them make it real.

So, just over six years after that first meeting in May 1982, Jack Nicklaus would experience some more-than-typical Cornish weather – in the Land of King Arthur, Camelot, pasties, cream teas, saffron cake and a 6ft 3ins "Pixie" called Hermon, the joker and jester, and his brother Martin - when his course at St Mellion was christened by the kind of relentless rain which would have tempted some Cornish boat builders to head for their sheds to start constructing a modern-day Noah's Ark.

Chapter 2

THIS WILL WORK – ON A WHIM

Cornish farming brothers Martin and Hermon Bond went out one day in their trademark wellies and flat caps and stood, in the rain, in the middle of one of their fields at St Mellion, a few miles from Saltash in the south-east of the county.

It was the early 1970s. They looked round at the land as far as they could see, through the drizzle and the rolling mist. Then they looked at each other and said almost in unison: "I think this will work."

Those five words were their "business plan" for a golfing enterprise which was to become world famous.

"It was as easy as that," the brothers were later to admit. "We knew if we built a place where Mum, Dad and the kids could all go and where Mum would let Dad play golf, because the course was on his own doorstep, we were on a winner.

"That's the way we looked at it. It was almost on a whim. There's nothing fancy about it. We were sure it would work."

Of course, they were influenced in their decision by their forward-thinking father and mother – and a number of factors which helped them make up their minds.

The head of the Bond family – William Hermon Bond, or W H – had dropped this bombshell to his three boys – Jim, Martin and Hermon: "You know you fellas, you're going to farm yourselves out of a job!"

The Bond family had been doing very well, thank you. Pretty productive with pigs, sheep, grain and potatoes. Jim, the eldest of the three boys, was one of the biggest potato growers in the South West. He had already gone his own way with his farming expertise and decided to continue down that road.

But father's prophesy stunned Martin and Hermon. They remembered how their mother Amy had foresight as well. She had told them, time and time again over the years, they should be considering other ways of promoting the family business – and she led by example. She had started bed and breakfast in the family farmhouse at Tideford, midway between Liskeard and Saltash, way back in 1933. Even then, she saw how important tourism and leisure were going to be for Cornwall.

What were Martin and Hermon to do? They thought a lot about what father had said. They pondered. They were asking themselves what on earth they could do to avoid his frightening portent becoming a reality.

They and Jim played golf at Whitsand Bay, on the South East Cornwall coast up near Rame Head. In golfing parlance, the realisation for Martin and Hermon that they were, basically, farming themselves out of a future, working hard to get nowhere, was tantamount to missing an 18-inch putt on the final green at Augusta to win the US Masters. And this quandary came at a time when they were giving serious consideration to expanding their successful pig business – across the English Channel.

Hermon said: "We had plans to go into Europe. We were contemplating building a pig unit in France." Martin said: "It's true we were certainly in the expansion mode, there's no doubt about that. We were working with a farmer in Devon who had two or three hundred sows. We thought if we could do it in Devon, we could do it anywhere and move the whole thing forward in a much bigger way."

But father's words kept ringing in their ears. And what followed were what could only be called "signs" which gave birth to the dream of a farm diversification project the likes of which Cornwall, the South West and beyond had never seen before.

In 1973 Martin and Hermon spotted an article in a local newspaper. It referred to a report by a South Western Sports Council technical panel, produced in co-operation with Cornwall County Council's planning officer John Barrington, on golfing facilities, or rather the lack of them. It said that golf courses were an important factor for tourism and as many as 18 additional courses would be needed by 1981. One of the conclusions reached in the report was that there was a deficiency in golfing facilities in the south east corner of the county. And one of the major recommendations of the report was that at least one of the badly-needed new courses should be of national championship standard to provide high quality golfing facilities.

"It all just came from that," recalled Hermon who was renting Dunstan Farm at St Mellion. At roughly the same time, an estate next to Dunstan Farm came on the market, three tenanted farms, 250 or 260 acres.

Hermon said: "We just thought 'Hang on, that could be just about right for a golf course'." Martin added: "They weren't good farms to farm; the land was steep in places. It was like a basin, but the top bit was quite nice and we thought we could do something with that."

The farms were Wollaton, Lower Wollaton and Horsepool. The brothers rang their bank, Barclays in Liskeard, and said they wanted to buy the farms. Now, this was new territory for the

Bonds. Up until then they'd stuck to renting farms. The bank manager Bill Warman told the brothers to let him know how much they wanted to borrow. They needed £90,000 for three-quarters of the land and then another £40,000 for the remaining quarter. In total, £130,000, a lot of money 45 years ago.

It was around this time Martin and Hermon thought it might be a good idea to draw up a business plan. Martin said: "We just talked to each other in one of the fields one day. We looked out across the land and both said at roughly the same time: 'I think this will work'. That was our business plan."

When he heard the story years later, Jeff Chapman, the founder, owner and chairman of the Bennelong Group which owns Crown Golf, was flabbergasted: "I couldn't stand in the middle of a bunch of fields and say I thought there was an element of a golf course on the land. The vision Martin and Hermon had was just outstanding. Lots of people have vision or have good ideas but then they don't have the courage and the tenacity to be able to follow through."

And their accountant Peter Riley joked: "Knowing Martin and Hermon as I did, if there ever was an original business plan, and I doubt there ever was, it was probably a few words scribbled on the back of a soggy envelope."

So, the brothers decided to go big on putters, not pigs! "Once we opted for leisure and to build a golf course, all our energy was put into that, rather than expanding the pigs," said Hermon. "If we'd expanded abroad, that would have been a high pressure job – and we couldn't do both. We were moving into leisure, something we didn't know anything about, apart from mother's B&B, so it needed our full attention."

Martin added: "We came to the conclusion that leisure was a growth industry, that, as the working week grew shorter, people would be looking more and more for ways and means to spend this extra time. What was it going to be, pigs in Europe or the leisure industry in Cornwall? We decided on leisure - I think we did the right thing."

The brothers had a look at the other courses in the area and decided there was a need for another, but it would have to be something special. Also, the Tamar Bridge, spanning the river and linking Cornwall to England, had opened in 1961. It provided the crucial road artery which gave access to St Mellion.

For advice on how to create "something special" the brothers went to St Pierre Golf and Country Club at Chepstow in Wales where Bill Graham had pioneered the concept of combining golf and other sports and leisure facilities in the one complex. What Bill Graham told them gave the brothers a lot to think about, because what he had achieved was phenomenal – sports, indoor swimming pool, dining facilities and the rest.

They realised what they wanted was a "St Pierre" or the equivalent at St Mellion. That was what was needed to make it work. But Bill Graham had one advantage over them. He had taken over a huge house and parkland. The Bonds had no bricks and mortar and no undulating slopes which would conveniently lend themselves to being golf holes.

They had to start from scratch. Hermon had started playing his golf at Launceston Golf Club which was changing from just nine holes to 18. The architect for that was John Hamilton Stutt. Hermon invited him to come and see if he could design a course at St Mellion.

Planning permission was needed and one of the fiercest opponents was farmer Jim Maddever from Menheniot, a councillor on Caradon District Council, the local authority for the area which included St Mellion. He stuck strongly to the line that it was totally wrong to lose "good" farming land to this kind of development. The Bonds argued it was not good farming land.

They got permission for the golf course and had a plan for a clubhouse. They told their new bank manager Denis Walters they needed £250,000 to build it. He said £45,000 should do the job. They told him "no", they wanted a proper clubhouse and that would cost a quarter-of-a-million. Mr Walters was not best pleased but agreed.

Rachel Bond, Hermon's wife, remembered that he and Martin caught the golf bug and were playing regularly at Whitsand Bay. They were addicted to the game and went out playing nearly every evening, when they could.

"I suppose it all stemmed from there," she said. Years later, when they started thinking of diversifying and the prospect of building a golf course came up, Rachel's reaction was: "It was another challenge. I knew they couldn't do much more on the existing Dunstan Farm, they couldn't grow any bigger. So, golf would be something different.

"My job in the beginning was to make cups of tea and do lunches and that sort of thing when the architect John Hamilton Stutt came round. They used to sit round the dining room table and I just kept quiet and listened and learned."

So the work on the course finally started. There was a caravan where prospective club members could view the plans for the course and clubhouse. Hermon, Martin or Alan, Hermon and Rachel's elder son, would give them a guided tour. If it was dark, the tour was by torchlight. Rachel would be there to offer cups of tea from a flask.

"We were like kids really, looking out the window of the caravan to see the next car coming. It was fascinating to think that people were interested and wanting to join," said Rachel. "They came from other clubs because they could see that the course here was going to be a bit more of a challenge when it was built."

Alan and his younger brother Graham grew up on Dunstan Farm. It was a normal childhood – to start with. No golf course, just fields, rivers and streams to walk through and play in. But Alan remembered how all that changed when construction work started: "It was all very new, this was happening in Cornwall, at St Mellion, a small little village, a hamlet really. I remember the clubhouse being built and showing prospective members around. I had to walk people across two planks of wood to get access. Nowadays people would have a little bit of a fit, doing that, what with Health and Safety. Looking back, there was a certain innocence to it all."

When Martin's wife Angela first heard of plans for a golf course, this was her reaction: "I just thought: 'What are they up to now?' Because everything else had to go on as well, the farming had to go on."

Tony Lister was brought in as farm manager to free up more time for the brothers to concentrate on golf and diversification.

Chapter 3

EVERY SPUD WAS A BRICK IN THE CLUBHOUSE WALLS

The Bonds' farming enterprise was, in the early stages, subsidising the progression of the golf plans. But the brothers had to drive the bullocks out of a field to start digging a hole to build the clubhouse. Things went well, but the money was running out. In 1975 the brothers had to tell the contractors to stop work for a time because they didn't think they'd have enough money to pay for it and finish the job.

The bank interest rate was around 15% - and so was inflation. Not the best time to be building a clubhouse. But every single person who visited the building site was shown round. People could feel the Bonds' enthusiasm. That rubbed off on them and they, too, embraced the vision. Prospective members were happy to pay their entrance fees to join the club. One female member, who lived at Looe and never played much golf, became a sports and leisure life member. The annual fee for golfing membership, including sport, was £90. But she thought the £400 for life membership would do the project and the Bonds more good than it would her!

In September 1976 Barclays in Liskeard got a new bank manager, Trevor Furse. At St Mellion the clubhouse was still under construction – and the Bonds were looking to borrow more money to build an hotel.

Trevor went out to St Mellion to meet the brothers for the first time: "It was clear to me that the development was reaching a fairly critical stage. I liked what I saw but I couldn't see at that stage how we were going to see the end of this project. And, they had stage payments to make to the builders as the construction progressed."

But the long, hot summer drought of 1976 proved to be the Bonds' saviour. There was a potato "famine". Spuds were scarce and prices were high. So, when Trevor Furse saw the massive mountain of potatoes the brothers had accumulated he was re-assured the Bonds did have the wherewithal to finish the clubhouse and get the second nine holes done.

"They told me they'd had a good potato season. We went up the road to the yard at Bake Farm where there was a big shed. Inside was the most enormous mound of potatoes, the biggest heap of potatoes I'd ever seen. For some reason we climbed to the top – and it wasn't very easy because the potatoes were on the move.

"They explained that when the potatoes were stored they had to dust them layer upon layer to inhibit the growth of the shoots because the potatoes start to go soft as soon as the shoots begin to appear.

"They said the market for potatoes was very firm but they were going to hang on as long as they possibly could because as the year progressed the price could only go one way because they were aware that there was a national shortage."

Trevor added: "I think in the end they got rid of them all by about January. Whereas an average price may have been about £40 a tonne, they were getting something in the region of £150 a tonne. I can't remember how many tonnes were in that heap, but it must have been an awful lot."

The other Bond brother Jim, whose prowess in potato growing was legendary, had a crop at Triffle Farm, Downderry. Jim's son James said at one stage the price was £60 to £100 a tonne, but the Bonds reached £300 a tonne.

The brothers were "lucky" (shrewd is probably a better word) because the following year there were similar weather conditions and they had another bumper crop.

In both years the Bonds were due to pay a lot of tax on their big profits from the potatoes. Certainly tens of thousands of pounds and probably more than that. Hermon joked: "Can't we just dig a hole and put the bloody money in the ground so the taxman can't get at it and then we can go back later and dig it up."

But Peter Riley, their accountant, explained that there was as a perfectly legitimate way of keeping most, if not all, of the money: "Due to the tax rules at the time it was quite legal to roll the potato profits over into the development of the golf complex, to transfer the money into that. It was effectively transferring trading profits into a capital asset. It meant a very sizeable reduction, perhaps 70 or 80 per cent, in the amount of tax they had to pay, if not a complete elimination of tax on the profits."

This was crucial to the progress of the Bonds' plans. Peter added: "Being able to do that facilitated the St Mellion project because, without that, they would have been in some difficulty. It made a hell of a difference. If they'd suddenly had to write a cheque for tens of thousands of pounds for tax while they were getting St Mellion off the ground they would have had an awful problem raising the additional funds.

"They would have had to phase down the project quite considerably to something more in line with the earlier opinions of others. People had wanted them to put up just a small clubhouse with a bar and a changing room, not a country club with sporting facilities and a swimming pool.

"If they'd had to go for something much smaller, the whole project would not have gone forward at the rate it did. If you'd have started with a small wooden clubhouse for members or whatever and that was it, would they ever have got to the stage of putting a big complex there with the swimming pool, squash courts and a hotel? Probably the answer is 'no'.

"So the potatoes really funded St Mellion, got St Mellion going. Without them, the potatoes, the St Mellion project would not have gone forward in the way that it did."

Thanks to the first good potato harvest, within a matter of weeks there was enough money to resume work, although the price had gone up by about £10,000.

"We reckoned every brick we laid was a potato, the clubhouse was paid for by the potato harvest," said Martin.

Rachel and Hermon would often drive around in their Range Rover to see how the work was progressing. "We used to think: 'Gosh, this is a golf hole now. We used to walk through the mud here to feed the sheep'."

Chapter 4

THE FAMOUS BOND PIG HERD PAYS FOR THE HOTEL

Bank manager Trevor Furse was always very soft-spoken and he didn't often speak during meetings in the proprietors' suite in the clubhouse. But on this occasion, the financing of the proposed hotel next to the clubhouse was on the agenda and Trevor felt he had to make one of his very few contributions to the debate.

He said this to Martin and Hermon: "I think the time has come when you, perhaps, ought to think about selling your pigs."

The brothers' legendary Landrace pigs, perfectly purebred, were their pride and joy, so Hermon's reaction was totally predictable. "Bloody hell," he retorted, looking at Martin. Martin's considered response was simply: "We never thought of that." Then he leaned forward and added in a thoughtful whisper: "I tell you what, we'll think about it. We aren't going to dismiss it out of hand, we'll think about it."

Trevor wasn't satisfied with that. He felt he had to add a sentence or two which would persuade the brothers to search their souls over the future of their beloved pigs.

He boldly – and uncharacteristically - told them straight: "I think you have reached the crossroads where you have got to decide where your priorities lie. You've committed so much money to the golf course project, you need more money and you've got to think where your assets are going to be of most use to you."

Nothing more was said. But Martin and Hermon did what Martin told Trevor they would do – think about it. Trevor Furse's problem was finding a strong enough argument for loaning any more money to the Bonds because he couldn't see, at that stage, where repayment was going to come from. Trevor had done some deep thinking.

"Up until then they'd borrowed money to buy the farmland for the golf course and clubhouse and they'd also had to borrow money for any development that was taking place. At that time they were getting £40,000 or £50,000 a year in at the start of the golf year in membership fees which was a help but in the brothers' minds that was already earmarked.

"I was pondering on the pigs. I knew how devoted they were to their pigs and how zealous they were of the reputation that they had in the farming community, not just locally, but across the country, for the quality of the pigs that they bred."

But Trevor also knew from other bank customers who had pigs that they weren't making much money. That suggested to him that if ordinary production pigs weren't going to make much money, then that's going to adversely affect the sales of pedigree pigs.

The days, and weeks, went by. Apart from the commercial value the Bonds put on their precious Purebred Landrace, they had immense sentimental value. They also used to cross them with Large Whites. That made for extremely good bacon. They'd been breeding pigs all their lives – and father before them. To get rid of them all would be the end of an era.

It was some two or three weeks after Trevor Furse had spoken to the brothers that Martin rang him and said: "We thought about what you said and Hobsons the auctioneers are producing brochures for the sales."

Father, W H Bond, died aged 84 a month before the first sale in June 1978. But he totally approved of what his boys were doing, as would their mother Amy, that pioneer of B&B back in 1933. She used to tell her sons, regularly: "It's better to be envied than pitied." That drove them on.

The first sale totalled £54,000. A second sale in September that year netted £64,500. More than 3,300 pigs were sold.

"It was sad selling the pigs but we were looking forward and moving on and it wasn't the worst couple of days work we ever did," recalled Hermon. "I don't often cry, but that was one of the times I did. Pigs had always made money for us, but after that they didn't improve much. So, long term, we were quite thankful to Trevor for his advice."

Also, by selling producing livestock the proceeds could be rolled over into another enterprise without paying capital gains tax. The money allowed the bank to put a stronger slant on what its contribution was going to be to the hotel development, in the knowledge that the Bonds were dipping into their own pockets as well.

"The pigs were a major injection of capital for them," said Trevor Furse. "It was the first time they'd put any real tangible monies in themselves other than the potato monies."

Martin and Hermon continued to hold their regular "board meetings" to discuss the development of St Mellion - in the same area of land in which they drew up their business plan! To them, it was the best "boardroom" in the world. No walls, no doors, no ceiling. Just fresh air and wide, open spaces. They talked - with no interruptions, no note-taking – decided and voted. And, that was that.

FOOTNOTE 1: Martin and Hermon Bond were only able to get St Mellion off the ground, thanks to their elder brother Jim being brave and loyal enough to stand as guarantor – being prepared to put his neck on the chopping block.

Bank manager Trevor Furse explained: "As guarantor you've got all the risk for no reward. So, if the Bonds had made a pig's ear of it and gone bust, Jim's guarantee would have been called and maybe, just maybe, it might have been enough to sink him as well. It was a huge expression by Jim of his faith in his brothers' abilities. I think they always knew that without Jim's shoulder to the wheel they may not have ever got off the ground."

FOOTNOTE 2: Martin and Hermon held back a herd of approaching a couple of hundred sows at Bake Farm because they had a very good Italian pig man and wanted to keep him in a job. But then, in the very early eighties, when the pig man was thinking of moving on, they sold the whole lot to one buyer.

FOOTNOTE 3: The shaping of the original course was done by James Ware and his team from Talastone Gardens (Launceston) Ltd. It was Mr Ware's last big project before his retirement. Architect Peter Stubbs from Plymouth designed the clubhouse and hotel. The clubhouse main contractor was Carkeek & Sons Ltd of Plymouth and the hotel main contractor was Dudley Coles (SW) Ltd of Plymouth. Caradon District Council's planning and development officer Jack Harcombe, commenting on the completion of the course and clubhouse, said they were a very valuable amenity and would be one of the district's most valuable assets. And he added this: "Championship class golf will be played there and will attract national coverage by the media. I think that is as about as good an advertisement as we could get for the area."

Chapter 5

A BONDING AGENT

Legend has it that they once introduced themselves to a group of people with these words: "My name's Bond, Martin and Hermon Bond. Never shaken by anything or anyone, always stirred to win." That may well be folklore but they were "as one" in their public "appearances" – "Little and Large", a true double act, inseparable on the public "stage", working off each other with perfect timing - united by their ambition to reach their goal. And, like Ian Fleming's secret agent James Bond 007, they always got their man – Jack Nicklaus included!

They could each, equally, command the stage on their own. Hermon – the biggest-faced driver in the bag, in your face, speak first think later, often peppering his verbal shots with expletives. Loud, difficult, a jester, a winder-up of people. Blasting, smashing his way round the course of life, divots flying. Delicate chip shots and precise putting were not his style. He'd rather win the hole by taking a wood out of the rough 200 yards short of the green and the ball ricochet off a tree and plop in the hole. Hermon liked to project the image of a larger-than-life, thick as two short-shafted club heads, a simple farmer with nothing more than straw behind his ears – or between them. A bit of a Cornish Herman Munster from the Addams Family. He was so down-to-earth, he was almost subterranean. Hermon was as much at home and happy mucking out pigs as playing a round of golf with a Prince of the Realm.

Martin – a pitching wedge, taking in the lie of the land and much thinking before a word is spoken. Modest, quiet, the deep thinker, the delicate diplomat. He always thought about his shots before he played them. And often he had to perform a balancing act, going around replacing Hermon's "divots" and, sometimes, forcing Hermon back in "the bag" before he executed another wayward drive off the tee.

So, an intriguing double act who could also be individual, different performers. And the Bonds and their families remained the same people over the years, in spite of their growing success and influence. "Hermon didn't change, none of us changed," said his wife Rachel. "We were always just ourselves. Some people used to say to us 'Well, you haven't changed since you've had all this' and we'd say 'Well why? We're us. What's the point of changing? Where's that get you?'

"You didn't think you were high and mighty and you didn't think that of the famous people you met. We were the same as anybody else. You didn't put on any airs and graces. We can't change. None of us can change. We don't want to change. What do you want to change for? There's no point. You don't want to be blown up and think you're a cut above everybody else, because you're not."

The Bonds are a very practical breed. If a job needed doing, they just got on and did it. Hermon was more outgoing than Martin. Hermon would talk to anybody and everybody. Martin was more reserved. Hermon, as he was more or less living "on site", would always go and see the cleaners first thing every day and have a chat. To him, they were just as important as the club members or royalty. He appreciated the work they did and they appreciated him taking the time to talk to them. Nobody was any better than anyone else.

One of the people who got to know Martin and Hermon Bond really well was Peter Hunter. He was a roofing contractor and very close friend of the brothers. Here he shares his insight on the character of the two men, how they were influenced by their parents and a couple of yarns about how unpredictable dealing with the brothers could be.

"Martin was 'the brain', the strategist. He was the one who was totally business-minded. Hermon was often the ideas man, the one who could speak to anybody and find out their closest secret within minutes. If the brothers were going to do something, Hermon would go and do all the spade work first and then he would say: 'Leave it to you now Martin'.

"Martin was great in meetings but Hermon wasn't any good because he wore his heart on his sleeve. If something went wrong he'd burst, he'd blow up. Martin was the fastidious one who took a clinical look at things. They worked off each other in a wonderful way.

"They were a great team together and if you work together every day of your lives you're going to have rows, but I don't remember them having a single row.

"Hermon was a volatile character but he was quite proud of the fact that Martin could be 'like a volcano' if he lost it. I saw this a couple of times. If Martin lost his temper with anyone he was straight to the throat. It didn't last a moment but he would tell them bluntly what he thought. If you crossed Martin in any way at all, business especially, or you broke your word, he would completely cut you dead.

"They were very, very close as brothers and very proud of their ancestry and their mum and dad. They were close to the land. When dad went to bed at night he'd try to work out if he made, shall we say, two shillings, because that was a couple more 'bob' to put away for the family. And mother took in boarders.

"To start from that – and they maintained that same down-to-earth attitude. The MP at the time was Robert Hicks, a man with a wonderful vocabulary, but Hermon used to swear at him with every other word. 'Hicksie', as Hermon called him, loved the down-to-earth attitude.

"Hermon worked at projecting the image of a thick Cornish farmer and enjoyed putting the act on that he was as thick as two planks. I used to joke with him that he didn't have to do much acting to make it work! He used to say: 'You know boy, they all think us down here got bloody straw hanging out of our ears. They think we can't read or write'."

Peter Hunter did a lot of work for the Bonds particularly in those early days when the clubhouse and original hotel was being built. When deals were being struck on jobs to be done there was never much evidence in writing of what had been agreed.

The brothers would ask: "Peter, tell us how long d'you reckon this job's going to take?"

Peter: "I can't tell exactly, but allowing for weather and things, it might be, say, six to eight weeks."

Hermon: "Oh lovely then."

Peter: "But it doesn't matter how long I take."

Martin: 'On no, we're just asking."

Hermon: 'Right then boy, get on with it."

The three had probably taken three days to agree a price, but Peter said that was the usual phraseology. And then, any time he finished a contract early, he would be subjected to the "silver tea service" ploy. The Bond strategy was to invite him up to the proprietors' suite. Peter would be hoping he was going to get a cheque in full payment for the job. They'd sit down, the tea and cakes would be served – and then the small talk would start.

Martin, in a soft voice, said to Peter: "How are you?" Hermon, in a whisper: "You've done a lovely job there." The compliments were always the calm before the storm.

Martin: "We agreed the price and you said, if you remember, six to eight weeks. Well you're done and out in a month."

Peter: "Nothing to do with it. The men worked weekends, Sundays, and I paid them accordingly. I'm not going to discuss it. We had a price agreed."

Hermon: "We're not arguing about the bloody price, but like, being fair, there's a hell of a lot more work to be done here you know."

Peter said these "thinly veiled threats" - hinting that if he didn't drop the final price he wouldn't get any more work at St Mellion - were customary in his early dealings with the brothers, until he really got to know them.

"In the end, you had to agree to a percentage off, whatever that was, not to get the money but so that you didn't have any hassle. You didn't need to have the cheque then because once they got off the bill whatever they wanted off the bill and slapped your hand, that was it, the amount was settled," he said.

Peter once told them, after the amount was settled: "If you'd kept going for another 20 minutes or so you could have got another bloody few hundred quid off. I would have dropped the price. You were wearing me down."

Hermon was raging mad and turned to Martin: "Don't believe him Martin, don't believe him."

Peter said the Bonds were total businessmen. Once the deal was done their word was binding: "They should have had a sign outside their office saying something like 'Bond is our name and our word is our bond'. They were known for that.

"With the Bonds - and they quoted this to me many, many times – 'If anything goes wrong, remember it's a lifetime guarantee, not 10 or 20 years, so bloody well do it right the first time so it don't go wrong'."

Peter said there was another tack the brothers used to employ to try to knock down the bill for a completed job. All three would be in the proprietors' suite but the brothers would be talking as if Peter wasn't there. Hermon would say: "He done a lovely job there, didn't 'e Mart?" Martin: "He did indeed Hermon."

Peter, raising his eyes to heaven: "Oh let's not go through this bloody ritual again, just pay me the money."

Hermon: "Don't be silly, we've got to be fair with each other, you know that, we know you're fair."

Hermon would then write down on a piece of paper a price that he thought was fair - in his way of thinking. Then he'd slip the piece of paper across the table, like it was a secret document, to Martin and say: "I think that's a fair price. What do you think Mart? If you agree, we'll see if Peter will agree to that."

Martin: "You're being a bit bloody generous there Hermon, what's the matter with you? But if you think so, okay, tell Peter."

The brothers would then argue over who was going to tell Peter the price on the piece of paper. Peter would sit there, still saying nothing. The Bonds were waiting for him to speak, but he kept quiet. Then, all of a sudden, Peter would snatch the piece of paper from the table, screw it up without looking at it, throw it on the floor and say: "I don't want to see it because I know the price you've written on that bit of paper is less than we agreed."

The Bonds would argue that there should be 2.5 per cent off for something or other and, in the end, Peter would agree. But Peter learned how to play them at their own game. He would factor-in a bit extra when he was pricing up a job to compensate for the 2.5 per cent he knew the Bonds would want to knock off the final bill.

Then, in the presence of the brothers, he'd glance up and casually say: "Alright, I'll do it for you, but I'm not going to argue the price. I'll give you a price and that's it, I won't take a penny off."

When the job was done the three would meet and the Bonds would start negotiating. "An hour later I'd agree to drop the price and they were smiling, thinking that they'd beat me down, but I'd got the price I wanted," said Peter.

"I wouldn't do this with other people because their word was good, their money was always there when they said it would be there. Very, very straight people and the whole Bond family is exactly the same, it's gone through to the children."

FOOTNOTE: Of course Martin and Hermon would secretly admit that they knew what Peter was up to and they were happy to play along. It was all a bit of a game – as long as the Bonds had that word-of-mouth promise and a handshake on the lifetime guarantee. No shorter period of time was acceptable.

Their word was their Bond so to speak.

Chapter 6

SPRING HAS SPRUNG – AND IT'S URGENT

It was a day in early Spring and Edward Andreae-Jones was in his office at solicitors Blight, Broad and Skinnard in Callington.

Hermon Bond came up the stairs to Edward's office and with some urgency said: "We want you quick boy."

AJ, as he was known to everybody, jumped to his feet and said: "I'll get my notebook."

"You won't be needing that," said Hermon.

Downstairs, Martin Bond was waiting in the car outside. They drove down the main Callington to Saltash road and then turned off up a lane. Martin stopped the car and ordered AJ: "Now get out of the car - and come and see the first primroses."

AJ recalled: "To me, being taken out by them to see the first primroses of that year was important, significant, it was real value. They'd just seen something which they enjoyed and they simply wanted to share it with me. It was super. Let's face it, those primroses will be there in a thousand years' time – I won't be."

The moment was to hold even greater significance for AJ.

Within a year he'd developed problems with his vision through glaucoma and he was registered blind.

AJ met the Bonds for the first time when he went to the clubhouse to talk to them about the planning of the Jack Nicklaus course: "I was impressed that they were honest and straight-forward. They were 100 per cent genuine people of exceptional ability who never lost their affiliation to the soil. Farmers at heart, but entrepreneurs as well."

When AJ knew his sight was failing and he couldn't read his own writing he taught himself to write in capitals. That's how he overcame his challenge. But it was generally accepted he could no longer continue working in a conventional solicitors' office.

AJ was determined to find a way forward for himself. He went to see Martin and Hermon: "I simply told the brothers that the only way I could continue with their work was to work at the club as their solicitor. They kindly agreed and were prepared to let me adapt my work so that I could cope with my eye problem."

The decision by the Bonds to fit "a blind man" into their plans and, indeed, "the primroses moment", typified a much softer side to Martin and Hermon who, in the eyes of the public, were renowned for their toughness and determination.

AJ was the Bonds' lawyer for decades and St Mellion and Martin and Hermon Bond became a big part of his life.

"It was a voyage of discovery, a voyage of pleasure. I have been very blessed to have worked for so many years with the Bonds. It has been a way of life and there are very few people who have a job which is a way of life."

It could also, at times, be a roller-coaster. The Bonds asked AJ for his advice on a tax matter. There was the potential that if they didn't do something they'd end up facing a huge tax bill. AJ advised them on what the law was - but Hermon wasn't happy.

"I'm not bloody having it," Hermon protested. "It may be the law, but it's not bloody fair."

AJ tried to reason with him: "Hermon, what you are saying is, to the layman, entirely reasonable, the only problem is that the law doesn't agree with you. I can't help it. It's the law."

Hermon, stubborn as ever, wasn't going to let the issue rest. At every meeting after that he went on and on and on about it. Eventually he wore AJ down to the point when AJ decided to revisit the entire issue. He took a week to look at it again.

"I found there was a perfectly legal way round it," admitted AJ. "Now, if it hadn't been, to put it bluntly, for Hermon's bloody-mindedness and sheer persistence, we would have been hit by a massive tax bill."

AJ said Martin was remarkable in his own way. A very deep thinker: "He was a very gentle person until you got to a certain point and then he could come down as hard as Hermon. Martin used to run the finances and most of it was done on the back of scraps of paper. The point was it was always 100 per cent right. They both had something to contribute, they were both unique in their own way."

Martin may have been in charge of the finances, but Hermon played his part in keeping costs down.

"I introduced the tradition of meeting for lunch on Mondays," said AJ. "It was a sandwich and, in the early days, it was accompanied by a KitKat. But Hermon stopped the chocolate bar - because he said it was too expensive!"

FOOTNOTE 1: AJ never took any interest in the game of golf. He never hit a golf ball and never had the intention of doing so.

FOOTNOTE 2: AJ ended up with a double-barrelled surname because his father Willie, also a solicitor, said no one would ever find the family in the telephone book if they were just 'Jones'. Willie decided the answer was to use the surname of his wife-to-be, Minnie Andreae. And so the family name became Andreae-Jones.

Chapter 7

MIND YOU BOY, 'TISN'T GOING TO BE NO ORDINARY GOLF CLUB

Hermon Bond asked: "Well, what d'you think of that boy?" as he unrolled plans for a golf course and clubhouse at St Mellion across the trestle table.

It was a typical drab, dismal February day in South East Cornwall. A Saturday in 1973 in fact. The local MP Robert Hicks was holding one of his routine constituency surgeries in a tiny, cold room at the back of the town hall in Callington.

He was expecting his constituents to raise the usual topics – pensions, benefits, housing, planning, school transport. He had never met Hermon or his brother Martin before: "I saw the names Martin and Hermon Bond on my list but I did not have the slightest inkling what they wanted to see me about. I nearly fell off my chair because it hadn't reached my ear, as it were, that this scheme was being formulated, that there were plans afoot. And, it was such a contrast to the usual topics, problems and reasons why people came to see me.

"I was totally taken aback. It was incredible. But here were two local farmers who had this vision, and that's all it was at that stage, a plan to develop the St Mellion Golf and Country Club."

Hermon told the MP: 'Mind you boy, 'tisn't going to be no

ordinary golf club, plenty of them around, this is going to be something special."

Robert Hicks and the brothers talked through the proposals and they made one specific request to the MP - to find out what grants were available. As they said their goodbyes there was the statutory Hermon Bond pay-off line: "Well, remember one thing boy, us be only poor farmers, but us do know how to grow good grass."

The MP remembered the instant impression he had of the two men: "Hermon was a big man in all senses of the word and 'up front'. Martin was quieter and, I suspected, shrewder. But they were two farmers from a local family, farming on quite a big scale by South East Cornwall and Westcountry standards, determined to go through with this project and they were literally starting from scratch. But, it was clear that it was going to be a superb facility for South East Cornwall."

As for the possibility of government grants? Back in the sixties and seventies financial aid was available, mainly for business, commercial and industrial projects – and job creation. Also, the Westcountry Tourist Board offered grants. Robert Hicks obtained the list of possible grants available and forwarded it to the brothers.

But, one of the hallmarks of the Bonds' achievement was that they never received a single penny of public money. It was all down to them and Barclays Bank.

Robert Hicks said: "I think one of the reasons for that was their inherent mistrust of being tied up with conditions and so on. As farmers, they would have been recipients of grants through the Ministry of Agriculture. But that was for growing something or investing in a new barn or cow shed. And it may have been that they considered the amount of grant available as not being sufficient, given the conditions that might be attached to it."

The truth of the matter was very simple. The Bond brothers didn't like to be told what to do. And, obtaining a grant which eventually would have to be paid back made no sense to them whatsoever.

"Some of the possible grants were loans and they were tied up with red tape. We weren't having that. We decided to do it all ourselves, so we never had to thank anybody for anything," said Hermon.

And Martin added: "With the grants, you would be talking to people who didn't know what they were talking about anyway and we weren't too impressed with that. Also with grants, you had to wait months and months before you found out whether you would get a grant or not and you couldn't start the work until you got the grant. We just couldn't afford to wait for that amount of time."

Chapter 8

THE BONDS AND THEIR "LUCKY" BANK

The farming Bond family had always banked with Barclays at the top of Pike Street in Liskeard, looking out across The Parade towards what was then Webbs Hotel. And, when Martin and Hermon Bond took the life-changing decision to diversify into golf, they were blessed with some very good fortune and timely coincidences in the shape of Barclays Bill Warman.

Bill was to be a vital link in the chain of events which allowed the brothers and St Mellion to achieve their full potential. Some say that more than once the Bonds came within a whisker of losing their dream. It was Bill who put his faith in Martin and Hermon and it was Bill who put his job on the line to get the extra finances they needed to keep going – when the going got really tough.

Martin and Hermon said: "Bill moved mountains to help us achieve what we did. We respected him, he respected us and he was well respected by the very top boys in his bank."

Bill Warman was a chief clerk at the Liskeard branch of Barclays in 1965 when he first met the head of the family William Hermon Bond, or W H, and his three boys Jim, Martin and Hermon. And, as good fortune and coincidence would have it, eight years later, in June 1973, Bill was appointed manager of the Liskeard branch, just when Martin and Hermon needed to borrow the money to buy the land for the old course and clubhouse at St Mellion.

"They asked me to come and have a look at the land. I went out to take a look and said to them: 'What is this? A bloody sheep track'. But it turned out to be a very special bit of countryside in the end," said Bill. "I sent the loan application off to the local head office at Penzance and there wasn't any problem."

The Bonds borrowed £90,000 to buy the bulk of the land and then in October 1973 they asked Bill for another £40,000 to buy just under 11 acres in the centre of the land they had already bought. Just how close a working relationship the brothers had developed with their bank manager and the trust and confidence Bill had in them is clear from the way the deal was done. The request for the extra money was made down the phone and there was no face-to-face meeting to confirm the details.

Instead, Bill Warman wrote this to the brothers: "Following our recent telephone conversation I have pleasure in confirming that the bank are quite prepared to advance a further £40,000."

And Bill added these prophetic words in his letter: "There is no doubt that the purchase of this land, although it might appear expensive at the moment, will prove one of your best buys in future years."

Bill was only at Liskeard for a year before being promoted. In the early 1980s he was in Exeter as one of the bank's three local directors for the South West when the bank's local offices looking after the region were merged into the Exeter office and Bill was to renew his business association with Cornwall – and the Bonds, but more of that later.

Chapter 9

FILL THOSE BOOTS, IF YOU CAN BOY

"Come on Riley, keep up boy, for Pete's sake," Hermon Bond shouted back to Peter Riley, the Bond brothers' accountant, who was having difficulty keeping up. Martin Bond couldn't stop laughing.

There was petite Peter, in his business suit, in the rain, in the mud, in wellies, not his wellies, Hermon Bond's wellies. Peter didn't have any in the boot of his car when he went to St Mellion to see how the original course was shaping up. Martin suggested they walk down to have a look at where the 12th green was going to be. Vast amounts of earth were being moved. It was very muddy, so Hermon offered Peter a pair of his wellies. Hermon was around a size 12. Peter took a very neat size six!

"I distinctly remember kind of plodding through the mud with these wellies on, twice the size that I needed, and I had to keep stopping because my feet kept coming out of them. It took me ages to walk down to the green. And Hermon was stood there in the rain pointing this and that out and saying: 'Come on Riley, keep up boy, for Pete's sake'."

Peter Riley said the Bonds had to contend with a lot of negative reaction to their initial plans for St Mellion. A lot of people were very sceptical. They said it wouldn't work, the club would never get enough members, people didn't want that kind of "thing" (facility).

"But I was very for it, once I'd done some research and Martin had done some research and given me more information," added Peter. "I could see the possibilities there because there wasn't anything in the area that was the same. There was the potential to bring people out from Plymouth. It wasn't that far to go to St Mellion.

"Having done some homework and worked out the costings, I told the brothers: 'I think this will work. I think you'll get the right number of people'. I'd acted for them for two or three years and, knowing them as I did, I felt that these guys could do it. They'd got the personality to do it and the drive to push it forward.

"In fairness, if I'd had any quiet doubts myself I would have tried to talk them out of it. But no, I really felt the concept would take off and it would be a big success. It wasn't going to be easy. None of us thought it was going to be easy. There were bound to be a lot of hiccups along the way but I'd got the confidence in them that they could push it through."

Peter said Hermon would make off-the-cuff comments and say things that in today's politically correct world would be deemed inappropriate. He was a thinker and a worrier. Martin would think things through more strategically and was better at technical meetings with advisers than Hermon, who might just say the wrong thing. But Martin would go away and think things through and then raise any concerns: "I always thought they were a good balance to one another and that was another reason why I thought they'd push it through together. They worked very well as a team."

Peter added that the Bonds achieved something a lot of other people would have liked to but couldn't, even people probably better qualified than them.

"To create the size of businesses that they ultimately grew from virtually nothing is quite astonishing really. When you look at it at its peak, they had St Mellion, two other golf courses (Looe and Lanhydrock), other businesses as well, the farm business, a separate property development business, it is quite astonishing in that space of time.

"You don't build up a business like that, or an empire like that, and not have a lot of stress and aggravation, but I always felt we could have fun working together. There's not many clients you could do that with. With some clients it was aggravation all the time, but, with Martin and Hermon, we always used to have a laugh and a joke - the wellies is just one example.

"It was an incredible feat for them to get Jack Nicklaus to come to 'out in the sticks' the other side of Plymouth. It was amazing."

Peter Riley retired in 2002. He'd been dealing with the Bonds for close on 30 years.

Chapter 10

THEY WATCHED THE GRASS GROW – BUT ONLY UNTIL IT WAS LONG ENOUGH TO FLOG

The Bonds started building the original course, later to be known as the "old" course, basically themselves. As farmers they used their own farm equipment. They always prided themselves at being good at growing grass so, after they seeded the land to create the holes they'd proudly watch the grass come through and climb.

Then they'd sell it to neighbouring farmer Roger Bush. He would regularly cut the grass on what were to become the fairways and put it in his silage pits.

Gradually Roger became more and more friendly with Hermon socially. They shared a great interest in horse racing. They would seldom miss the local meetings at Newton Abbott and Exeter and they would also go to Taunton and even further afield sometimes. They gelled totally, 100 per cent and trusted each other implicitly.

The same close friendship also developed with Martin. All three talked on the same wavelength and, business-wise, all three became more involved as the brothers expanded their initial dream.

Chapter 11

A 16 HOLE GOLF COURSE – I DON'T THINK SO

It was new territory for Martin and Hermon Bond – building a golf course on farmland they'd bought near St Mellion village. They'd had to borrow heavily to buy the land – and then they had to build the holes and the clubhouse.

They had constructed 16 holes - so just two holes short. But they'd overspent on a few things and run out of money. They went to the bank manager and told him the bad news – they needed to borrow more to finish the job.

The manager just happened to be the mild, modest, soft-spoken, laid back Trevor Furse, who only ever stepped out of his comfort zone to call the shots when, instinctively, he knew, it was time to do so.

Trevor listened intently to the details of the overspend on this and that. Then he leaned back in his chair behind his desk and casually announced: "I suppose I'd better give you some more money because I don't know of any successful 16 hole golf courses!"

That story is told by Australian Jeff Chapman, the owner and chairman of the Bennelong Group which owns Crown Golf, the biggest golf course operators in Europe and now owners of St Mellion.

"Martin told me that story and he told it sort of against himself, but it says something about the relationship the Bonds had with their local community and the trust and support that they had," said Jeff.

Jeff Chapman recounted "the tale of the 16 hole golf course" when he came to St Mellion in June 2009 for the official launch of the re-opened St Mellion International Resort. More of that later.

Chapter 12

TONY JACKLIN AT ST MELLION - NEVER

Opponents of the original golf course at St Mellion claimed it would never attract the likes of Tony Jacklin. How wrong they were. The 18 holes opened to club members in September 1976 but an exhibition match was held in June 1977 to officially announce the arrival of the new course. The players were Tommy Horton, Eamonn Darcy, St Mellion pro John Yeo and - former British and US Open champion Tony Jacklin. These stars were not there just to christen the course. They were also there to cast a critical eye over it.

Hermon's son Alan caddied for John Yeo in what was a "skins" game. Each hole has a set value or a "skin" but, when players tie on a hole, the value of that "skin" is added to the value of next hole. If several holes in a row are tied, the value of the "skin" can become quite significant.

Alan said: "Unknown to John and me, the three tournament professionals were planning to split their winnings. They didn't include John. Each hole was tied up until the 10th which is a driveable par four over water.

"John had deliberately three-putted on the ninth for a bogey six which meant he would tee off last at the tenth. So, he had the advantage of seeing what the others did before he played his tee shot. Two of them hit a three wood and one of them an iron. None of them made the green.

"John hit a driver onto the front right of the green. The others chipped on. I attended the pin, which was back-middle. John made the long putt for an eagle to win all 10 'skins'.

"There was a huge roar from the crowd and a look of astonishment on the faces of the pros. Very amusing."

Chapter 13

GATHERING THE TEAM

During 1976 and 1977 Martin and Hermon went talent spotting, looking for people to run the day to day operation of this new golf club. They made some very astute appointments, recruiting Bill Powell as the first General Manager, David Webb as Golf Club Secretary and Martin Watson who would eventually lead the team at the club.

Here is Martin Watson's view of how things evolved under the Bonds and it gives a rare insight into what today is known as HR and PR – Human Resources and Public Relations.

Staff salaries at St Mellion were fair, but there were plenty of perks over and above that which reflected the loyalty the Bonds had to their staff. Martin Watson, who was originally taken on as food and beverage manager, worked in several positions over a number of years, gradually climbing the management ladder to become first General Manager and then Managing Director of St Mellion International Hotel Golf and Country Club.

At his interview at St Mellion he was given this stern warning by Hermon Bond: "Boy, if you work for us you can upset who you like, but don't you upset my missus." Martin brought with him his wife Susie and their two young boys. But it didn't work out for the couple and eventually Susie went back home with the boys to near Chepstow and Martin started a relationship with the head receptionist Sally Willis.

Martin decided to tell the Bonds what had happened: "They helped me out. They got me through. They must have seen some potential in me because they helped me financially get through it. They used to say: 'If you've got any problems boy, you just come and see us'.

"I used to go and see Martin Bond because he was always known as the Chancellor of the Exchequer, he was the one who signed the cheques. Martin was in control of the finances."

Martin Watson married Sally and they lived on site rent free. The first house the couple shared next to the big timeshare barn was connected to mains water, had storage heaters and the phone was linked to the clubhouse. The Bonds paid for everything including the rates, apart from the electricity bill.

When Martin needed wood for the fire, Martin Bond would say: "Leave it to me." Next thing the wood was delivered, pre-chopped, ready to go on the fire.

Martin and Sally also lived in the house behind the 15th green. It was a double barn and the second barn had been converted with an office and play room/utility room downstairs and en-suite bathroom upstairs.

Martin Watson got an invite through a friend of his to a Round Table boxing night in the old Cornwall Coliseum and he took the brothers with him.

"If you ever went out with them socially you would not be allowed to put your hand in your pocket. I would go to the bar to get the drinks and it was almost as if you had this fatherly figure with you all of a sudden. This hand would come from behind you and discreetly put a note in your hand. It would be 20 quid to get the drinks. If you were in their company you would not spend a penny.

"I maybe saw the best of them but for all their bravado the Brothers Bond as I sometimes called them were incredibly generous.

"Everybody gets a cash flow crisis every now and then and I would go and see Martin. The next day he'd appear and say: 'There you go boy' and slap a little brown envelop down. I'd ask about paying it back and he'd say: 'Of course you don't pay it back. That's a little thanks for what you do'."

Martin Watson said he learned an awful lot from Martin Bond, who was a great teacher of how to deal with people. One of the things he taught Martin Watson was how to react to complaining customers.

"He always used to say to me if somebody's complaining, just agree with them and tell them they're totally right, because if you agree with them it takes all the thunder out of them and they've got nothing else to fire off at you.

"We had a system and rules to deal with people who were really serious complainers. I'd tell them to speak to Hermon, Hermon would tell them to speak to Martin (Bond) and Martin would tell them they'd better speak to me. By that time they'd be fed up with complaining and give up."

As the years went by, Martin Watson always remembered what Hermon had said about not upsetting Mrs Bond: "I never, ever upset Rachel Bond. I probably had the best working relationship of any of the staff with her. I always found her absolutely delightful to me. She never, in all the years I worked there, called me Martin. I was always Mr Watson."

Martin Watson was surprised that Martin Bond remembered the first time they met - at St Pierre Golf and Country Club in Wales - because Martin Bond, who didn't drink, had been drinking!

"Martin and Hermon had lunch in what used to be the top ballroom. The owner Bill Graham sent them in half a bottle of wine. Martin had somewhere between half a glass and a glass and told me years later that it was the first time in his life he'd ever been tiddly. All the years I knew them, I never saw Martin drink anything but lemonade and lime. But he and Hermon used to love seeing anybody else get drunk."

David Webb, played a huge part in the early development of golf at St Mellion and for many years was the face and voice of the club as neither of the owners were remotely interested in being centre stage.

Many celebrities have catch phrases and David followed the trend with his famous opening line of "On behalf of Mr Martin and Mr Hermon Bond"- he prefaced every public speech with those words whilst waving first his right hand in perfect time with the "Mr Martin" and followed in sync with the left on "Mr Hermon".

He was much loved and respected not only in the club but in the wider golfing community too. He carried out his duties with sensitivity, diligence and charm. He always had time for people.

No account of St Mellion would be complete without mentioning Peter and June Kelly, both long-serving loyal members of staff. Peter and June epitomised the family values espoused within the team and the club.

Hermon and Rachel Bond were personal friends of Peter and June and the couples would regularly holiday together. It says a lot for all concerned that the lines were not blurred when it was time to go back to work. No favours were expected - nor given.

Chapter 14

WE HAVE WAYS OF MAKING YOU MOVE

Weekend golf breaks in the early eighties on the Old course were proving very popular with groups of players travelling from all over the country to enjoy themselves.

Two such golfers left their cars – a very flashy Jaguar and a brand new Range Rover – parked side by side right outside the main entrance to the clubhouse. A person could just about walk through the gap between the two vehicles.

There was a function on that Friday night which meant the food and beverage manager Martin Watson didn't get away until the early hours of the Saturday morning. He almost fell over the cars as he left so he went back into reception and left a note for the morning staff to match the number plates with the guests' names and room numbers and get them to move their vehicles.

"I assumed it was weekend residents who'd arrived late on the Friday night, perhaps around midnight, so it wasn't a great problem, as long as the cars were moved first thing in the morning," said Martin.

Workaholic that he was, Martin was back in by 9am on the Saturday. The two cars were still there, getting in the way of everybody going into and coming out of the clubhouse main doors. Martin queried it with reception staff. They said they'd asked the car owners to move their vehicles and they said they would. But they hadn't - and had gone out on their round of golf.

Martin checked with the starter at the first tee Peter Kelly to estimate where the golfers might be on the course. They were probably on the 4th or 5th. This was in the era before golf buggies so Martin set off in his car around the course to track down the culprits.

"I asked these guys to move their cars. It turned out they were a couple of 'Hooray Henrys' in a group of eight staying for the weekend. They denied any knowledge of the vehicles so I came back up and spoke to Peter Kelly. He confirmed it must be them.

"So I went back out on the course again in my car, this time with Peter. He pointed the guys out to me and I asked them again. One of them said in a very posh voice: 'Yes it's my car but I'm not going to move it now. I'll move it after the first nine holes before we move on to the 10th'."

Martin wasn't going to have an argument or a fight on the golf course so he went back to the clubhouse. It was at that stage Hermon Bond appeared on the scene, unaware of the developing impasse. It was about 9.30 or 10.00am and St Mellion was catering for two wedding receptions. It was going to be an exceptionally busy day. And these two cars were threatening to disrupt the ordinary running patterns of the business and upset the two brides if, on the most important day of their lives, they had to manoeuvre their white, flowing dresses between the obstacles to get inside to enjoy their receptions.

"Hermon was outside the clubhouse and asked me what was going on and I said the guys who owned the cars had promised to move them when they were walking from the 9th green to the 10th tee," said Martin.

"The two men came round and walked straight past so I said to

Hermon: 'That's the guys'. Hermon was wearing a cloth cap, a shirt, his trademark tartan trousers and wellies. He could have been anybody. Hermon shouted to the chap: 'Hey, Mister'. The bloke was not too impressed but eventually Hermon got his attention and said he wanted him to move the car."

For the purposes of the rest of the dialogue, the golfer is nicknamed Henry. Henry: "I'm not moving my car. There's nowhere to park." Hermon: "There's plenty of parking round the back of the hotel." Henry: "I'm in the middle of a round of golf." Hermon: "If you don't move it, I'll move the bloody thing." Henry: "You can't move it." Hermon: "I can."

Hermon then casually waved his arm in the direction of a member of staff Tony Barriball. Now, if there were digger driver world championships, Tony would be in the finals and would probably win the trophy. He was the expert behind the wheel and levers of one of these machines. His touch was so delicate he could make them dance. Some said if they could speak and could hold a note he'd have them singing everything from the classics to the latest hits.

Tony appeared from nowhere in an intimidating machine which had a bucket on the front and jaws which would open up like a huge mouth. It was a grabber and lifter. He drove it right up to the back of the spanking new Range Rover and stopped, just in time.

Hermon: "Would you like to move your car now sir?" Henry: "You wouldn't dare." Hermon shouted one word: "Tony."

Tony Barriball edged the digger forward. The car driver dived in front of the digger, between it and the back of his Range Rover. The owner of the Jaguar certainly got the message and drove his car away very swiftly. And it finally dawned on the Range Rover owner that he and his car would come off worse in this particular confrontation if he didn't back down, get out of the way and move the car.

Henry: "I'm leaving the hotel. I've never been treated so rudely in all my life." Hermon: "About time you were then boy."

So, off Henry went to pack his bags and leave. Martin Watson and "HB" as he affectionately called him sometimes, went inside and upstairs. Hermon was giggling as they watched Henry pack his bags, load his car up and disappear. But then Hermon suddenly panicked: "Has the bugger paid his bill?" The group of golfers had seen off a considerable quantity of wine the previous night and that had been paid for. Hermon decided he wasn't bothered if the Range Rover driver hadn't paid for his room. Its monetary value paled into insignificance compared to the "priceless" quality of the scenario he'd just been a part of.

"The Range Rover driver left quicker than he arrived," said Martin Watson. "We never saw him again. Very amusing."

To Henry, the man in the flat cap and wellies may have conjured up an image of a country yokel who was minus a few bolts and only needed strands of straw sticking out of his mouth – and ears – to complete the bizarre picture and even more outlandish circumstances.

It was an image Hermon cultivated, but he was afraid of neither man nor beast – nor Hooray Henry. Just a farmer's son from west of the River Tamar, but a match any day of the year for a City Slicker.

Chapter 15

STARS OF STAGE, SCREEN AND TELEVISION AT ST MELLION

The Bonds met scores of famous people over the years, mainly because of the fund-raising events held at St Mellion by the Lord's Taverners sports charity for young people.

For many of the famous names, playing golf with Hermon and Martin Bond was a little bit different because the Bonds were so down to earth.

Hermon said: "It was nice to meet all these people. You can take them or leave them, just as you want. But when you saw them on television or whatever you look back and think 'I played golf with him once'. It was quite nice to talk to them."

Martin said: "Ronnie Corbett was a great chap. He was tremendous, his attitude, he was a very, very nice person to be with." Martin was sitting next to Ronnie at a dinner and the comedian was about to do his party piece. "He was like sitting on eggs because he was worried if the microphone was going to be good enough, was it going to be okay. You would have thought a man who had done it so many times would have been quite happy but he was really nervous to make sure that everything was right. He was wonderful company."

Jimmy Tarbuck came to St Mellion on several occasions. The

brothers would play Jimmy and the club's director of golf David Webb. Frequently, the brothers lost and they had to fork out £5 each to the winners. Martin: "Tarbuck was a hustler, but very good, a good player and good fun."

The former MP for South East Cornwall Robert Hicks never claimed to be a good golfer. He comfortably admitted that his golf swing was more like a batsman striking the ball past mid-off hoping for a boundary.

But he did win a prize at one of the Lord Taverners annual celebrity functions at St Mellion, the Texas Scramble.

"I was the so-called 'celebrity' with Martin Bond and Hermon's son Graham and an American Clarke Ikestead and we won the tournament. I expect I only helped with the putting as all the others could hit the ball so much further than me". Martin Bond remembered Robert Hicks putting everything to help win the trophy. The MP used to take all his shots with his pipe still in his mouth but, probably, when he had a few professional lessons, first from pro John Yeo and then pro Tony Moore, he was advised to drop that particular trait of his game.

Also his back swing wasn't very full – the lessons didn't do much to alter that. He was made a life member at St Mellion and used to play once a week with the same two companions – Ian Rawlings, the retired orthopaedic surgeon who did the first of his two hip replacements, and Brian Fisher, the former managing director of Plymouth City Bus.

Chapter 16

RACHEL PROVIDES BLANKET COVERAGE

It was like something out of an episode of Fawlty Towers. It was September 1978. The 24-bedroom hotel at St Mellion was just about finished in time for the Great Britain and Ireland versus the United States of America PGA Cup Match. The paint was still drying in the rooms to be occupied by the players of the two teams.

The day before they were due to arrive, everyone was in the thick of it, putting the final, finishing touches to the rooms and doing things like making the beds - sheets, pillows, blankets.... blankets!!!??? To Hermon Bond's horror he realised they did not have anywhere near enough blankets. The Trago Mills out-of-town shopping centre near Liskeard didn't have the right ones, but Trago's branch in Falmouth did. He dispatched his wife Rachel "to get a car-load of blankets." She didn't know Falmouth, but she had to get down there and back as quickly as possible. She went and cleared the shelves of all the blankets Trago had. So the hotel was finally finished – the beds were made - and the rooms were ready to be occupied.

Martin and Hermon Bond had been invited to host the event. But they realised tournaments wouldn't happen without a hotel, so they decided to build one, next to the clubhouse.

It was intriguing to see the American golfers, surrounded by the numerous members of their entourage. The place was crawling with high-fliers, the likes of the President of the USA PGA, the main people of American golf at the time. Attracting the PGA Cup Match came through Colin Snape, the top man in the Great Britain and Ireland Professional Golfers' Association. He actually came along and asked the brothers would they like a tournament.

The Bonds were delighted, although they admitted later that they were totally apprehensive because of their lack of experience and their naivety. They hadn't a clue what they were letting themselves in for. The icing on the cake was Great Britain and Ireland beating the USA for the first time in 21 years! Martin and Hermon presented the cup.

Martin said: "We never expected someone to come along and invite us to have a tournament. It was run exactly the same as the Ryder Cup, over three days."

Hermon added: "The greenkeepers were trying to get the course just right. We had to file off the blades of our machines to cut the greens lower. It was some fun and games. Maybe not up to American standards, but it was good."

The club put on a dinner for 160 at the close of the event. It also went very well. Rachel Bond recalled: "The match was our first big thing really. It opened up players coming here from America. I always remember, it brought a lump to my throat. The Royal Marine Band were there, playing, marching up and down the 18th. There we are, standing up on the balcony, watching. I thought: 'Oh my, we've arrived'."

During 1977 and 1978 the Bonds had their first tentative contact with officials from the Benson and Hedges International Open. There followed an initial meeting – and the officials also came to St Mellion to have a look at the golf course and facilities.

During the previous year - 1976 - the clubhouse and course were proving successful and the golfing side started moving forward. Companies wanted to hold golf days and corporate membership grew from that. The United Friendly Insurance Company had one of its bigger golf days at St Mellion. The setting was ideal. The clubhouse offered the space for large groups to meet, socialise and have a drink and a meal. The golfing days were modelled on what was done at the St Pierre Golf and Country Club in Wales. St Mellion was a family club.

But it was always the intention of the brothers to see golf become the "big potato". St Pierre had the Dunlop Masters......the Bonds aspired to that kind of golf tournament on their course.

Chapter 17

LET THERE BE LIGHT – AS LONG AS YOU PAY

The first things the Bonds opened at St Mellion were the pro shop and a beautiful snooker room with a lovely carpet on the floor. But it had a rather strange system for lighting the table, a bit like a coin-operated electricity meter.

Peter Hunter, a friend of the Bonds and one of their contractors, was in there playing snooker. The light was just fading and Hermon Bond marched in. He'd been out in the fields and left mud all over the brand new carpet.

"What do you think this bloody machine's for?" shouted Hermon, pointed at the slot. "You don't play in the dark. Put 20p in the machine."

Peter thought it just summed up the entrepreneurial mind-set of Hermon and Martin: "They thought as much of that 20p going in the machine to pay for you to have enough light to play snooker as they would about costs if you were doing a major contract for them."

Chapter 18

WOULD YOU LIKE SOME MINT SAUCE WITH YOUR LAMB, SIR?

Hermon Bond was a very good snooker and billiards player and had the trophies to prove it. It just happened that the club's general manager David Webb knew Ray Reardon, six times world champion, so it was decided to set up some exhibition matches at St Mellion.

In February 1979 the first venture at pairing together two of the world's top professionals for a three-day series of 11-frames-a-day challenge matches was a great success. Alex "Hurricane" Higgins, then the current B&H Masters' champion, took on Ray Reardon.

Ray brought Higgins to St Mellion, but the fiery Irishman's reputation went before him and Ray announced on their arrival: "There you are boys, he's all yours, he's nothing to do with me anymore."

In the afternoon practice sessions, when Higgins was getting used to the table, Hermon challenged him to a frame. Higgins gave him a 60 point start – and won. Then an 80 point start – and won. Then a 100 point start – and won. There wasn't a fourth frame! But Higgins was due some "winnings" from Hermon, because Hermon never missed the chance for a bet or wager.

During the interval in the exhibition match that night, Higgins confided in Martin Bond that he didn't think he was entertaining the crowd very well. Martin said nothing. But "Hurricane" came out for the first frame after the interval and stormed round the table. He made a break of 108 in eight minutes! Martin Bond, and the other 300 spectators, had certainly been entertained to an absolutely astonishing feat.

After the match that night, Higgins went clubbing in Plymouth. He returned to his room at St Mellion's hotel and opened the door to find that Hermon, humble in defeat, had thoughtfully left Hurricane's "winnings" in the room – a sheep, young, alive and jumping up and down on the bed!

Ray Reardon recalled: "Hermon owed Alex a couple of hundred quid but when he came back to his hotel room instead of finding his cash on the table he found a sheep on his bed. And a lovely sheep it was too. It hadn't been sheared. There was a note from Hermon which said something like: 'Ran out of cash, please accept this in lieu of – one sheep'. I don't know what Alex did with the sheep. I'm surprised he didn't take it out and sell it."

So it's not clear how Hurricane handled the situation or whether he liked mint sauce with his lamb. But he certainly had an extreme love affair with mustard.

It was a tradition that, at the end of the matches, which could be eleven o'clock or midnight, the players would have a meal in the restaurant. On one night, for a change, Alex Higgins didn't go clubbing in Plymouth. Hermon Bond was sitting beside him when the restaurant manageress Di Pile served Alex his steak.

Di asked Alex: "Would like mustard with your steak?" Alex: "Yes, yes, yes, mustard, mustard." Di brought the English mustard to the table. Alex spread it liberally all over his meat. "You couldn't see the steak for the mustard. It was plastered with mustard," said Di.

Hermon, being Hermon, looked at Higgins and blurted out: "Hey boy, Hurricane, what the hell you doing with that steak? Do you like a bit of steak with your mustard then?" Higgins said he did – and he ate the whole thing. Di's opinion was: "I think he ate it out of cussedness in the end. Alright, it was English mustard, but it's still quite strong."

The then boxing promoter Barry Hearn brought many of the famous players down to St Mellion. Hermon and Barry never missed the opportunity for a wager. On one occasion the "prize money" was a pig and it was won by Barry. But, as Hermon still had an outstanding bill from Barry for something else, Hermon decided to deduct the value of the pig from the invoice before he paid up.

The exhibition matches were incredible events. Snooker stars who most people had ever only seen on television, were friendly and approachable. They were happy to have a frame with local players.

Three hundred spectators a night enjoyed the snooker matches. They sat on rows of individual chairs on tiers constructed of planks and scaffolding. It was all a bit precarious, too much for one group of spectators, about half a dozen of them. Their chairs fell off the back row. The silence of the snooker room was shattered. The spectator on the end of the row somehow managed to crash out through the fire-doors which slammed tight shut behind him. He staggered round the building to the main entrance to get back in. Security staff challenged him and asked him for his ticket. He told them: "No, I've just fallen out the fire-doors." Their reaction: "Yeh, we've heard it all now." They did, eventually, let him back in.

Other snooker stars who played in the exhibition matches included Jimmy White, Denis Taylor, Tony Mayo, who also gave Hermon a head start in practice frames, Steve Davis, Terry Griffiths and John Virgo.

Chapter 19

THE STILL BALL TABLE GAME AT ST MELLION

The world of professional snooker will always be grateful a Welshman decided to take a risk and go against the advice of his boss. After spending 11 years down the mines, Ray Reardon spent almost eight years as a police officer and was stationed in Sheffield when he decided to become a professional snooker player. The station chief superintendent told him it was a very ill-advised move with no security and he would lose his police house and have nothing. If he didn't win the world championship, what was he going to do?

"But, you know," said Ray, "sometimes you've got to take a risk in life. I thought I can do this and I knew the standard of play in the world professional championship and I couldn't see anybody in there that could really beat me."

So Ray did turn professional and won the world championship – six times. Becoming a pro was also a good thing for snooker enthusiasts in Cornwall and the South West because Ray came to St Mellion to play exhibition matches. Ray moved to the South West in 1972 and, through his love of golf, went on to become president of Churston Golf Club at Brixham in Devon. "My lifestyle is – if it's fine I play golf, if it's wet I play snooker."

Ray always held very strong views on the pressures sportspeople face in different disciplines: "They talk about tennis players being under enormous pressure. What a load of rubbish. They're very lucky that they are playing a moving game, not a still game. You haven't got time to think about pressure, you haven't got time to think of the shot you're going to play.

"It's a reactionary game, you have to be exceedingly fit, very clever and have a high degree of skill. I'm not knocking it. But when you talk about temperament, come on, golf, snooker, a still ball game. It's waiting there for you to stroke it or to hit it. It's daring you. And then you've got time to think and when you've got time to think your nerves come into play. Then you come under pressure. That's when you find your heart isn't where it should be. It moves for some unknown reason and when you're playing a shot and you've got your left hand extended and when you can feel your shirt moving at the back of your muscles (there's no wind about, all the doors are closed, there's a roof on the place) it's your nerves.

"And that's when I used to get up from the table and do my shrug because that's how I got rid of the tension. But playing the game was an enjoyment. Leading players learn to win playing in front of lots of people and on television. So, if you remove either of those two things, or both, they can't play because they need motivation.

"I love motivation. I can't play with no audience. It's useless. I've got nothing to prove."

There was always a good audience to motivate Ray at St Mellion. He had met David Webb who was the Churston Club secretary and later went to St Mellion to work for Martin and Hermon Bond.

"Hermon got David Webb to bring me down to play local people, the best of the West if you like, exhibitions. We had snooker weekends once a year. We did that for a few years. Then Alex Higgins came on the scene. He'd won his world titles and Hermon wanted him down at St Mellion.

"David asked me to bring him down for a weekend. I said I'd do it for David, I'd get Alex down but for me to get him down I'd have to take him home the night before and he'd have to stay at my home. Because, Alex being Alex, if I said to him I'd meet him somewhere in the morning to bring him down, he'd never be there, he'd be unreliable, you'd never find him.

"I told David I'd bring Alex down to the hotel, ask for him, introduce Alex to him and him to Alex and add: 'He's all yours. I wipe my hands of him'. That's what I did and that first night Alex went missing. He hadn't been there four hours."

Hurricane was fast round the snooker table, hence his nickname, but he was in as big a hurry round the golf course, more often than not with a bottle of Vodka in his bag of clubs. On a par five on the old course at St Mellion he teed off and hit a nice drive down the middle. Ray Reardon was one of the other players: "Then the rest of us teed off. We all walked down to our balls and, by the time we got to our drives, Higgins was on the green putting out. We are still 280 yards away from this green and Higgins is on it, putting out by himself. Etiquette and standards went out the window as far as Alex was concerned. There weren't any. He couldn't care less. He was 'Hurricane Higgins' on the golf course as well as at the snooker table.

"When you think of what he was and who he was. We make a lot of excuses for great players, geniuses sometimes I suppose, but he broke all the rules in the book. He could be as nice as pie but was also a Jekyll and Hyde. He was an amazing man. He could be lovely, warm, friendly, affectionate to old people, families, visit hospitals. And the next day, different, you couldn't even talk to him."

Ray could probably fill a book solely on his memories of Alex Higgins. He played Alex in the Pontins snooker final. It was a two-session final and Ray had a very good first session, so good he needed only one frame to win the match. When Ray came down in the hotel lift to go across to the arena for the second session, Alex was in the bar with John Spencer and other players.

“They saw me and I said: ‘Hi chaps, see you later, it won’t take long’. Higgins was upset about me saying this and was talking about going into the second session and stuffing that Reardon bloke.

“When we were sitting in our seats in the arena ready for the second session one of the Pontins hostesses asked me if I’d like to have a drink with Pontins. I said that was very nice and I’d have an alcoholic drink after the first frame but I would like a nice glass of ice cold water.

“Then she went across to Alex and asked him the same question and what would he like. He told her: ‘I’ll have a nice, long orange juice please....and put a triple Vodka in it’. A frame later he was walking back to the hotel.”

It was a different story when the two met in a match in Sheffield: “Alex turned up with two black eyes. He potted me off the table. It was the best of nine frames. He won five-two, easy, no problem. Incredible.”

On another occasion Alex was in Manchester. He decided to jump out a window but forgot he was on the first floor. No black eyes, but a broken ankle.

Ray recalled: “Two days later he’s playing in the first round of a tournament in the Hotel du Ville in France, a big, posh five-star hotel. The table was in a lovely arena and in comes Alex, hopping on one leg. He won the match. What a star.”

At St Mellion, Ray got to know Martin as well as Hermon. He admired Martin immensely: “Martin was a lovely man, quiet, unassuming, he enjoyed his life and was a very shrewd businessman. But Hermon was the one who liked the fun of sport, if you like."

Hermon would challenge Ray at the snooker table, and there was always money involved: "I'd give him a huge start, but he couldn't win. £50 a game, £100 a game. It was like he was trying to get back the fee he was paying me. But it ended up costing him double really.

"Hermon was wonderful, a charming man. He was quite an amazing man. He had this warm affection about him somehow. He made you welcome. And when you shook hands with him it was unbelievable. He had the biggest hands you've ever seen or felt. I've got fairly long hands and strong hands. But my hand would go inside his hand and he would envelope my hand and his fingers would go around my wrist. That's how big they were, like shovels really."

Ray would have to say to Hermon: "Please don't squeeze my hand so hard, I've got a match tonight."

Hermon: "I know, I'm paying you."

Ray: "Don't squeeze or you'll have to abandon the match."

Hermon: "Ah, that's different."

Ray said Hermon would instantly let go of his hand as if he'd had an electric shock.

"Hermon was a great host. He was a great sort of kidder, he liked practical jokes, but nice jokes. I loved him. I used to say to him: 'That's my boy'. And his wife Rachel was charming, a great host. They were a lovely family all round."

Chapter 20

TREVINO IS COMING TO ST MELLION TO DEFEND HIS B&H TITLE – OR IS HE?!

It was 1979. St Mellion Golf and Country Club was getting ready to host, for the first time, the Benson & Hedges International Open in May. American superstar Lee Trevino was due to come to South East Cornwall to defend his B&H International Open title won at Fulford the previous year. But, would he turn up?

Trevino, one of golf's greatest, flamboyant characters and entertainers, could demand virtually anything to guarantee his appearance. The top men in his backroom team knew that and were geared up to fulfil his every wish and desire and the B&H people were keen to oblige if possible.

But as the tournament start date grew much nearer, no one was expecting the bombshell Trevino was about to drop. He let it be known to Len Owen, the director of special events for Benson & Hedges, that he was expecting to occupy a suite of rooms at St Mellion. He was insisting on the luxury of a suite of rooms so he could chill out before and after his rounds of golf.

There was only one problem with that. St Mellion didn't have any suite of rooms! Just a modest 24-bedroom hotel, mainly paid for by the Bonds' sale of their precious pigs. The absence of a suite of rooms was something no one was too keen to share with Trevino. He was just told everything would be in order by the time he arrived. There followed lots of pretty frantic behind-the-scenes activity.

But, what did Martin and Hermon Bond do? They simply held an impromptu, not-in-any-way-an-emergency "board" meeting, over a lunchtime pasty. Was the reigning B&H champion not going to come to St Mellion because the hotel facilities were not of the calibre demanded by one of the world's most famous golfers? That was inconceivable. He was the defending champion, the big crowd-puller.

The Bond brothers came up with the answer before they'd munched and crunched on the last of their pasty crusts. This was their solution. At the end of one of the corridors of the hotel, they'd take the doors off the last two rooms, one on each side of the corridor, and put a partition and a door in the corridor to turn the two rooms into a makeshift "suite of rooms".

The double bed was taken out of one of the rooms and replaced by a settee and other furniture to make the room into a lounge area. It's thought the door in the corridor was one of the two doors taken off the end-of-corridor rooms. It almost certainly was. The Bonds wasted nothing.

When Trevino went into his "suite of rooms" he exclaimed to his agent and manager Derrick Pillage: "What the hell's this!" Derrick recalled: "It was very much a last-minute job. When Trevino arrived and came up to his, so called, suite of rooms, the paint was still wet when he opened the door to his accommodation.

"When Tre went in, I just had to tell him what had happened. Tre just burst out laughing. But that was Martin and Hermon at their very best. They never gave in to anything. They'd never be beaten."

Lee Trevino remained forever amused and bemused, because he had two bathrooms in his "suite of rooms". Back in those days, that was something special!

Chapter 21

THE BITTER BLOW OF THE BLACK OUT

It seemed almost unbelievable that a course and club so young got to stage the 1979 Benson & Hedges International Open. The Bonds had been trying to attract the tournament for some time. They had discussions with B&H special events officials Len Owen and Derrick Pillage, encouraging them to bring the tournament to St Mellion.

They must have been using the right words and giving out the right signals because they were invited by B&H to visit Fulford to see exactly what would be expected of them, if they were to produce a tournament of the standard and stature required.

The organisers of the B&H were looking for something new – and St Mellion was new. The fact that the course had staged the PGA Cup Match in 1978 was a good feather for the Bonds to have in their cap.

The B&H said "yes" and the brothers were ecstatic. They were excited too, at the prospect of national television coverage and the publicity that would give St Mellion. There was a lot of hard work to be done preparing for the event. A huge area had to be levelled out and re-turfed for the tented village. The Bonds did everything they could to accommodate the tournament.

The convoy of ITV lorries and trucks arrived and all the cameras and equipment were put in place. Then the crew came out on strike. The plug was pulled on the eve of the first day's play. The crew and the vehicles pulled out the next morning. This was the start of what was to become a 10-week industrial dispute.

Jon Bond, Martin's eldest son, recalled: "I was nine years old at the time. I remember clear as day all the lorries arriving and then they all went. I got the impression this was something quite major. The whole idea had been to get Press coverage, television coverage, and it disappeared."

Laurie Higgins from Yorkshire Television was in charge of all golf coverage for ITV. Len Owen was Benson & Hedges special events manager: "I had a message to go and see Laurie in his caravan. When I got there he was virtually crying his eyes out. There was to be no television coverage at all because of a strike. It was a huge blow and it upset Hermon and Martin. I always remember the Press doing more interviews than they normally do with us because we were suddenly really important, an important news story because there was no TV coverage."

The producers apologised to the Bonds. The brothers were very sorry for everybody concerned, including themselves.

"We were so close. They were all set up. The cables were out, the cameras were up," said Martin Bond. "You can imagine how B&H felt. They were advertising their brand. That was the job of the golf tournament. We could feel for them as well. But it was a terrible blow for us."

Hermon was less diplomatic: "Now we're buggered."

But there was the bonus of a lot more newspaper coverage because the television cameras were pulling out. Derrick Pillage, who was responsible for promotion and public relations for Benson & Hedges at that tournament, said this was the lowest point of all his years of association with golf publicity, but he came up with an idea.

"I got hold of Plymouth Sound (the local commercial radio station) who were on site and all I had to do was bring in players to be interviewed. The night before the interviews I would go around and get the players' favourite piece of music, so when the presenter asked each player for their favourite piece of music, the radio station already had it there, ready to play in.

"The coverage on Plymouth Sound was excellent and that was linked to London so we had it going out all over the country. I think we had more publicity that way than we would have had if it had been televised nationally."

Because the 1979 B&H at St Mellion was going to be "a one off" away from its home of Fulford, the loss of national publicity through ITV coverage was a hard knock to take.

David Moon, St Mellion golf manager, said: "The strike was nothing to do with the Bond brothers, but the lack of television coverage had a massive effect on the tournament. Knowing Hermon, I wouldn't have liked to be in the room when that news got broken to him. The air around the golf course should have been green, but it would definitely have been blue."

David added that the Bonds were visionaries to get a European Tour event, especially on the old course which, although at the time it was a good golf course, there were other great courses around as well: "But, the lack of television coverage didn't dissuade them at all from their vision to get tour golf down here."

The local Member of Parliament at the time was Robert Hicks. He said it was a great shame that an opportunity to show off St Mellion and its facilities to the nation was lost.

"There was great disappointment. Here we were in the Westcountry getting a genuine national golfing tournament for the first time and it was tremendous to have all the Ryder Cup players coming down to play, the leading UK golfers and some

Europeans and Americans including Lee Trevino. Also, we had the Australian Greg Norman, the White Shark.

"It wasn't televised but it was still an important event because it attracted quite a significant local following from spectators who would also then be aware of this facility here in South East Cornwall."

The event demonstrated for the first time the positive impact St Mellion could have on the local economy. Robert Hicks said Maurice Bembridge, who won the tournament, stayed with his wife and two children at The Tavistock Inn at Gunnislake and Seve Ballesteros's entourage virtually took over The Coachmaker's at Callington. There were numerous other examples of leading golfers staying locally, spending money and contributing to the local economy.

"Plus, we had all the spectators and everything that goes with hosting a tournament of that calibre. The spin-off, the ripple effect for the local economy was very significant indeed."

Englishman Maurice Bembridge won the trophy with an eight under par, 272. Second, two strokes behind, was Scotsman Ken Brown, who one local newspaper journalist likened to a schoolboy in short trousers. Ken has matured a lot since then, but he still looks as young and fresh as ever, and no televised golf coverage should be without his astute and often amusing contributions.

As we said in our preface to this book it is not a "score card" of golf, a book full of statistics, but, on this occasion, we make an exception. Below, you will find some other names from that historic occasion. We mention them because you will already have found, or will find, some of them featuring, for a variety of reasons, elsewhere amongst these pages.

Tony Jacklin came in fifth with a three under par 277. Back in joint 12th was Nick Faldo, with four other players, on level par, 280. At joint 17th with one other player came Manuel Ballesteros, brother of you-know-who, on one over, 281.

Lee Trevino finished joint 19th on two over par, with six others, on 282. At joint 31st, another Scotsman Sandy Lyle, with six others, on four over par, 284. Coming in at joint 42nd was German Bernhard Langer. He, with five others, finished with a six over par 286. And, at joint 57th, with two others on +9, 289, a Spaniard whose ability to swear in English improved dramatically once he'd met the Bond brothers, Severiano Ballesteros. At joint 66th, with 10 others who failed to make the cut was Australian Peter Senior.

The 1979 Benson & Hedges International Open at St Mellion was the first and only time the original course was to host the B&H.

However, the Bond brothers accepted at the time that everything hadn't been quite first class for the event. Because of the lay-out, some things weren't really in the right place. Although the old practice area had been levelled out and re-turfed for the tented village, it was too far away. Everything was, in a way, make shift. It just wasn't right for first class sponsors like Benson & Hedges. The B&H officials concluded that the tournament didn't work as they thought it would and they took the event back to Fulford which was always the intention anyway.

Martin Bond summed it up like this: "It was quite a good tournament but you could see that it was not the same quality as it was at Fulford. It's fair to say the course was not of the same quality the professionals were used to playing on. So, when the B&H told us it wasn't quite what they had wanted, that was fine. We could understand that, accepted it and went on from there."

The Bonds were pleased to have done the best they could, under the circumstances, and they were encouraged by the thousands (30,000 over the four days) who turned up to watch - and surprised by the number of non-golfers who came along.

Of course, when the Bonds started building the Nicklaus course, the Benson and Hedges special events people began looking towards Cornwall again.

Chapter 22

THE BONDS AT DUNSTAN FARM

Hermon and Rachel Bond's wedding was on June 2, 1959, just a few months after they'd got engaged in December. The reason for the short engagement was purely "business". The Bonds wanted the tenancy of Dunstan Farm at St Mellion, way back then, for farming purposes only. But to clinch the deal the landlord insisted someone from the Bond family had to live in the Dunstan Farm farmhouse as soon as possible. So Hermon and Rachel got married, so they could live on the farm. Of course, Dunstan Farm, which the Bond brothers bought many decades later, was to prove pivotal to the creation of the Nicklaus course.

Hermon and Rachel had two sons Alan and Graham who both grew up on the land that was to become so famous later as an International Golf Resort. Their reflections are contained in later chapters.

Chapter 23

THE MEMORIES OF MARTIN'S WIFE AND CHILDREN

"Well, the custard's lumpy, what do we do about it?' – that's how Angela Bond, Martin's wife, reacted when she heard little titbits about how Jack Nicklaus was talking about not having enough land or wanting to change things.

Angela's laid-back approach to it all probably stemmed from the fact that Martin was taking it all in his stride and had a firm rule about not talking "shop" at home – at least not past the bottom of the stairs.

Angela met Martin when she came on a family holiday to stay at Martin's mother Amy's B&B at Trerulefoot. Romance blossomed, when Martin found the time in between his hectic farming commitments, and they married.

Angela said the move towards diversification into golf and leisure was a big challenge: "I was just thinking: 'What are they up to now?' Because everything else had to go on as well, the farming had to go on. So Tony Lister was brought in as farm manager.

"Martin and Hermon were working up to ten o'clock every night at a caravan meeting people who wanted to join the golf club. Our two little ones, Jon who was born in 1970, and Chris, who was born two years later, used to go and sit at the bottom of these huge piles of earth while the course was being built. We would take picnics and Martin would join us if he could. It was great fun.

"For the first event we did at St Mellion we all mucked in and poured cups of coffee and whatever. Alison, our daughter, who was born in 1976, was stuck in a carrycot behind the reception desk. Later she helped WH Bond, William, officially open the clubhouse."

Angela said she was kept busy with a young family and Martin didn't bring the job home with him: "One of his sayings was: 'Never take work past the bottom step of the stairs'. And he didn't and I didn't ask. He was home and it was nice to have him home."

When Martin told Angela he and Hermon wanted Jack Nicklaus to design a course for them she thought: "Here we go again! When we went to the States we were going for a nice holiday, it wasn't just a business trip."

When the course was officially opened by Jack Nicklaus on the 10th of July 1988 Angela was very keen to follow Nicklaus, Tom Watson, Nick Faldo and Sandy Lyle round the course: "I'm not really into hero worship or that sort of thing but it was a spectacular day – and we got wet through."

During the Benson & Hedges years on the Nicklaus course, Angela, like many others, was particularly taken by the young, dark, dashing Seve Ballesteros.

Angela summed up her feelings: "I admire what Martin and Hermon have done. It's amazing. Before St Mellion they'd had pigs and potatoes which were time-consuming and then they did something else which was time-consuming in a different way. And it all stems from, in particular, their mother Amy being very strong-minded. I think that's gone through the family. She was the brains, the organiser, and father, W H, William Hermon, was the worker.

"It's the work ethos and ethic of the Bond family. The word Bond means peasant and worker. Martin and Hermon made a brilliant team. Martin would sometimes have to 'pick up the pieces' after Hermon had said something to somebody. But he did it without it being too obvious and with patience. He didn't suffer fools gladly. He didn't say anything unless he'd got something to say. Generous, thoughtful, caring."

Martin and Angela's elder son Jon remembered that in his early teens he'd be working on the farm and also at St Mellion, helping at the tournaments, painting the stakes which were used to carry the ropes for crowd control: "Later we realised it was better to put the stakes in the ground first and then paint them because you didn't need to paint so much of the stake."

He was also a score runner, taking the results from the Press box to BBC radio commentator Renton Laidlaw.

When Jon's father and Uncle Hermon went to the States to meet Jack Nicklaus, Jon was more interested in the fact that they were flying by Concorde or what was growing in the field in front of the farmhouse. But he did get to fly Concorde on a family holiday a few years later.

Jon's favourite memory of Uncle Hermon was him driving into the yard at Bake Farm, which the Bonds had been tenants of for years.

"He said in some colourful language: 'Why's the end of that building falling down? Get the land agent out and get it fitted up'.

"I said: 'Well, you own the farm'. They'd bought the farm but he omitted to remember that. The 500 acre farm was his and the land agent was, in fact, himself. That was just how Uncle Hermon was. There had to be somebody to blame and it certainly wasn't going to be him."

Jon said his father believed in sheer hard work: "He had lots of very, very good ideas but they were backed up with some really hard work. He was able to keep his head in some difficult circumstances over planning issues and things like that. Having seen him go through that and watching what happened, I don't think we would put ourselves through it. We've seen how high the hurdles can end up being."

Jon said his father and Uncle Hermon made an excellent team and that had gone through to Jon, Chris and Alison: "Us three are very together but very different and you can use each person's skills for different situations. That's what father and uncle did so well. Hermon would sack a member of staff, say Tony Barriball, six times in one day when he was building the golf course but Tony didn't leave because he knew when father turned up he would 'reinstate' him.

"As much as the Bond family did it, you can only do it with the people who work for you. People like Tony Barriball, who worked for us for nearly 40 years, every day of the week, and several other people like that through the years who were Bond through and through. If you cut them with a knife it would be Bond blood in there. You've got to have people like that to help you get through. They were as much instrumental in carrying it through some of the difficulty times.

"The Nicklaus course is in my mind one of the best in the world. It is outstanding. It's a great tribute and testament to the hard work of father, Uncle Hermon and those around them - and it will be there for a long time."

Jon's younger brother Chris was just three years old and full of uncontrollable excitement when the original clubhouse at St

Mellion was under construction. The footings had been dug and the blockwork was done.

"I found a little brown cow on the site of the footprint of the building. One of those tiny Britain toys. It was a heifer. I brought it home and used it in my farm set. She became part of the herd, but I never gave her a name. That's my earliest memory of St Mellion," Chris said.

Many years later, what did Chris make of his Uncle Hermon? "A complete character, larger than life. He'd fill up any room. As soon as he walked in everyone knew he was there. If there were 30 or 40 people in the social club at Callington, everyone knew he'd arrived. He didn't say anything, they just knew he was there. A great presence, a massive presence."

Jon added that his uncle took great pleasure in winding him up: "He used to put the six pence pieces in the huge Christmas pudding the family shared and everyone used to get a few in their piece. But one year there were so many in the piece I had, it might have been 20, it felt like my teeth were falling out because I kept biting into coins.

"The next year I was expecting the same, so I was really careful and then I was quite disappointed when I didn't find any. But Uncle Hermon had rolled up a pound note, put it in instead and made sure I got that piece. I've still got the note, it's got Christmas pudding stains all over it."

Hermon was the extrovert, Martin was the quiet thinker. Chris put it this way: "Dad was always the calming influence and would get to the same end as Uncle Hermon but through a different route. Uncle was the hammer and chisel, dad was the sandpaper. Dad had a brilliant mind. You could see, even in his latter years, as he walked across the fields with the dogs his mind was ticking all the time – and he'd pretty much always be right. That's probably why it all worked for him and Uncle

Hermon at St Mellion because, although they were brothers, they were very different people.

"What they did at St Mellion was mind blowing, to the complete extreme. To go and get Jack Nicklaus, the Tiger Woods of that era, drag him back to little old Cornwall, ask him to design a course on the worst bit of land you've ever seen in your life and him say: 'Ok then'. It's just beyond comprehension. That's how they were. They were just driven by doing the best things really. It had to be the best, the best course in the country, the best person to build it.

"They took rough farmland and created this massive facility which was completely unique and at least 10 years ahead of its time. Entrepreneurs to the end, absolutely incredible."

Chris added these profound words: "If you're doing what you're doing, you don't perhaps appreciate what you have done. People would ask members of the Bond family about meeting so and so, doing this and doing that, building this and that, and the answer would be: 'Well, at the time we just did it'. I think that's always been a family thing – we just get on and do things. It's no big deal until someone mentions it.

"But to look back and see all the photos and memorabilia about St Mellion, it's great to think it is known world wide."

Alison Bond was the first girl in the family for years and years, several generations. She was pictured as a small child with granddad W H Bond outside the clubhouse when W H officially opened the building. Not for him a fancy curtain to draw back to reveal the plaque commemorating the occasion, just a bit of cardboard stuck on with tape which he pulled off the wall.

"I've seen the picture and in a way you build a memory on that image," said Alison. "So much so that we made sure the plaque was removed when the clubhouse was altered and made copies of it for dad and Uncle Hermon's wife, Auntie Rachel."

During the tournaments and Pro-Ams Alison met lots of famous people but it was all part of it.

"A lot of the time it was just saying 'hello' but when you think 'I've been kissed by Seve Ballesteros'. I was working at reception at the time and dad introduced me. I'd watch Dad standing up at tournament presentations - and that would not be his favourite place to be by any means."

Alison added that she was very proud of the massive achievements of her Dad and Uncle: "I think, in the world that it is now and everything so fast and a lot easier with communication and everything else, if you look back to when they actually did it, it makes it even more impressive.

"I know they wouldn't have known any different but for us to look back on what they did, they were forward-thinking. They wanted to build something massive and did it to a really high standard. But they didn't make a big thing about it.

"And we didn't know any different. That's what we were born into. For us, in terms of W H Bond, you work the hours to make sure things happen."

Chapter 24

ALAN BOND – ANOTHER BOND, ANOTHER EXTRAORDINARY LIFE

Alan Hermon Bond was a stunningly handsome Cornishman - 6ft 4ins tall, at his fittest and best 225lbs of solid rock, fair hair and sparkling, shining, piercing blue eyes. Eyes not unlike those of his hero Jack Nicklaus. It came to pass that these pairs of eyes were to meet one day – as the two men sat on a bench at Nicklaus's Muirfield Village golf course at Dublin, Ohio. Alan had got there, in a roundabout way, thanks to Starsky and Hutch and Kojak.

Alan, elder brother to Graham, had come a long way – in miles and professionally – from his days on father Hermon's Dunston Farm at St Mellion in South East Cornwall. His maturing good looks were matched only by his smile, strong character and determination to achieve his goals and ambitions, thanks to the love and influence of his father and mother, Rachel.

Alan was extraordinary. He wasn't a Hermon. He wasn't a Graham. He had an immense individual presence of his own. He was, in no particular order, enthusiastic, sharp, knowledgeable, warm, funny, sincere, soft-spoken, humble, gentlemanly.

Alan looked back with affection to his childhood: "It was always interesting, even before the golf came along. Dad and Uncle Martin worked very well together as brothers. Brothers would fall out over this and that, but I don't remember much of that. I just feel lucky that, through mum and dad, I had a good upbringing. I know what right and wrong is. If I choose to do something that's not quite right, I know I'm doing wrong. A lot of kids these days, I don't think they know what right and wrong is."

People often asked Alan why he went to the States? His reply: "I watched a lot of Starsky and Hutch and Kojak when I was a kid." Those posing the question would often laugh at Alan's answer but, seriously, Cornwall was too quiet for him. On the television, America was big and exciting and Alan had dreams to go there. But there was no magic carpet or free rides.

"So I worked for 25 pence an hour for dad. I would just work all the time on the farm, doing anything. We had pigs, so I had to take care of them which is not very pleasant in the summer time. There was always something to do on a farm. Then I went over to Uncle Martin's farm at Trerulefoot and he paid me the same. I earned £250 at 25p an hour, that's 1,000 hours. I thought I was rich!"

Freddy Laker had just started the £99 one-way flights to America. So Alan, in his very late teens, packed his rucksack, bought his ticket and flew across The Pond. He went to Miami, where everyone was a stranger and he didn't have a job.

"I realised what money I had left over wouldn't go that far so I was looking around for work and got it – on a golf course, on the green staff at Bay Hill, Arnold Palmer's course in Florida. They didn't want to employ me because they didn't think I, being English, could keep up in the heat. But I was told to slow down by the other workers because I was making them look bad," said Alan.

"Then I ended up at Jack Nicklaus's Muirfield Village at Dublin, Ohio. I slept under a bridge that first night, washed in the river the next morning, hid my rucksack behind the main sign, walked through the front door and asked for a job in the kitchen. I didn't have any work visas at the time, so they didn't want me to work in the restaurant as such. They told me to go downstairs to see the caddy master. I got hired for caddying and met some of the caddies there and they put me up in their place. That's what I did until the end of the summer. I didn't know at the time that my dad and uncle were negotiating for Nicklaus to design a course at St Mellion. It was a sheer coincidence that I happened to end up at his place."

Alan came back to Cornwall and then returned to Muirfield in April the following year. He was caddying on an exhibition day when Nicklaus played three holes with one group and three with another group and so on. Jack was now aware of who Alan was, but they hadn't met face to face. However, and Alan doesn't know how it happened, he found himself sitting on a bench and next to him was Nicklaus himself.

"There was nobody within 180 yards. He was just asking me questions. I was overawed. He's my hero and you're young, naïve and you're sitting next to a legend. It was very big for me. When you meet Nicklaus he's shorter than you think he is and his voice is very high-pitched. It's a different image from when you see him on television where he's larger than real life. He has small, blue, piercing eyes that stare right through you, which is intimidating. But, if you stare and look right back at people like Jack they respect that. They're so used to having their own way, they like to listen to people who stand up for themselves as well.

"Muirfield is a very impressive place. There are no leaves on the fairways. They have blowers that blow the leaves off. The water's blue. It's all manicured. There's one type of grass. The greens, the bunkers are fantastic. Not like anything you see growing up and playing golf in Cornwall or England.

"Nicklaus just looked at me and said: 'Would your dad like something like this in Cornwall?' Of course I beamed and said 'Yes'."

Later, when Alan's parents, brother Graham and Uncle Martin came over to meet Nicklaus at Muirfield, Alan soon got the feeling that re-creating what was there back in Cornwall was definitely something the Bonds could – and would - do. Everything they saw excited them and gave them ideas about what they could achieve.

"Dad and uncle got Jack at a good time. I think he was looking to expand. I don't know how many offers he would have had but I believe this was his second course in Europe. The first one was in Spain and that one didn't go very well," said Alan.

After the original course was built at St Mellion, Alan took up golf and played the course with his father. But the Nicklaus course was going to be something else. Alan saw it for the first time when he came home after being away for about five years. By then, it was built and finished.

Alan recalled: "The bus dropped me off in the village early in the morning and I just started walking across the course. It was absolutely unbelievable for me to see what I remember as a kid as farmland and to see what was here. I stopped and turned around and thought: 'I'm going to have dad show me this. I can't be walking round here by myself'.

"Dad did take me round – pointing things out, explaining everything. I could see him looking out the side of his eye just to see my reaction. I was amazed by what I saw. I'd travelled quite a bit and I'd seen other places and this stands up to pretty much anything you could see in the world. When you see what was here in the first place, to drill the sides of hills, to have a building site to put a hole in. Thoroughly impressed and proud that this was something that my dad and uncle had done. Here we are in Cornwall. Stuck out in the middle of nowhere but look what's been achieved."

Hermon wanted Alan to stay and work, and he did for a year,

as assistant manager in the club – years earlier he'd been to Torquay College to study hotel and catering management. But Alan, in his mid-twenties, still had, what he called "a little bit of travel lust." His parents, Hermon and Rachel, were bitterly disappointed and unhappy that he returned to the States. Alan understood how they felt, but he still had places to go, things to see, things to do.

Uncle Martin was able to take a more detached and less emotional view. He told Alan: "You've got to make yourself happy because if you aren't happy you can't make anybody else happy and, in those circumstances, you ain't worth anything to us here." That made Alan feel better, but he always appreciated what his parents had done for him.

"Dad took me out to Portugal and we played nine holes with Henry Cotton and I had a lesson. It would have been nice to stay with him for a month or so. I hit the ball good but, at the end of the day, I wasn't anywhere near good enough. But I still wanted to be 'in golf' so that's why I caddied," said Alan.

He became a professional caddy on the PGA Golf Tour in 1985. The first tournament he won was the Memorial at Nicklaus's Muirfield Village with David Edwards who he also caddied for to win the RBC Heritage Classic at Hilton Head, South Carolina. Alan won the Canadian Open with David Frost and the Australian Masters with Bradley Hughes. He also caddied for Jack Nicklaus, Tom Weiskopf, John Daly, Jose Maria Olazabal and about 60 others and went on to work with Scottish professional Martin Laird.

This is how Alan summed up his caddying career of more than 30 years: "It was exciting and the travelling was exciting, a different town every week. It's not a hard job, but not everybody can walk off the street and do it. A lot of it is judging the player's emotions. They change once they get inside the ropes. They're very emotional. Some guys will keep it in and others will blow up and let it all out – and you're right there! So, you're ideal to be blamed or whatever, even if it's not your fault. That's all fine if they get it out of their system and hit the next one closer. That's what it's all about. The better they did, the more money I'd make. You get a salary and a percentage of their winnings. So, the better they do.... I'm definitely my guy's number one fan, so if you're rooting for him to hit it in the water, it's time to go and get another job."

And this is how Alan defined his father and Uncle Martin and what they achieved: "The image they liked to portray was a couple of Cornish boy farmers just mixing it up. There was a lot to that. That's where they were from. They started off as Cornish farmers and then they had to diversify because they could see farming wasn't going to be that good and I think my gran had told them they had to change and go into something else.

"They certainly did that! I've travelled quite a bit and I've caddied, not all around the world, but I've been to Africa, to Thailand, Australia a few times and all over America. The Nicklaus Course at St Mellion stands up to pretty much anything I've seen in the rest of the world. This is an absolutely fantastic resort. I'm very proud of my uncle and my dad."

Alan lived in Dallas, Texas, with his wife Kay and their daughter Anna Grace. He died, at home, in November 2017, aged 56, after bravely battling Acute Myeloid Leukaemia.

A memorial service to celebrate Alan's life was held at St Mellion Church on 3rd January 2018 which was attended by family and friends. Many a happy tale was exchanged at the reception held later that day at the Club.

Co-author Paddy Flavin recalled how Alan would always make time to dine with him and his wife Sue whenever they visited a tournament at which Alan was working. In fact the Waste Management Open in Phoenix and The Northern Trust Open in

Los Angeles became annual meeting points invariably with Alan staying in their apartment. A dear friend much missed.

Chapter 25

AFTER THE FIRST B&H in 1979

Under the stewardship of Martin Watson and David Webb the club continued to thrive by growing membership numbers, hosting weddings, parties and other functions. Corporate golf days proved to be a good source of revenue due to the burgeoning reputation of the course as a true Championship venue. The Brothers entrusted the day to day management to their team as they had a much loftier vision for the resort. With the addition of a Time Share Village to the site St Mellion was fast becoming a destination resort.

In 1983 and 1984 St Mellion hosted the Tournament Players' Championship. The 1983 winner was Bernhard Langer. Jaime Gonzales won in 1984.

The championships were arranged by the Bonds and the PGA. In the first year, the Bonds put up the prize money - £80,000. The timeshare village was under way. There was planning permission for 50 properties. The Bonds built the first six themselves, but selling timeshare wasn't their scene, so they brought in the well-known building company Henry Boot of Sheffield. The firm helped finance the second Tournament Players' Championship. It put up the prize money, £95,000, and the Bonds put in the same, if not more, in terms of meeting all the costs of the event. The publicity was good and a lot of spectators came to watch.

Chapter 26

GOOD TIMING

One fine morning Professor James Mowbray (more about the professor bit later), a member at St Mellion, was playing the original course when he came up to the top of a hill, looked down and saw some building work going on.

At lunchtime he saw Hermon Bond and asked him what was going on. Hermon said they were building a timeshare village and produced a brochure which had been typed on a typewriter with a ribbon which should have been replaced three or four years before.

It was 1983 and later that year, in October, James and his family came down to decide on which timeshare property they wanted and which weeks: "They were building the first four houses and we decided we wanted number four, the one which sticks out in front of the others. It was the best. We rushed to get the weeks we wanted before anybody else got them - the half-term weeks in May and October, for 80 years."

So James Mowbray holds the accolade of being the first owner at the St Mellion Timeshare Village by being the first person to buy any weeks. He also became the chairman of the timeshare owners' group.

James first came to St Mellion during the 1979 Benson & Hedges because he was on holiday with his wife Sheila and their sons at Maker, on the Rame Peninsula in South East Cornwall, something they'd been doing for many years. Another holidaymaker, who had become a friend over the years, told him about the B&H at St Mellion.

"He said it was on a new course and we went that afternoon, the Saturday, and again for the final day on the Sunday. It was lovely weather. St Mellion back then was still the farms and an awful lot of the course was composed of the edges to the farm fields and in the middle were three or four buildings which were the centre of the farm with the golf course round it.

"Lee Trevino thought the whole thing was a great joke from start to finish. I stood behind him on the 17th tee and there was a tree in the middle of the fairway, a bit of farm hedge and the club professional's house sticking out beyond that. Trevino said: 'It's crazy, but it's made for me'. He hit one of his Lee Trevino 'bananas' which bent round everything. I was amazed."

James added that he now had another golf course to play when he came down on holiday and gradually he got to know Hermon and Martin: "Together they were farming brothers, brought up in farming. The growth of them as businessmen was quite amusing to look at because they weren't typical businesspeople. Their potato crops paid for the clubhouse. This place was born and bred on potatoes. It was a remarkable thing. Their vision was tremendous."

James played golf regularly with Martin and Hermon, but also with their brother Jim: "He was the best golfer of the three, but he had a problem at St Mellion because he looked very much like Martin although he was a little bit heavier.

"Jim told me he didn't like being around here too much because people thought he was Martin and would come up and talk to him, thinking he was Martin. He felt a bit bashful about that so he tended not to come here to play golf very much in case he was mistaken for his brother Martin."

ROYAL FOOTNOTE: Back to the professor bit. James Mowbray was Professor of Immunopathology at St Mary's Hospital Medical School, London. Immunopathology is a branch of medicine concentrating on immune responses associated with diseases. One area he specialised in was cases of women who suffered repeated miscarriages, most commonly attributed to an immunological cause. Princess Diana was the sponsor of one of the big gynaecological obstetric charities and some of the work done in the gynaecology department at St Mary's and in James Mowbray's department.

The Princess was coming to look round his department. The visit was being organised by the Queen's gynaecologist Sir George Pinker who told James to do his best to keep his complicated work as simple as possible so Diana could understand it. But Diana had done her homework and had even phoned Sir George on the eve of the visit to find out more about James.

"I was a bit worried, but Diana was absolutely fine, as bright as a button," said James. "I was showing her round the exhibits on display for the day and explaining things to her. It became very apparent very quickly that I wasn't going to get the chance to finish a sentence. She knew what I was going to say. She was very knowledgeable.

"The only thing she was unsure about was her gait. The floor had been polished to a shine for her visit and she told me she was concerned that she might slip in her stilettos and go 'ass overhead' in front of the Press and media."

Chapter 27

I'LL DRINK TO THAT!

The Brazilian golfer Jamie Gonzales came to St Mellion for the 1984 Timeshare Tournament Players' Championship. Not that many people knew much about the young player, but by the end of the first day, they did. He was in the lead.

That evening he went to the bar – and he was drinking quite a lot. And it wasn't pints of shandy. It was hard stuff, like Tequila. St Mellion bar staff were confidently predicting that Gonzales wouldn't repeat his performance on the second day because of the impressive amount of alcohol he'd put away.

But, by the end of day two, there Gonzales was, still ahead of the rest of the field and, that evening and night, in the bar again, drinking heartily. At the end of the third day he was still in the lead and enjoying himself in the bar.

On day four, in his final round, he made a mess of things on the 17th. He needed a four on the 18th to tie with Mark James, which he did. And then he won the playoff.

Amateur golfers who enjoy a drink may take some heart from this story. Perhaps they should try it and see if it improves their game. Maybe it would be more advisable to go into the club bar on an evening during a professional tournament and count the number of pros leaning on the bar counter. Usually the total is zero!

Chapter 28

NICKLAUS COMES TO CORNWALL TO CLIMB "THE MOUNTAIN"

"This is going to be a big bucks job." - That was the initial reaction of Jack Nicklaus on his first of many visits to St Mellion to design a championship golf course for the Bond brothers Martin and Hermon. It was the summer of 1982, just a few weeks after they had gone to America to tell Nicklaus face-to-face that they meant business. But the land they had might as well have been on the moon.

Hermon said: "It was like a mountain. It would have been easier to design a course on the moon. So we thought we had better invite him, personally, to come and see for himself before we got too far down the road. We knew he would probably have never seen anything like it before."

Nicklaus had already sent top people from his team to take a look but, nevertheless, he agreed to check it out. Martin said: "I think, when he met us at the club for the first time, he wondered where we'd come from! But I think it was a challenge to him and, after seeing the land, he knew it was a challenge."

Nicklaus was to embrace the St Mellion dream - as a challenge to relish. The brothers' meeting with him back in May that year at his Muirfield Village Golf Club, Dublin, Columbus, Ohio had been social, warm and friendly. But this was different. Hard, straight, tough talking. This is how the conversation went: The Bond Brothers: "This is what we want, can you do it?" Nicklaus: "Fine, it's going to be very expensive. This is a big bucks job. Do you realise what you've taken on?" The Brothers: "Yes. You design it. We'll build it." And, of course, they did, but only after a very committed Nicklaus went out of his way to play his part. He gave a talk to local people, invited guests, parish councillors and others. He was very relaxed and forthcoming, had pictures taken with everyone and he was very accommodating. He wasn't "licking up" to people because he was never like that. Those who met him saw he was determined and committed, just like the brothers he was designing the course for.

At the time one member of the Press wrote that £25,000 a hole was the minimum estimate for a worthwhile course, but the one Nicklaus was designing at St Mellion was to be £100,000 a hole! (And the rest) It was a lot of money. Hermon added: "I mean, we moved mountains, and that's what we did – made valleys into flat areas of land." The Bonds had asked Nicklaus to do a job for them and it didn't prove too hard to get him to do that job, simply because he wanted to.

Martin added: "We had some so-called experts there but they soon fell by the wayside. It boiled down to Jack and his people he wanted there and Hermon and me. That was it, there was no one else. We didn't use 'the experts', we used mainly ourselves. Sometimes it can be a problem doing it yourself. We should have stood one step back perhaps, but we didn't. We met Jack Nicklaus and organised it ourselves. I think he knew he was doing it for us and that was the way it went."

Chapter 29

WHAT HAPPENED BEFORE

The brothers had wanted to expand St Mellion and to do that they needed to build another golf course. The "old" course had been up and running for about five years and all the club's sporting facilities were in place. They'd had the Benson and Hedges International Open for one year only in 1979, but the event wouldn't come back again because the course wasn't of a high enough standard or tough enough to challenge the Tour players. The Bonds thought they'd better do something about it. So then it came down to who was going to design the second course? They thought they might just as well start at the top. Nicklaus was the man for the job.

"It was a name and we thought a name would help give us publicity, put us on the map, which we needed, specially being in Cornwall," said Hermon. Along with Martin, he decided to have the best. There was no good having a mediocre designer. They wanted a name that would make people sit up and want to come to St Mellion. They insisted on going to the top golfer and designer. Back then, Nicklaus was in his prime. Nicklaus didn't know it, but his first UK course would be at St Mellion. The brothers had made their mind up. Going after him would never be a road too long. Their target was fixed. Their goal was set. They were not to be thwarted. It wasn't a question of taking the risk that he might actually say "no". They never thought for a second that he would reject them.

So Chuck Perry, a leading member of the Nicklaus team, came to St Mellion to see if the land would suit Jack's purposes. He was at the time Jack Nicklaus's business partner and the president and chief executive officer of Golden Bear International. To the relief of the brothers, who owned 260 acres at St Mellion, Chuck formed the opinion there was enough land available to do the job. That was music to the ears of the brothers.

But, sometime later Jay Morrish, another member of the Nicklaus team and a very good golf course architect, came to take a look. He turned to Martin and Hermon and announced: "You haven't got enough land!" It wasn't what the Bonds wanted to hear and it could have been a very serious set-back, but the brothers were determined. Nothing was going to stop them. They bought Dunstan Farm which Hermon was renting at the time. The 160 acres was an old Pentillie Estate farm that had been sold to the Fisons Pension Fund. The Bonds didn't need it all, but they bought the lot anyway.

Their lawyer Edward Andreae-Jones said: "We had to go out and buy the whole farm. It was wise to buy it all. If we'd gone and said we just wanted that particular bit they'd have realised we wanted it for a purpose and charged us the earth, so we bought the whole."

Ten acres of woodland was also acquired from Prince Charles via the Duchy of Cornwall. The Duchy land steward was Jack Hickish who was based at the Duchy offices in Station Road, Liskeard, just beyond the railway station. "Jack Hickish knew what we were after. We went to his office and sat round a table, talked about it and did the deal there and then," said Hermon.

And there was more land again, a couple of acres from Mushton Farm for the 5th fairway and some land from Keason Woods. Martin and Hermon also bought 14 acres on the edge of the village of St Mellion from Raymond Martin. The deal was they'd buy a tractor from Ray on condition he sold them the bit of land.

The land was needed for the 10th green area. The extra land totalled around 200 acres. It brought the entire acreage of the St Mellion complex and courses to more than 450. The brothers often had a chuckle about Chuck Perry's initial view that the original 260 acres they had would be enough.

The Bonds, through their local bank manager in Liskeard, re-established contact with Bill Warman, by then a regional director of Barclays. The procedure the Bonds had to follow when it came to financing the Nicklaus course was that any applications for loans – and some of them were pretty substantial – went to Barclays Bank in Liskeard, then the Exeter regional office and, if need be, to the bank's head office in London's Lombard Street.

"Locally and at regional level we were very supportive of any application by the Bonds and I don't think in head office there was a great deal of people against it," said Bill.

"There was an adage in the old days that people coming up in banking were always taught. It was: 'You shouldn't put a man on the bottom of a ladder if you aren't prepared to see him off at the top'. Kicking a man off a ladder half way up doesn't do anybody any good. What good is half a job to anybody.

"You might think the clients can do that job for £2 million, it's bound to be alright. But if something crops up, like they hit rock or granite somewhere, you can't say: 'Oh well, we lent you £2 million, sod it, we're walking away now and its money down the drain'. It's just not the way to do business.

"So once a business was on the bottom rung of the ladder we were going to stay with them if it was possible. You had to use your common sense."

Bill said knowing the Bonds from earlier was a vital factor.

"People are everything. People are what you deal with. Knowing the brothers from my brief time as manager of the Liskeard branch was helpful. If you start from a position where you know the people and you know what's going on, you can make an informed decision. Perhaps, now-a-days, if you put all the facts and figures on a computer you may not get the same decision because you don't know the people involved. In the old days it was a relationship and you backed people to do what they were trying to do."

Bill added that when Jack Nicklaus decided to put his name to the Nicklaus course, he was going to get it right. He wanted to spend more than Martin and Hermon wanted to spend. There was pressure for more money to be spent than was originally budgeted.

"There was a risk attached to it. But it wasn't that much of a risk if you could see yourself what was being done, you knew who was behind it and you knew the complex."

There was one particular occasion when the Bonds needed a very, very significant amount of money. Bill had to tell them it was outside of his area of control and he would have to refer it up the line to head office in Lombard Street.

"I told the brothers all I could do was represent the case as strongly as I could. I knew at the other end that the people up there in London were thinking it was a lot of money. But you make your own track record too. You're dealing with London perhaps every day on behalf of customers like Westland Helicopters and Brittany Ferries and, if you've got it right many times before, those in Lombard Street are more prepared to say they'd agree it if I thought it was alright.

"If I wasn't sure that Martin and Hermon were making bloody sure that everybody else was working to the limit to support them, then that would decrease my certainty that I should be supporting them myself.

"I wouldn't say that the bank bailed the Bonds out. I wouldn't put it like that but certainly there was no question that, like many, many, many businesses, when you start off, you budget, you know what it's going to cost and sometimes for reasons outside your control you get over budget."

Bill added that, many times, particularly during the construction of the Nicklaus course, he left his office in Exeter to drive down to St Mellion to see first-hand the challenges the Bonds were confronted with.

"Either they ran into a type of countryside that was harder to excavate than anybody thought and it cost them a lot more, or they would strike a spring somewhere which would add to the cost. There was never a time that they were telling lies about their problems, but I needed to see the problems for myself.

"The Nicklaus course did cost a bit more than the Bond brothers wanted it to cost, but in the end Jack Nicklaus was very pleased with it. It's a real cracking golf course."

Bill said there was never an occasion when he thought the project would fail: "There were times when I thought we were running up a bit of a fair figure and that sort of thing but once you got down to 'why' and realised the money wasn't being wasted.....if they hit a chunk of granite and it was going to cost X thousands of pounds to move it to make a fairway and you're half way through doing it, there's not much you can do about it but crack on!"

"So I was always ready to help them and always strongly supportive. I look back and I'm very pleased to have had a hand in something that turned out to be a success. And that, really, is what life's all about. It isn't knocking people down, it's about helping them get on the way. One of the most satisfying things is if you're lucky enough to get involved in a business and you can make money for your employer, in my case the bank, and make somebody else money - then what better job could you have."

Meanwhile, Martin and Hermon were impatient and wanted to get on with things, but buying the land took time. But, they got there. Everything was in place, so they sent this message to Nicklaus: "We've got more land."

This all happened before Martin and Hermon, their wives Angela and Rachel and Hermon and Rachel's younger son Graham flew Concorde to Kennedy Airport for the historic meeting with Jack in Ohio in May 1982. The visit was also a chance for the Bonds to try and absorb the magnitude of the task they were taking on. They were to have their eyes opened very wide as to what could be achieved.

Chuck Perry told the Bonds that meeting Jack was only part of the plan. They needed to see what he'd accomplished with some of his other courses. Flights were arranged for a 1,500 mile, three-day round trip to Austin Texas, Birmingham Alabama and West Virginia.

"We were very impressed because the Americans don't do it by halves and these were all championship courses. We expected them to be top class – and they were," said Hermon.

"We just thought, if only Jack could do something like that for us, then our vision would become reality," commented Martin.

Martin modestly summed up the involvement of Jack Nicklaus in St Mellion: "I honestly believe there was nothing smart in what we did. We were just fortunate that he wanted to come this way. I honestly believe that there's nothing that Hermon or I did to make it happen. We could build it up into all sorts of things but I do really believe it was a question of 'right time, right place'. It was a great coup for us, and Cornwall, to be the home of his first course in the United Kingdom. It was American ideas and American design. I think the owners of other golf clubs were afraid of it. They weren't prepared to pay the fees, the price, that was the problem. It sounds blasé, but with having Jack Nicklaus as the course designer, it was just another day's work."

And Hermon said this: "He was somebody we were employing to do a job, that's all it was to us. It's Jack Nicklaus, fine. He was a wonderful golfer but he was also a golf course architect who we were paying to do a job. A lot of people seem to be afraid of celebrity-type people. But, he was a normal boy as far as we were concerned – and a very nice one too. I think he appreciated that we had no airs or graces and were ordinary, hardworking Cornish people, but I think at times he wondered where he had landed up."

AMERICAN VISIT FOOTNOTE 1: During the Pro-Am before the Memorial Tournament at Muirfield Village, Hermon and Rachel were standing by the 18th green when Lee Trevino finished his round. Hermon said: "Lee, do you remember me?" Trevino, fast as a bullet, replied: "Hello Mr Bond. How's your brother?" It made their day to think that Trevino had remembered them from three years before at the 1979 Benson & Hedges at St Mellion.

FOOTNOTE 2: May 31 - Hermon and Martin played the tournament course at Muirfield Village exactly as it had been laid out for the final day's play. Hermon's son Alan caddied for them. According to Rachel's scrapbook, Hermon went round in 91, with a two at the 12th and a three at the 14th.

FOOTNOTE 3: June 2 was Martin's 48th birthday and Rachel and Hermon's 23rd wedding anniversary.

FOOTNOTE 4: The Bonds had planned to sail home on the QE2 but the Prime Minister Margaret Thatcher had commandeered the luxury liner for the Falklands Conflict, so they flew home as they had flown out - in Concorde.

Chapter 30

GOING TO THE TOP – IN THE MIDDLE OF THE NIGHT

It was proving to be a very long night in the corridors of power at Westminster. It was a very late sitting. Members of Parliament were going through the voting lobbies quite regularly – vote after vote.

Walking through together, chatting, were Environment Secretary Michael Heseltine and Minister of Agriculture Peter Walker. South East Cornwall MP Robert Hicks saw his opportunity to pounce and, potentially, bring to an end a lingering impasse and avoid a delay of perhaps 18 months in a decision on the plans for the Jack Nicklaus course at St Mellion, along with the housing development.

"I'd been bullying their junior ministers for months for a decision, so I decided that here was my chance to go to the very top," he said.

Robert Hicks looked on Messers Heseltine and Walker not only as colleagues but also as friends. So he interrupted them, very nicely of course, and explained the situation at St Mellion.

The proposals for the Nicklaus course and up-market housing to help finance it were going through the planning process. But times had changed since the approval of the original plans for the Old course and clubhouse because, by the early eighties,

County Structure Plans were in place and the proposals by Martin and Hermon Bond were contrary to the Cornwall Structure Plan.

Caradon District Council approved the proposals in principle but, because the plans went against the structure plan, Environment Secretary Michael Heseltine had to decide one of two things. Was he going to "call in" the application, which meant taking the decision out of the hands of the local authority and getting his department to rule on the plans? Or, was he going to leave the decision to the local council?

The former would mean a public inquiry and a delay of, perhaps, a year to 18 months, in the final decision being made. And all this was in the balance at a time when Mr Heseltine was advocating speeding up the planning process and leaving decision-making to local authorities.

The Bonds were waiting, impatiently, to hear which way Michael Heseltine was going to go. Hermon, in particular, was getting very frustrated. He would, regularly, badger the MP, with an ample splattering of expletives: "What's goin' on up there boy? Can't they make their minds up?"

One reason for the delay was that the Environment Department had to consult with the Ministry of Agriculture because grade 2 farming land was involved in the scheme.

Robert Hicks explained: "A stalemate had developed which dragged on for months. There was this hiatus, a delay, a real classic 'Yes Minister' episode, no one prepared to make a decision. Junior ministers passing bits of paper around over the issue and getting nowhere. This was perhaps for me the only 'lowlight' in the story of the development of St Mellion because I realised the implications of the delay. The expansion was a necessary, essential step forward and nothing was happening. I was getting very frustrated because Martin and Hermon were on my back, quite rightly as constituents, because obviously the delay was affecting their timetable and, no doubt, their financing of the project, particularly in respect of the housing because that was to help finance the golf course."

So, the MP saw his chance to confront the two top men – in the middle of the night.

"They were either very sympathetic to me or feeling a bit tired as we dragged our way through the lobbies voting that night, but they promised me that they would have a look at it together," he said.

"I shall never forget it. Within 24 hours I actually had a telephone call, not from Peter Walker's private secretary, but from Peter himself, saying that the Ministry of Agriculture had withdrawn, what was technically called, their provisional objection over the question of the farmland and that Michael Heseltine had decided not to 'call in' the application.

"I remember ringing Hermon to tell him the good news. He was surprised and flabbergasted but obviously extremely relieved. It was a highly significant moment."

Chapter 31

PROTECTING THE TAMAR VALLEY

Not everyone locally was enamoured with the idea of granting planning permission for a second golf course together with an extensive housing development.

The Tamar Protection Society was one of the most vociferous objectors to some of the major proposals for St Mellion. Jack Spiers joined the organisation in the mid-to-late seventies and went on to become its chairman. He and his wife actually joined the club purely to use the swimming pool. He remembered meeting Hermon Bond when he went to the caravan before the clubhouse was built to register their names.

But when the Bonds wanted a second golf course, the Nicklaus course, Jack and the society objected strongly.

"The thing that got up my personal nostrils was how was it that a second golf course could be developed at quite considerable expense and who was paying for it. Then, of course, eventually it all comes out that it is all on the back of planning permission being granted for housing. That is the thing that got to me and it still does to a certain extent that there seemed to be nothing in Caradon District Council's planning rules, regulations and strategy that actually permitted housing on golf courses.

"Here we had a case of a golf course being granted planning

permission and the way they financed it was basically 120 houses. And no sooner had they got planning permission than they sold the freehold off and raised money. You could say that was fairly shrewd thinking. You could see with retrospect that it was quite a smart move and now, looking back with hindsight, that sort of move to raise money is now sort of common practice. But in those days, back in the early eighties, it was somewhat novel".

"We, the Tamar Protection Society, weren't objecting to the actual establishment of the golf courses themselves. It was the bolt-on development that was being proposed and what relationship that had with running a commercial golf course."

Jack Spiers became even more apprehensive when the Bonds wanted many more houses, a five-star hotel, a third golf course, a golf academy and, as part of the deal, they would provide a bypass for the village, a shop and quite a few more "goodies" to aid St Mellion village.

This was on top of the society's concern about the impact of, particularly, housing on the landscape and the environment of a sensitive area.

Notwithstanding that St Mellion had become one of the biggest employers in SE Cornwall directly employing over 150 staff and creating many more jobs for several local businesses, Jack Spiers queried the benefit to the community in terms of infrastructure and facilities: "What value if any, what benefits have there been to St Mellion village due to this development. The theory that development round the golf course might have aided the village or benefited it is some way has patently not come true."

But Jack was happy to give credit where credit was due. The Bonds were pioneers: "I never fell out with them personally. Although they might have gritted their teeth if I turned up at meeting and said: 'Oh my God, that bastard's turned up again' there was never any antagonism between us. I think we both recognised our relative positions.

"If hindsight tells you anything which, of course, it didn't tell you at the time, is that there have been quite a number of golf courses granted permission, and I think of Bowood out at Camelford, and again housing has been permitted but not on the same scale as St Mellion.

"Planning policies have been altered and there's all this business about trying to encourage diversification in the countryside so, in a sense, if farmers came along and wanted to diversify their land into race courses or livery stables and farm shops, to a large extent they now get the green light. But, again, they can't get planning permission for six houses down the end of the lane to help finance it. So we're still back to that initial conundrum.

"As to the wider picture, one again has to concede and I would say with a certain amount of admiration the golf courses are kept nice and trim and clean and tidy. They look green and it's all sort of now part of the landscape scene. To that extent I suppose one could argue that St Mellion is a credit on the plus side but the residential development still grates.

"There's obviously been quite a lot of spin off from the club premises and the golf course because when there are these big tournaments, people want to stay so bed and breakfast establishments have enjoyed a certain amount of added business. They've benefited as have a certain number of local traders.

"So there you have it. Mixed thoughts about it really. To look down on it as a golf course it does look pristine and pleasant but you have to avert your eyes from what I still regard as the unwarranted and unseemly residential development that surrounds it."

Jack added that Martin always seemed to be the more cool and collected of the two. Hermon was the front person, the one you had the dialogue with and you always knew where you stood with Hermon.

"Whether bullshit baffles brains would be an apt description I don't know but Hermon was a big person in the sense that he had quite a big physical presence and he was able, I think, to do quite a lot of bulldozing to get his way. He was certainly no slouch when it came to persuading people to back his enterprise and go with him."

Chapter 32

ENVY BETTER THAN PITY

The Bond family was, and still remains, ambitious – full of drive and determination, always progressing. One down side of that is it can create jealousy and envy among others. There was a feeling of resentment against anyone who was "thriving". The mother of the three Bond boys, Amy Bond, used to tell them: "It's better to be envied than pitied." As Martin and Hermon were moving their golfing plans forward, that phrase echoed in their ears.

"It gave us that fillip to move on and do a bit more – in spite of," said Martin and Hermon. Mother died when she was 70 after an illness which had kept her indoors. Unfortunately she passed away before Martin and Hermon created the St Mellion complex and all that followed from it. But the way Amy Bond brought them up – and the advice she gave them – played an important part in what they achieved.

Chapter 33

LOCAL JOBS FOR LOCAL PEOPLE

Agriculture was going through a huge evolution. Farms were getting bigger but small dairy farms were disappearing. Employment opportunities in the rural areas of South East Cornwall were virtually non-existent.

And, right in the middle of it all, at St Mellion, the Bond brothers, who had taken the brave decision to diversify into golf and leisure, had arguably become on the largest employers in the area.

They scooped up people from a rural background who otherwise would either have been unemployed or have to commute into Plymouth for work. The jobs were so local that many members of staff lived in the village and were able to walk to and from their place of work.

Roger Bush, who worked with the Bonds, remembered when staff numbers at St Mellion reached 160, including green-keeping staff: "Of course the joke is if they'd applied to build a microchip factory instead of a golf course they'd have probably got £5 million worth of funding from Europe and created six jobs.

"I think their success was that they were local farmers themselves, they knew what the local environment was like and they wanted to take the local people with them. But they found it very, very difficult to come to terms with people who objected to their plans. I don't mean planning officials or councillors, I mean local individuals.

"I always used to say to them that some of the objectors they'd got were not a problem because they didn't carry an awful lot of weight. So I told them to live with the objectors that they'd got but they still got very, very up-tight about local objections. They were always anxious to bring local people on board from day one."

Initially, that wish didn't always come true. Some villagers had objected to the development of the golf and country club. Perhaps they didn't like the idea of change. There were plenty of doubters - it would never get off the ground, the Bonds were acting as front men for somebody else etc., etc.

But many of them relented later and joined the club and, also, initial objectors ended up having jobs in the complex. When the Bonds sold St Mellion they were employing 200 people, many of them local.

Penny Baxter, who was born into the local Brooking family, has spent all her working life at St Mellion: "Hermon was a large gent. Big bone structure. 'Scary' may be a bit of a vicious word, but he had his moments. He would really fly off the handle sometimes. Whatever he was thinking just came out of his mouth, he didn't actually stop to think before he said anything.

"Martin wasn't the barking type. He was the calming influence on Hermon. He was just a far more gentle person. But they were both men who knew what direction they wanted to go in and knew what they wanted. So there were times when neither of them would take any messing from anybody. Martin just did it in a different way. Over a period of time, working with them far more, you got to know them better and, for me anyway, Hermon never meant anything by it. His bark was worse than his bite.

Underneath, you actually had a really gentle man with a heart of gold.

"Hermon was very proud of what, as two Cornish pig farmers they were going to achieve, what they wanted to achieve, what they were prepared to do. He didn't care who knew his background, he was proud of it. And he didn't care what he said of who he said it to. I don't think he ever thought there was anybody who was more important than him.

"Hermon and Martin worked well together and they achieved loads. They were very brave to even think of attempting it. But it was a dream. It is something they always wanted to do and there's not many people who will take on something of this size. To even think of approaching somebody like Jack Nicklaus, can you think of that? Just going for it, basically. Give them their dues. It was Nicklaus who they wanted, and by God they got him. You've got to have some respect for men like that."

As the prosperity of the area grew only the meanest spirited of the locals continued to object to the proposals to develop the club.

But Steve Moss was one of the many who backed the Bonds and St Mellion all the way. Steve, a carpenter, became maintenance manager and facilities manager and had many stories to tell of his time there, most of them hilarious.

Steve was a member of the Saltash and District Round Table which held its big annual bonfire on the driving range. All the timber rubbish from the site was collected throughout the year for the fire.

"It was all done on the Bond family's land. It suited them. They could have a good burn-up and be very philanthropic about the whole affair and we charged car parking, let the fireworks off, risking life and limb, and raised lots of money for charities.

"Hermon used to park his Range Rover up on the mound in a very regal fashion, close to the fireworks. He wouldn't get out, so if he wanted to speak to me he'd drive down through all the fireworks to have a quick chat," said Steve.

Hermon and Rachel Bond lived in Dunstan House overlooking the Nicklaus course. The ceiling of the drive-through porch was made of heavy duty vinyl kitchen flooring, put in place by Steve Woolley and Steve Moss. It was what Hermon wanted. So the two men had to lie on the roof of a van which was driven into the porch area so they could put the flooring in place.

"It was what you would lay on the floor in an industrial kitchen but Hermon loved it as a ceiling in his drive-through porch. He'd make quite a thing about it and would point it out to people," said Steve.

Steve added that the house was massive but you couldn't get away from the fact that its occupants were farmers: "The rooms are vast but Hermon and Rachel were never happier than when they were in the smallest room, Hermon sitting in a battered old chair, which probably came from the old Dunstan Farm farmhouse, the horse racing on the television. He was in paradise."

Hermon was known for his striking Cornish tartan trousers that he wore with pride. Steve said he wanted the carpet in the bar to match his trousers. So he had carpet specially designed by Axminster. It cost lots, but it was a statement. The carpet was all about Hermon.

Another loyal Bond man was Cornishman Dave Glover who stood 6ft 3ins tall and weighed about 15 stone. At that height and girth he was big enough, on a physical level, to match Hermon Bond. Dave said he could always have a laugh, joke and muck around with both brothers, but particularly Hermon.

One day Dave was tending to the pigs at the farm at Trerulefoot when Hermon drove up in his band new car: "Hermon come down moaning and shouting about something. Then he chucked a bucket of water over me – just for a laugh. I chased him and I got him with the hosepipe. I turned it on and squirted it all over him. Then I put it right in the driver's window of his Ford Granada. He forgot his window was open and I got his car streaming.

"My dad John started shouting at me: 'Dave, stop, stop'. But Hermon told my dad: 'I can't blame him John, it's my fault, I started it'. Still, Hermon didn't like it very much. But he knew what I'd be like, what I'd do after he threw the bucket of water over me, so he was waiting for something to come back at him. He was probably happy that I came back at him there and then, instead of thinking something up to catch him out later."

Dave described Martin and Hermon Bond as more like uncles to him than bosses or an employer: "They was lovely. It was a good relationship. Martin would tell me off if I did something wrong but I can't say nothing bad about the Bonds because they were good. They were brilliant people."

Dave holds the accolade of being the Bonds' youngest "employee". He started his association with them as a four-year-old, mucking out pigs and lifting four-inch concrete blocks.

Dave was born in a room in his gran's house in Saltash. The family moved to Trerulefoot, between Saltash and Liskeard, when Dave was a year old and he's been there ever since. The schools Dave attended included Pencalenick School at St Clement, Truro, which helps children with learning and communication difficulties.

"I had a little bit of trouble reading and writing. But Hermon and Martin helped me out a lot with that and, in the end, they took me on and I went on from there like, you know," said Dave.

"I didn't enjoy school, I was always wanting to be on the farm really. Any time I could have off school, I would take it. It was like the time the Bonds sold their pigs. I must have been in my early teens and Hermon and Martin wrote me a letter asking me to help out so I took the day off school.

"They took me on full time after I left school. I did anything and everything. I did all sorts, the pigs, the spuds and bringing the hay and straw in. When they built the Nicklaus course I learned to drive a machine and I was moving earth for the course," added Dave.

His father John worked for the Bonds doing various jobs from tending the pigs to corn drilling. Mother Sylvia used to hand-pick potatoes for the Bonds. Later, machines picked the spuds and the Glover family would help sort them in the barn. Sylvia did her bit to build the original golf course, raking the stones off the land. The whole family, a bunch of tough, hard-working folk, was involved at St Mellion and were proud to have played their part in its creation.

So, why did Dave Glover later become known as "Dave The Shed Glover"? Simply because he made a business out of building sheds, he was built like a shed and could lift sheds. He went on to weigh 24 stone and pull two double-decker buses, with a combined weight of 21 tonne, across Plymouth Hoe to raise money for charities. He's raised tens of thousands of pounds for the Children's Hospice South West and other charities.

His thinking was: "I'm lucky, I'm growed up, I'm old enough. My boy John's growed up and I'm lucky again. Then there's these little kids who doesn't live to grow up. That's what I think about."

Chapter 34

THERE'S BIG MONEY IN MUCK-SHIFTING

The Nicklaus course was under construction, basically round the edge of the Old course. The St Mellion golf complex was a building site. One abysmal morning in 1984 the Bonds invited the MP Robert Hicks to come and take a look at the progress. It had been raining constantly for the previous 48 hours. There was mud everywhere. It was misty and foggy.

They jumped on board Martin Bond's Range Rover. Martin drove, Robert Hicks was front seat passenger and Hermon was in the back. They drove round talking about this, that and the other, who on Caradon District Council, the local planning authority, was with them and who was against them, Plymouth Argyle Football Club, Plymouth Albion Rugby Club, what the English cricket team was up to and such like, men's chit chat.

They'd come down the 12th and 13th and were on the 14th.

Through the mist and fog Hermon spotted out of the corner of his eye a massive earth-moving machine high up, right on the horizon. He stubbed Robert Hicks on the back with one of his huge, solid fingers and said: "Here boy, how much money does our Prime Minister earn then?"

The question was totally out of all context from the previous conversation. The MP was taken aback. But he thought about it and told Hermon Margaret Thatcher was probably getting about £80,000 a year.

Hermon lent forward again and this time poked his brother Martin in the back as he drove through the mud: "Hear that Mart. The bloody driver of that thing up there gets more money than our Prime Minister."

Of course, Hermon was notorious for his colourful language and, on this particular occasion, he wasn't doing down the truck driver or, necessarily, the PM. He was merely making the point, in his usual combination of cutting and explicit language, just how much the construction of the Nicklaus course was costing him and his brother.

The machine driver was probably Bob Steele, a specialist giant bulldozer operator, across from the States to play his expert role in the moving masses of mud and earth to help create the Nicklaus course. The principle dumper truck drivers were from the Wadsworth Golf Construction Company, America's premier golf course builders. The firm had something like 600 drivers and course "shapers" and some of them were at St Mellion to "shape" the Nicklaus course. Some of them, including Bob, were, indeed, earning more than Margaret Thatcher.

Of course, there were other people working on the course. Their contribution was invaluable, and they weren't on the same pay packet as the boys from the States. People like Hermon's son Graham, who was doing two jobs, working on dad's Dunstan Farm but doubling up on the diggers. He would transport soil, operate some of the smaller machines and, occasionally, to his extreme delight, get behind the wheel and controls of some of the bigger pieces of equipment, the 50 tonne machines, the ones which were usually reserved for the exclusive use of the likes of Bob Steele. The small crew of "locals", literally a handful of men, was led by St Mellion's main machine operator Tony Barriball. Sometimes farm staff would be brought in to help out.

The Bond philosophy was – the job needs doing, so every hand to the plough, every shoulder to the wheel.

Food and beverage staff were not spared either - Martin Watson who was the general manager at the time, recalled what happened when Jack Nicklaus was due to make one of his initial visits. The original idea for the lay-out of the 12th on his course was to carve a hole half way up through the bank of trees to the left. Nicklaus wanted to be able to visualise where the 12th green would be. The best way to do that was to tie a flag to the top of one of the trees so it could be seen from the area of the proposed 12th tee.

Martin Watson set off with Hermon Bond and one of the greenkeepers with a standard flag usually used on the greens. Hermon ordered Martin up the tree. It was about 25 feet tall and quite a thin tree, not much wider than the cup on a green. And there wasn't much to hold on to.

As Martin neared the top, clinging on to the flag, the tree started to bend - and bend and bend. Martin hung on to it as the tree made a complete arc shape. It gently lowered him down and he was able to step off it on to the ground.

"It was hilarious. Hermon was swearing at me, calling me a prat, probably worse than that," said Martin. "He said I'd ruined his tree. We still had the top of the tree on the ground, so I suggested we tied the flag to the tree and then let go of the tree, which is what we did.

"That flag was up there for years. It's probably still up there, you just can't see it."

Principally though, in the summer months, the work was left to those more suited to the outdoor life. Graham Bond and Tony would start work on the site at 6.30am, at the latest, and go through to 9.00pm or 9.30pm. That was Monday to Friday.

Saturday was 6.30am-ish to 6.00pm and Sunday was up to around 1.00pm. Dedication and determination, inspired by the dream which they were gradually turning into a reality. The pair were good time-keepers, even when they had the occasional "morning after the night before" after the odd pint or two.

Four years later, Robert Hicks was to tell the story again, in moderated language, of the machine driver who earned more than the Prime Minister. He was speaking at the presentation of the St Mellion Trophy after Jack Nicklaus and Tom Watson took on Nick Faldo and Sandy Lyle to officially open the Nicklaus course. And it brought the house down because it was just so "Hermon Bond-ish".

But, to Robert Hicks, the story meant much, much more: "It epitomised not only the Bonds' determination and tenacity to 'nail down' Nicklaus for what was the first Nicklaus course in the UK but also the tremendous financial investment they were making and that implied tremendous courage.

"Also, Jack Nicklaus is a perfectionist. He wanted everything to be just right in terms of levels, gradients and where the grass 'bubbles' should be to catch your drive and that sort of thing. So it was a tremendous investment for South East Cornwall which these two local farmers, together with their bank, were making. It was the Bonds and their bank, and they did it. It's there, testimony to them, these two brothers.

"Martin and Hermon's story is incredible. They had that initial vision but also the determination and tenacity, because there were ups and downs, and the courage to see it through. They delivered. What a tangible legacy to leave.

"It means today we have a real centre of expertise and excellence here in South East Cornwall and with Crown Golf's investment in the site, it's going to progress even further."

Chapter 35

ALWAYS THERE FOR MARTIN AND HERMON

The winter months had not been kind to the team constructing the Nicklaus course. There were too many wet days, far too many, and the work was getting behind schedule. Jim Bond – elder brother of Martin and Hermon – came across from Triffle Farm, Downderry, to take a look.

Jim announced, without invitation or hesitation: "Well bugger it, we'll do the 18th for you, we'll put that one in, we'll do that one."

Jim's son James remembered: "We went up there with all our own men, about six or seven of them. We had our potato machines, like de-stoners and what have you, tractors, trailers, whatever was required, and we did the 18th fairway. We basically de-stoned it, raked it with a big, wide stone rake on the back of a tractor, piled the stones in a heap, came in with a tractor and loader, picked them up, stuck them in a trailer and took them away to wherever they wanted them. We also used hand rakes on the banks."

Jim's original intention was to do just the 18th for the hell of it, but James added: "We ended up staying there for six weeks. We also did the 1st, 15th and the 16th and some work on other parts of the course. One of us would disappear for the day and do whatever we had to do back at Triffle Farm."

Jim, like his brothers, a keen golfer with a handicap of seven, was always there for Martin and Hermon when they needed him. When they set out to provide golf and leisure facilities at St Mellion, Jim promised them: "If you ever want or need any help I'm here, be it money or muscle, I'm here."

Jim was into potatoes. He got the spud bug in his teens with his father and things were going well. Martin and Hermon were big on pigs. Jim decided to stick with potatoes. Martin and Hermon opted to diversify.

Jim, the eldest by six years, went on to become the biggest potato producer in the whole of the South West. He had 230 acres and was producing, regularly, about 5,000 tonne of potatoes a year. Martin and Hermon went on to create a golfing mecca at St Mellion.

James explained why the brothers decided to take different paths: "At that time the spuds were carrying father and us along nicely. But I think, with the pigs, the trade was getting tighter and tighter, it was beginning to get more difficult, so Martin and Hermon were looking at where they were going from there."

Jim Bond was indeed true to his word – money or muscle. The potato harvests of 1976 and 1977 helped finance the original clubhouse. Jim had a crop at Triffle Farm and Martin and Hermon had a crop on their land.

James recalled: "I think top price was £300 a tonne, normally it would be £60 to £100, so it really was big money. You were talking maybe tens, even hundreds of thousands of pounds."

James is very proud of what his uncles created at St Mellion – and the part his father played in it: "Looking back at it, it was a hell of an achievement and it certainly put East Cornwall on the map. There's a legacy there because you've got a premier sporting facility, but at the time it was just a case of getting on with the job.

"Having started it and got on the roller coaster, they had no choice but to stay with it. They couldn't half do it. There were always those who said it would never work, but it did. If there's one thing within this family, we're all tarred a bit with the same brush. If somebody says you can't do something, that's a red rag to a bull and we'll prove to them that we can."

Jim Bond played the Nicklaus course with Jack Nicklaus in a pro-am and won a hole, which pleased him no end. James liked to think he played his part in that because he used to give his father informal golf lessons.

Jim Bond died in January 2006 after a series of strokes.

Chapter 36

THE STAND-OFFS

It was, without doubt, THE defining moment in the relationship between the Bond brothers and the man with the golden hair who they regarded as a professional consultant being paid to do a job. Martin and Hermon actually had the "balls" to tell Jack Nicklaus "No". He was an icon of the golfing world who, because of his standing and status, wasn't used to people saying "no" to him. And the Bonds never had and never would fall into the category of "yes" men.

It was about a year into the three-year construction of the Nicklaus course. The great golfer and course architect was on one of his regular visits to St Mellion to observe progress. He was wandering around the site as the various holes took shape. With him were the Bonds and a group of people including his own entourage. They arrived at the 14th which was not an easy hole to create to his design.

"We'd spent no end of time digging through rock," recalled Hermon. "It was hard, really hard. We had a 50-tonne machine digging for weeks to make the hole in the hill." Nicklaus looked round and announced: "No, I've decided to design the green to be 30 yards further up the hill" The Bonds were flabbergasted.

Martin beat Hermon to it – and he didn't mince his words: "What was that? You aren't, you aren't changing it, we dug a hole, laid the drainage, stone and root zone mixture. It's going to stay here."

Nicklaus: "Oh no, but we can do better...."

Martin: 'You should have thought about that earlier on Jack. We aren't going to change, we aren't going to change it."

The talking was firm, straight and blunt. Hermon swore, but not as eloquently as usual! The atmosphere was so thick and tense, it would have been difficult to find any kitchen implement which would have successfully cut through it. The result was that what had been a group of over a dozen people dwindled very quickly to just three – Martin, Hermon and Jack Nicklaus. The others dispersed, anticipating an embarrassing and, perhaps, damaging bust up.

"They knew things weren't right between us. It was funny, we looked around and there was nobody there," said Martin. That didn't deter or shake the brothers. Martin and Hermon stood firm. Hermon told Jack: "We aren't moving the hole. You said it should be there. We've spent £40,000 or £50,000 digging a hole to put it there and that's where it's going to be."

The Bonds continued to stand their ground. Jack Nicklaus stormed off in one direction. Martin and Hermon stormed off in the opposite direction, affirming to each other: "No, we aren't going to change it." Martin recalled: "We couldn't afford the time to change the hole. We weren't going to anyway, whatever happened. That was it. We had followed Jack's original design." Hermon said: "Looking back on it, we didn't look at it as a turning point, something that could have taken the whole project one way or the other. I know I blew my top, but we were only stating our point of view. We had gone too far down the road with expense and time. We weren't having it. That's what Jack designed and that's what we built."

But Hermon's son Graham, who was there that day, definitely considered it as a defining moment in the relationship between the Bonds and Nicklaus: "Back then, Jack lived in a world in which what Jack said, everybody did. It was evident that it was unusual for anybody to say 'no' over what he might consider a small item, £50,000 to dig a hole, or having to buy some more land. I think it probably surprised and shocked him that people would actually say 'no' to him. He did respect that. He didn't take umbrage or anything like that."

After strutting off in opposite directions, they later met up in the clubhouse and then went to the Bonds' office. They knew they had to move forward. Nicklaus came around to agreeing with the brothers that the 14th should go ahead as originally planned. He accepted their judgement. The air was cleared. Everything was fine.

This incident, like many others in Martin and Hermon's story, has produced more than one version of exactly what happened. That's understandable, given the passage of time.

Len Owen, who was the manager of special events for Benson & Hedges, recalled how Hermon told him about having a right go at Nicklaus over the 14th: "Hermon said every time Nicklaus came to St Mellion he would change his mind about the layout of some of the holes. He would decide to 'turn round' a par three by putting the green where the tee was planned and the tee where the green was planned. On one particular par three Nicklaus turned it round three or four times. Decisions like that would cost time and money.

"When Nicklaus wanted to change the 14th Hermon absolutely exploded. He worshipped Nicklaus as the greatest golfer in the world and a true gentleman, but he went for Nicklaus and he swore and swore at him and shouted at him: 'I don't care who you are, no, we're not doing it. I've had enough of it now'.

"Hermon told me everyone else there was subdued – and Nicklaus walked off 20 or 30 yards and stared into the distance. What Nicklaus was thinking I don't know, but he may have been analysing what had happened and how he'd never seen Hermon like that before, swearing at him. He took quite some time thinking, perhaps 10 minutes, but 10 minutes is a long time in those circumstances.

"Being the man that Jack Nicklaus is, and Hermon recognised this too, he walked back with a big smile on his face and put his hand out to the brothers and said: 'It's alright Martin and Hermon, I agree with you, we will work it out'. The situation subsided. I think all those who were there really thought, not that the project wouldn't be completed or anything like that, but that relationships were going to be bad for some time but, apparently, it all just went away, even though Hermon had blown his stack. They all had dinner together."

Hermon's wife Rachel had this view of what happened: "I think Jack respected them for the stance they took. To think they had a mind of their own. Here were people that didn't bow and scrape to him all the time, where perhaps a lot of people would have. If Jack hadn't realised it before, he realised it then. These boys meant business. They knew what they wanted."

When the 14th was finished the Bonds were more than happy with the par three - a beautiful short hole. But in none of his many interviews about the course did Jack Nicklaus, perhaps out of diplomacy, politeness and in deference to the brothers, ever mention his quandary over the 14th and the tough stance taken by Martin and Hermon.

However, Nicklaus did, when the 14th was finished, stand on the tee, put an arm round each of the brothers, and say: "This is some nice hole boys, isn't it, I think we got it right!" Perhaps Jack hadn't forgotten the earlier stand-off? Perhaps this was his apology to the brothers for pushing them to their limits on the lay-out of the 14th? Perhaps he was “doffing his golfer’s cap” in the direction of two of the most extraordinary, difficult and determined men he had ever come across?

Suffice to say, this is what Nicklaus wrote about the 14th in his aerial course guide to his St Mellion course: "This was the hole I wanted to skip on the course. I was trying to find a way to not build this hole because I didn't know whether we had enough room to build into the hillside. We were worried about this hole but, in the end, it turned out perfectly and looks as though it's always been there."

Chapter 37

AND, WHAT ABOUT THE 18TH?

There was a similar “stand-off” incident, although nowhere near as serious, at the 18th, over moving at least one or two of the little hills round the green. Jack Nicklaus had flown in for one of his visits and he had his entourage with him. Peter Hunter, a roofing sub-contractor for the Bonds and a close friend, recalled what happened: “I saw Nicklaus, after having a discussion with the brothers, walk off in deep thought up the 18th fairway and back again.”

Hermon and Martin had said to Jack: “We hope you’re happy now Jack. We’ve done everything. We hope you’re not going to alter anything else.” Nicklaus replied: “These little hills, those humps round the 18th green, I’m not sure about them.” Hermon, being Hermon, told Nicklaus: ‘If you want the bloody hills shifted, you shift them yourself Jack.”

Peter Hunter thought this of the situation: “Apparently no one ever said things like that to Nicklaus but by that time the brothers had had enough. They’d done everything he’d asked for and they were not going to do any more.”

The hills are still there!

Jack Nicklaus - always the ultimate perfectionist. With that title comes the right to change his mind over his original conception of, not only the 14th and the 18th but, according to one top golf writer, numerous other holes at St Mellion. In "Golf World" in September 1983, the assistant editor Robert Green wrote that Nicklaus redirected a river and moved sections of thick forest, notably on the long 12th. Three holes from the Old course – the 6th, 10th and 18th – were remodelled to incorporate in the new course: "Nicklaus totally re-arranged the front nine from his original plans. The 1st became the 9th, the 2nd the 8th and so on. With the back nine, including the 620 yards 12th, he felt that even for the professionals there was too much emphasis on length, so he had to rethink that as well."

One thing is certain, an awful lot of earth was moved to create the course. One estimate is around 1.5 million cubic metres, or approaching three million tonnes of earth, give or take the odd cubic metre or tonne.

When Jack Nicklaus came to St Mellion to see the completed course, he said this about the entire project: "This may have been the most difficult piece of property that I have ever worked with. I had special difficulties here. It's so hilly and so narrow that I thought at first I couldn't get a course in at all. Normally, I have to excavate flat land to make mounds. Here it's so hilly that it was necessary to take earth from the hills to make the fairways and still leave enough mounds to form good viewing galleries."

He was very pleased with the end result: "I think it's going to be a very, very good golf course. I think people will enjoy playing it. It will be a little bit more difficult than the other golf course and of course the Bonds wanted to have a tournament golf course, one that was internationally-known and one that would attract a lot of people – and the serious golfer.

"I think when we have a tournament here, on what is a spectators' golf course, it will be better than any other place I've seen in the world. Simply because of the type of terrain and the elevations, the spectator will be able to be 'above' the golf with unobstructed views."

The co-authors have played the Nicklaus course – Paddy Flavin former Director of Golf & Leisure at St Mellion - numerous times, Michael Taylor only the once, and that was enough for an occasional hacker!

Chapter 38

UNBELIEVABLE BROTHERS

"Defining moment, crucial, pivotal" – words used by Roger Bush to describe the decision by the Bonds to get Jack Nicklaus to come to St Mellion.

Roger, who was a close friend and business associate of the brothers, said the most significant thing they ever did was to go after Nicklaus to design their second course.

"When they made the decision to contact Nicklaus and physically go and do it, that was a defining moment. You've got to put it into perspective. This was two guys from Cornwall, farming stock, they weren't bankers or financiers or entrepreneurs in those days. To make that decision themselves, no one else influenced them. It sounds easy now, but you've got to remember that St Mellion was Nicklaus's first venture into golf development in England," Roger said.

"These two brothers actually had the vision and courage to go out and grab hold of this guy and that in itself cost money. You don't talk to Jack Nicklaus without paying money and it costs you money to even find out that he's going to say 'no'.

"In the whole picture of what the Bonds achieved at St Mellion there were many, many things but my lasting memory was when they said they were going to the States to see Jack Nicklaus. It was crucial, so important and pivotal to what happened from then on."

Roger said Nicklaus gelled straight away with the brothers: "Okay, I know there were some pretty harsh words during the construction of the course, but make no mistake about it at all, he admired them."

Roger added that the timing of the brothers was perfect: "Nicklaus could have gone anywhere in the world he wanted to, but categorically, without any shadow of doubt, the thing that drove Nicklaus to St Mellion was the challenge, because there was no land and the course had to be created out of the side of the hills, but also the enthusiasm and respect that he had for Martin and Hermon. He knew full well he was going to be dealing with two blokes with their feet on the ground who would be there every time that he came over, not with some corporate entity or bank that was funding most of the golf courses that he built. He was actually dealing with real live people on the ground, which he thoroughly enjoyed.

"One stroke of luck the brothers had was Nicklaus winning the 1986 Masters, after they'd built the Nicklaus course. That was the icing on the cake. It helped raise the profile of St Mellion."

Not only did the Bonds get Nicklaus to design the course but they also got him to come back in two successive years and bring with him arguably the second-best player in the world Tom Watson to play against the two best players in Europe at the time, Faldo and Lyle.

"Martin and Hermon pulled that off! Today you couldn't orchestrate that if you tried. It was unbelievable, an enormous coup."

Chapter 39

NICKLAUS THE PERFECTIONIST – BUT ALWAYS FAMILY FIRST

St Mellion will always hold a very special place in the heart of Jack Nicklaus. There are numerous reasons for this, some professional, some emotional, some just plain Jack, the man, the husband, the father, the grand-father and the generations beyond. As a golf course designer, he was meticulous and incredibly demanding. He was that way because, when each and every single design project he was involved with was finished and done he wanted to be able to take justifiable pleasure and pride in the outcome. Of course, not everything he touched with his input turned to gold, but most of it did, and St Mellion was gold star plus.

St Mellion was a milestone for Nicklaus, his first course in the United Kingdom, and a challenge which, he admitted, was the likes of which had never confronted him before. The "ups" and "downs" of the land he was commissioned to transform into a world-class golf course would have been unsurmountable by most, if not all, but Jack.

It was always going to be dubbed "The Course that Jack Built" but it was a three-man job and the team behind them - Nicklaus, the Bond brothers Martin and Hermon, a small army of professionals from The States, the home-grown talent and a band of willing helpers and volunteers. Jack always went out of his way to praise the Bonds for making the golf course possible. For them it was pure faith in their dream - and chucking something like £4 million at it.

Nicklaus, who had by that stage already designed more than 40 courses around the world, said the brothers made it clear to him they wanted a championship course on which a major event could be played. They demanded it, and he delivered it. Each of the 18 holes offered a unique challenge, because each of the 18 holes was based on 18 of the best kinds of golf holes he had ever played on the world's finest courses. A whole world of golf in a corner of Cornwall.

Perhaps the reader can gain an insight into the challenge faced by Jack when one considers the following example. There was an overgrown valley at St Mellion, covered in trees, some of them fallen, with a stream invisible in the undergrowth. Jack Nicklaus was able to picture in his mind what that fairway and green would be like. Incredible vision. He wasn't in the skies in a helicopter, looking down. He was just standing there, on the side of the hill, looking round him, thinking "what can I do with this?" What he did was create the par four 5th by damming the stream and introducing a water hazard. Players have to clear the long, wide lake with their drive. Loved by those who do, hated by those who don't, it's regarded by many as the best hole on the Nicklaus course, particularly when played from the back tee.

Jack visited St Mellion at least nine times during the construction of his course and he genuinely looked forward with anticipation to his visits. He was always guaranteed a sincere and genuine welcome by Martin and Hermon. As the work progressed Nicklaus could visualise probably the finest galleried golf course on the globe – no need for step ladders and periscopes - and, when it was completed, he forecast that, one day, it would stage the Ryder Cup. He continued to firmly hold that belief. But Jack's incredible achievement is to have created a course which was attractive to the best professionals in the world and also local amateurs and club members. The end result was way beyond the expectations and aspirations of Nicklaus and the Bonds. It matched what a golfer would find at Muirfield Village and Glenn Abbey and the Australian Golf Club in Sydney.

Of course, getting it right at St Mellion was vital to Nicklaus's success as a golf course designer across the rest of Europe. Potential customers from numerous countries were queuing up at the time. Nicklaus confided that if potential customers liked what they saw at St Mellion he'd be very busy on the Continent, if they didn't like it, they might walk away in considerable numbers.

Nicklaus was, like the Bonds, always a great family man. His devotion to his wife Barbara and their five children and their numerous offspring was paramount. When the European Tournament Players' Championship was being staged at St Mellion in September 1983 he agreed to be there for just one day to play in the pro-am. However, he didn't turn up, for family reasons: "It conflicted with the high school and college football schedules of my sons Gary and Steve and I simply won't miss games they're playing in."

Chapter 40

THE GREEN, GREEN GRASS

Greenkeeper Roy Battishall was comfortable looking after the original course at St Mellion, cutting the grass, tending to the greens, keeping the bunkers right and so on. But the Nicklaus Course was going to be something special. It was a totally different ball game.

Roy was sent over to the States to be trained by Nicklaus's staff on the exact way he wanted the greens and how he wanted them drained – and much more.

Roy and his wife went to Nicklaus's course at Muirfield Village Golf Club, Dublin, Ohio. He spent months visiting several Nicklaus courses "learning the ropes". Roy's visit was personally organised by Jack Nicklaus who was very "hands on" when it came to getting things right for his course in Cornwall. Roy became course manager of both courses at St Mellion until his retirement in 1994.

Roy's contribution to the progress of St Mellion as an internationally-recognised golfing venue cannot be under-estimated. Paddy Flavin, who had the pleasure of working with Roy, said of him: "Roy's quiet demeanour hid his steely character and he always told the Brothers what they needed to hear rather than what they always wanted to hear."

When he retired Roy became an active full-playing member of the Fossils, St Mellion's Senior section. Roy suffered a fatal heart attack in August 2006 while playing his beloved course, the course he tended with such loving care during his working life.

Chapter 41

GRAHAM – THE FARMER AND MUCK-SHIFTER

Graham Hermon Bond, the younger son of Hermon and Rachel, was just 12 years old when the "old" course opened. He didn't fully appreciate what was going on and the scale of it all.

It was only years later, when work started on the Nicklaus course, that Graham realised the magnitude of the long-term project his father and Uncle Martin had started.

The land concerned was hard to work with. Now-a-days computers work out how much soil had to be taken from one area to another and how many loads would be required. Back in those days the calculations were much more hit and miss.

Graham was working on his father's Dunstan Farm but he was also doubling up working on the diggers on the construction of the Nicklaus course. He would transport soil, operate some of the smaller machines and, occasionally, get behind the wheel of some of the bigger pieces of equipment, the 50 tonne machines.

"I enjoyed the muck-shifting," he said.

The course was actually built with a small crew, led by the main machine operator Tony Barriball. Sometimes farm staff would be brought in to help out.

"Once the Nicklaus course was finished and opened as an international venue, I would see on a regular basis the international stars of golf, sport and entertainment. When you're not used to that environment, it was exciting to see these people at the club," Graham said.

Graham was still doing seasonal work on the farm but more and more time was being devoted to helping the head greenkeeper Roy Battishall. It was a roller-coaster of a time for Graham. And, like many others, he remembered the good times, not the bad.

Graham with his wife Clare have gone on to grow a very healthy business of their own at Lanhydrock Hotel and Golf & Leisure Club near Bodmin.

Chapter 42

COME AND SEE THE COURSE THAT JACK'S BUILDING

Work started on the Nicklaus course at the beginning of 1983, but on the afternoon of the 14th of October 1984, a remarkable event took place. Club members were invited to take a look at the work in progress - and they flocked to St Mellion for the chance to walk the course with the top men working on it.

Martin and Hermon Bond valued the club membership immensely and felt they owed it to each and every one of them to see how things were going. It was a proud moment for everyone who turned up - and an historic occasion.

On that memorable day David Webb, spokesman for the Bonds, introduced several people to the club members before the guided tour. Perhaps the most important were Jim Lipe and Bob Steele, the two resident Americans at St Mellion during the creation of the course.

Jim Lipe was there as the architect for Golf Force, with a Masters degree in landscape architecture. He had been designing golf courses for many years. Jim was the scratch golfer who carried the St Mellion name into the last 16 of the British Amateur Championship in 1984.

Bob Steele was a highly-skilled heavy machinery operator. He led the team of machines reshaping the countryside for the course. Bob had worked for many years with the Wadsworth Golf Construction Company, the world's largest golf course construction company which did a lot of work on Nicklaus-designed courses.

David Webb also introduced an array of other very important pieces of the Nicklaus course jigsaw: Head greenkeeper Roy Battishall. The Bonds had arranged for him to go to America for eight months in 1982-83 to study American methods of greens-keeping. Roy worked at the Nicklaus courses at Bear Creek and Muirfield Village. Roy was therefore trained and ready for his future role as course manager.

Jim Ware, of Talastone Gardens Ltd, East Penrest, Lezant near Launceston, the main contractor for the project. The company had built the first golf course at St Mellion in the early seventies.

Hermon Bond's farm staff, who were farmers one day and golf course builders the next. Worth a special mention are Tony Barriball, who led the team with such energy and enthusiasm, and Graham Bond, Hermon's younger son.

After all the introductions, David Webb handed over to Jim Lipe who took the members round the 18 holes. David said it was, indeed, a very special day which, he believed, only came about because of the very close working relationship which had developed between the Bonds, Nicklaus and his team.

"The relationship and friendship between Jack Nicklaus and Mr Martin and Mr Hermon was unique. I happen to know that he held the brothers in the highest regard," said David.

"One thing that sticks in my mind from the very early days was when he said to the brothers 'If you need me personally for anything, just pick up the phone'. I doubt very much if Mr Nicklaus would offer this service to many clients in his world-wide operation."

Chapter 43

LADIES FIRST – AT ST MELLION

Women golfers christened the Nicklaus Course in 1987 when the British Ladies Open Championship came to St Mellion. Peter German from ING Golf rang to ask if St Mellion could stage the event. The Bonds were very pleased to host it and the sponsor was Richard George from Weetabix.

The course was brand new, just growing into shape. It was summer time, August. It was a tough challenge and Alison Nicholas took the trophy. The event gave the brothers an idea of how things could be done in the future.

Amongst the other competitors was big-hitting Laura Davies who tied for second place with Muffin Spencer-Devlin from the USA. Rumour had it that Laura became distracted because her mother slipped on the newly laid banking and injured her ankle.

The Wheetabix British Ladies Open Championship was one of the highlights for Thelma McEvoy. Thelma was a member of Looe Bin Down Golf Club and its ladies captain in 1977. But in 1986 about 40 male and female members left Bin Down at the same time because of the controversial measures taken by the then owner, builder Ken Wood. He had closed half the course because of a development dispute with Caradon District Council and he had also made part of the clubhouse his home. All 40 members joined St Mellion at the same time in October, including Thelma and her husband Bob. Thelma was St Mellion ladies captain in 1993.

"Even though St Mellion was a proprietors' club, you still felt special, because the brothers always spoke to you, always stopped and had a yarn," said Thelma. "If somebody took the lady captain's parking space they would personally be told by the brothers: 'You do that again, you're out'."

Chapter 44

GROWING INTEREST

Once the Nicklaus course opened, it rapidly became popular with amateur players locally, nationally and internationally. James Mowbray, a St Mellion member and timeshare owner, said: "There were two golf courses, long summer nights, people playing golf for 12, 14 hours a day and every two people was another buggy hire. There was a lot of money coming in."

Initially, quite a few people in the golfing world laughed a bit about St Mellion's location. They said it was out on the end of a peninsula at the end of Britain and it was too far from anywhere. But James said this: "St Mellion started appearing on the golfing map and people were coming to play the Nicklaus course. The Japanese would fly 6,000 miles to play here. They said it was cheaper than playing in Tokyo."

James felt the Bonds never took sufficient credit for what they achieved: I said to both Hermon and Martin: 'Look, you've done a great job for East Cornwall, don't forget it, you've done it. You may not have noticed it, but it is important'.

"It is an enormous legacy. They were great innovators. They were people with a vision of what might happen. I don't think they'd any idea that it was going to be as much as has happened. They were two gentlemen, and everybody knew them and they knew everybody, they knew all their members".

"They were very good at trying to help people, quietly help people, help the members and so on, but not be averse to making a few bob along the line. They had hearts of gold. They didn't blow their trumpets, they just got on with it."

Of course, the enormous investment made by the Brothers had to provide a return on their capital outlay.

"They so enjoyed the development of St Mellion, it wasn't about money, it's just that they had this vision of making a decent golf complex. They were unique. The great thing that they've left behind them is happiness. You don't find people who moan about Hermon and Martin. And the brothers enjoyed themselves. They thought what they were doing was fun," added James.

Chapter 45

NICKLAUS INTERNATIONAL AIRPORT

An airport on Viverdon Down, a few miles to the north of the golf complex! The Nicklaus Course was open – and what a way to attract people to it and the other facilities at St Mellion.

The Bonds knew exactly what line the runway should take. They instructed Willett Ltd, a Trafalgar House company, to investigate. A team came down to see if it was feasible, if it could actually be achieved.

The firm's commercial airline division came up with an alternative runway alignment. Both proposed runways had a take-off and landing distance of about 6,500 feet – adequate for a Boeing 737. In May 1989 Ted Morgan, a director of Willett, warned the Bonds of "the problems which lie ahead", mainly in relation to the terrain and slope of the land, which was owned by the Pentillie Estate.

The brothers had always thought the communications "down this neck of the woods were dire". Without airports you would die. They were thinking Plymouth Airport could be sold to finance a new airport for the region at Viverdon Down. It would have been much bigger and better than anything in the South West at that time – Plymouth, Newquay, Exeter.

Hermon said: "It would have been ideal. When we visited

America, everyone had their own small airport. We flew in to stay at The Greenbrier Hotel and Resort in West Virginia. The airport was just down the road there, and they brought in thousands of customers that way."

Martin said: "This is the sort of thing we could see happening here. We thought, the nearer we could get people to come to us by plane, the better. But, over there, they have plenty of room. We didn't have plenty of room. That's the difference."

The Bonds didn't take this particular project very far down the road. It was to be one of their ideas which never saw the light of day.

Martin conceded: "There would have been a fair bit of noise and I'm sure there would have been hell up if it ever came into the public domain."

Hermon said: "More than likely we were already causing enough trouble in other quarters, so we thought we'd leave it quiet. But, if we'd done it, we'd probably have called it 'The Nicklaus International Airport'. It would have sounded great."

Chapter 46

THE SHOTGUN ROUND

Derrick Pillage was playing a match against an American Clarke Ikestead, who was a very low handicap St Mellion member, and Hermon had a bet with Derrick that Clarke would beat him.

"The bet was for something ridiculous or stupid like £10," said Derrick. "I was three up when we came to the 9th green where Hermon was waiting to find out how the game was going. When Hermon found out I was three up, he told Clarke to buck his ideas up and then disappeared," said Derrick. "We halved the 10th hole and just as I was about to hit my tee shot on the 11th, there was a loud bang from behind a hedge. Someone had discharged a shotgun and the sound completely spooked me. I lost that hole and the next, waiting for the shotgun to go off again.

"But I won the match on the 17th and Hermon wasn't very happy: 'Here you bugger, I didn't fire that gun. Who told you I fired that gun?' But the joke was, he was saying all this and what's he doing at the same time? Unloading the gun while he's arguing with me. That was Hermon. There was no malice in it, just fun."

The name Derrick Pillage is synonymous with golf. He was in charge of promotion and public relations for Benson & Hedges for a few years, managed some of the game's biggest names and helped organise the famous St Mellion Trophy matches in 1988 and 1989.

He first saw the Nicklaus course when he was in Plymouth to visit his mother. He decided to take a look at the course as it was taking shape.

"I was standing looking at the first hole thinking what a great hole Nicklaus had built when I heard this voice behind me: 'Here, what you doing here?' It was Hermon. I said I'd just come to see the place. 'Well, get in the bloody cart then,' said Hermon. I said: 'You can't drive that thing round the course'. He said: 'Bugger you, I own it. Get in the bloody Range Rover and we'll drive round'. So we drove round the entire course. At the end Hermon said to me: 'What do you think of that then?'."

Derrick's answer to that question was: "It was one of the greatest ideas ever in British golf. To get Nicklaus over to this country was revolutionary."

Derrick played off a low handicap and always enjoyed his rounds with Hermon, although they would always be unpredictable: "In one round I was three up after three and we got to the par three 4th. Hermon announced we'd play off the back tee for £10 nearest the pin. Hermon played his shot to within four feet. I'd never played off the back tee before and I missed the green on the left. 'You owe me £10', said Hermon.

"When we got to the next tee Hermon started laughing and kept laughing. He confided that when he was recovering from back trouble he used to practice every day off that back tee at the 4th. He'd hit maybe 50 balls so he knew exactly what he was doing and which club to use. That was Hermon Bond all over!"

Derrick added that the Bond brothers were the most wonderful people - great, great people: "They were part of my life and I will never say a bad word against them. But I did love the way they went about things, that's just the way they were.

"You couldn't beat them. I've always said I wouldn't like to play poker against them. Tough cookies. Came up the hard way. Their great line to me was: 'You don't pay to come into Cornwall, you pay to bloody go out'."

Derrick and the actor Stanley Baker formed Golf Management Ltd. The first player/client they had on their books was Malcolm Gregson.

"The second player I managed was Lee Trevino, who I notoriously renamed in 'Golf Illustrated' as Lee Trevano. Then there were Bernard Gallacher and Brian Barnes. They were the first four and we ended up with 42 players worldwide including Japanese and American. It was a great 21 years and a lovely life.

"I managed Sandy Lyle from the age of 17 all the way through. What the public and a lot of pros didn't understand is that he always gave the impression of being a simpleton, but he had the best golfing brain of anybody I ever managed. He knew what he was going to do. He may have been built wrong at 6ft 3ins with an inside trouser leg of 29 ins, legs like tree trunks.

"I could write a book about Sandy's jokes and mistakes like when he won the Suntory tournament sponsored by the Japanese brewery company. (World Match Play Championship in UK in 1988) It's got to be the best faux pas ever in the history of golf. He stood up with the trophy and said: 'I'd like to thank the Chinese for putting on such a great tournament'."

Derrick Pillage, the head of promotion and public relations for Benson & Hedges for many years, was always a bit of a wordsmith, but he set aside the corporate speak when it came to summing up Martin and Hermon: "To me the brothers were like Yorkshiremen. If they liked you, they liked you, if they didn't like you, you knew it. That's what I found with them. If you were a friend, you were a friend – and a friend for life.

"St Mellion was part of my life and it's in my heart and will never be taken away. There's love in my heart for Martin and Hermon, they were just hilarious. They were lovely, humble, wonderful people. My love for the Bonds was as powerful as anything. Hermon and Martin were totally different characters, chalk and cheese but, God, they loved each other. I'll never forget the Bonds and my wife Sally feels the same."

Chapter 47

GET NETTED

The first few luxury houses built in Dunstan Lane on the edge of the Nicklaus course had a view many golfers would die for - looking down over the fairway and green of the first hole and also the tee and fairway of the second.

The homes were much sought after - by those who could afford them. They were well designed, extensive, beautifully finished and surrounded by expansive gardens and lawns.

So, what a delight for the owners. They could sit in their gardens, take in the view and watch golfers of all abilities coming down the first, putting out and heading off down the second.

However, it wasn't such a delight to be sitting in your garden enjoying the sun, sipping a G&T - and having your glass shattered - by a stray golf ball. Time to run for cover – and a brandy to settle your nerves.

So, safely indoors, calmed down and relaxed. And on comes a programme about the rise in house burglaries. Suddenly a window in your television lounge is smashed – it's not a burglar, it's a golf ball!

This was the downside of those lucky to live on that stretch of Dunstan Lane. Players teeing off at the 2nd would slice their drive, if they were right-handed, off to the right in the direction of the houses and gardens. For left-handers it would be a hook, but just as dangerous for the home dwellers.

Residents complained that it wasn't safe to sit outside, and their privacy was being invaded by golfers climbing up the slope and, like a naughty child who's kicked their football into your garden, asking: "Please can I have my ball back?"

Some homeowners got out the binoculars to try to identify the consistent culprits. There was talk of people wearing hard hats, the sort you find on a building site, or crash helmets. Would some form of air raid shelter, or golf ball shelter be the answer?

Of course the perfect solution was a safety net to shield the first couple of properties from the wayward missiles. But it wasn't quite as simple as that – and the story goes back to sometime much earlier, when the Bonds applied for planning permission for the houses in Dunstan Lane.

Caradon District Council's planning officer Alan Hartridge argued it was bad planning to have housing – as proposed in Dunstan Lane – away from the village. He'd seen the original plan outlining where the houses would be.

"I asked what would happen if a dog was running across the green after a cat and a child was running after the dog from one of the houses and there were golf balls flying around?

"I also asked about golf balls being sliced. People sitting in their garden having their gin and tonic and golf balls coming their way?"

Hermon told Alan Hartridge: "You don't know what you're talking about. Nobody could hit a ball like that." But Hermon and Martin Bond agreed to erecting some netting down by the

2nd tee, not up next to the proposed houses, which would have looked a mess.

Alan Hartridge took advice on that and was told it should be alright. So netting was erected at the 2nd tee. But when the houses were built and residents moved in, they started complaining about golf balls in their gardens and hitting windows.

"These were residents, who were members of the golf club, who bought those houses, complaining about other members putting golf balls through their windows. Hermon didn't think they would ever do that," recalled Alan.

The council sent along its planning enforcement officer John Rowe. He had been a policeman and a leading member of Looe Bin Down Golf Club where he played golf with Hermon and his other brother Jim Bond.

"Finding golf balls landing in your garden was alright if you collected balls but it could be a bit dodgy if one of them hit you," said John.

Alan Hartridge said the issue then was to make sure any additional netting wasn't a real eyesore, resembling a military establishment or the fencing at the atomic weapons base at Aldermaston near Reading. Hermon didn't think it was a major issue. As far as he was concerned almost everyone was happy, apart from one or two residents. Alan Hartridge suggested at one stage that the Bonds go around and talk to the residents and see the damage that was being done and try to see if they could sort it out without having to involve the planning system. And, it might be possible to extend the existing net around the tee.

Hermon was having none of it: "They don't know what we're trying to achieve here. They can't see the big picture, they've got their own little axe to grind or they're bloody jealous."

John Rowe commented: "What was needed was netting about 30 feet high until the trees that had been planted grew up. The netting was to have come down after so many years, but it was still there when I left the council!"

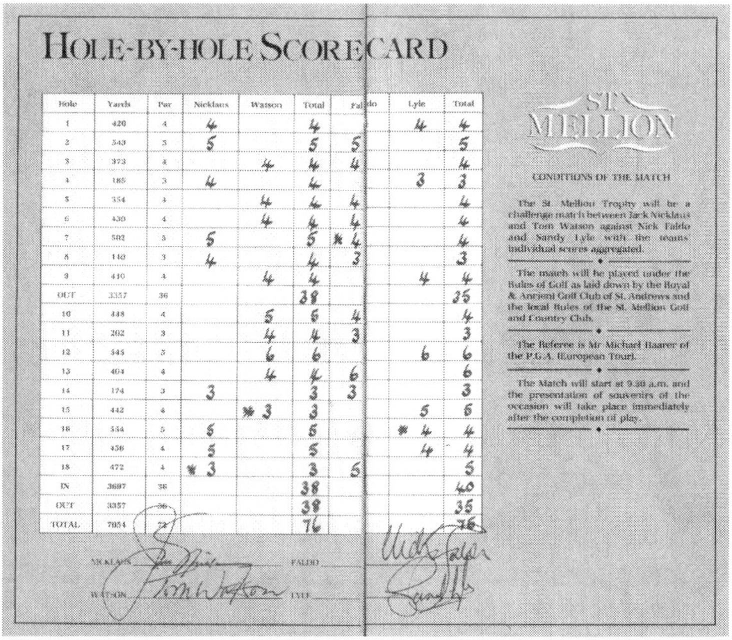

HOLE-BY-HOLE SCORECARD

Hole	Yards	Par	Nicklaus	Watson	Total	Faldo	Lyle	Total
1	420	4	4		4		4	4
2	543	5	5		5	5		5
3	373	4		4	4	4		4
4	185	3	4		4		3	3
5	354	4		4	4	4		4
6	430	4		4	4	4		4
7	502	5	5		5	* 4		4
8	140	3	4		4	3		3
9	410	4		4	4		4	4
OUT	3357	36			38			35
10	448	4		5	5	4		4
11	202	3		4	4	3		3
12	545	5		6	6		6	6
13	404	4		4	4	6		6
14	174	3	3		3	3		3
15	442	4		* 3	3		5	6
16	554	5	5		5		* 4	4
17	456	4	5		5		4	4
18	472	4	* 3		3	5		5
IN	3697	36			38			40
OUT	3357	36			38			35
TOTAL	7054	72			76			75

NICKLAUS ________ FALDO ________

WATSON ________ LYLE ________

ST MELLION

CONDITIONS OF THE MATCH

The St. Mellion Trophy will be a challenge match between Jack Nicklaus and Tom Watson against Nick Faldo and Sandy Lyle with the teams' individual scores aggregated.

The match will be played under the Rules of Golf as laid down by the Royal & Ancient Golf Club of St. Andrews and the local Rules of the St. Mellion Golf and Country Club.

The Referee is Mr Michael Haarer of the P.G.A. (European Tour).

The Match will start at 9.30 a.m. and the presentation of souvenirs of the occasion will take place immediately after the completion of play.

Hole by hole Scorecard from St Mellion Trophy Match July 1988

All photographs were kindly loaned to the Authors by the Bond family and are reproduced here with their permission.
We should also like to recognise the photography of:
Mervin Biggin LMPA
Gordon Belman
Phil Sheldon

Martin Bond - Jack Nicklaus - Hermon Bond
"Planning the Course"

Martin Bond - Jack Nicklaus - Hermon Bond
"Planning the Course"

Celebrating Seve's victory in the 1994 Benson & Hedges International Open

John Shrewsbury- HRH Prince Andrew- Martin Bond- Hermon Bond
"The Royal Match"
Photo by Mervyn Biggin LMPA

Martin, Jack & Hermon "Studying the finished course"

Martin, Nick Faldo, Sandy Lyle, Hermon. "to the victors the spoils"

Upper Picture -Hermon Bond
“at pig sale”

W H Bond and a very young Alison Bond
"Opening the Clubhouse"

Pictures of the Match against La Baule Golf Club
"a friendly exchange"

Chapter 48

EVEN THE DUCKS THOUGHT IT WAS ALL A BIT TOO MUCH

Had all the rain clouds in the Northern Hemisphere come together in the skies over the British Isles? It certainly seemed like the blackest of them all, heavy-laden with the stuff, had gathered above one small corner of South East Cornwall.

It was Sunday, the 10th of July 1988. It's one of those surreal moments. Do you remember where you were on the 10th of July 1988? If you were at St Mellion or watching sport on television, you remember, without hesitation, that you were there or somewhere fixated in front of the box – and you will never forget it.

Arguably the four best golfers in the world at the time had gathered at St Mellion to officially open Jack Nicklaus's first golf course in the United Kingdom – the Golden Bear himself and Tom Watson, who were to take on Nick Faldo and Sandy Lyle. Watson, Faldo and Lyle turned up at the personal invitation of Nicklaus. The occasion deserved a better day – sunshine and sunhats. But it was umbrellas and waterproofs. And did it rain! And did it rain!

It wasn't even weather fit for ducks. The very famous ones on and around the large, filled to capacity pond beside the 18th green had had enough at one stage and sought shelter and sanctuary from the perpetual precipitation.

Had it been a tournament match, it would have been cancelled or postponed. Or, if they'd even made a start, they'd have been called in after the first few holes. Nick Faldo's estimate was, if officials had been on duty for a tournament event, he'd have been back in his room having a shower after just three holes. Sandy Lyle had flown down from Scotland to Plymouth the day before, after finishing runner-up in the Scottish Open at Gleneagles. He, his caddy and the Press flew in an aircraft nick-named the Vomit Comet. They arrived at St Mellion around 10.00pm. The next morning, Lyle must have been wishing the Vomit Comet had developed a technical fault and been delayed for 24 hours.

It was going to be like playing a round of golf on a lake. The built-in watering system to cover the greens, tees and fairways wasn't needed! But Jack Nicklaus said: "We're going to do it. We're going to play it." The wind exacerbated the horrendous conditions, but it was the unrelenting downpour that made the day so challenging for the players, their caddies, the 50 marshals on the course and the television crew. By the time the four golfers approached the final hole, there was only one television camera still working. It had been the intention to just film a few holes between breaks in the other sporting events to be televised that day. The weather was so bad nationally that St Mellion received uninterrupted live coverage for the entire duration of the golf. This was achieved by the cameramen alternating the positions of the few cameras on site.

It was a long round, just over 5 hours. One reason for that was the players had to wait for the cameramen to catch up with them before they hit their next shot. It could take up to 10 minutes between strokes.

The four drenched players finally waddled up the 18th. A quartet of drowned ducks, squelching their way home. Nicklaus was thinking: "I wish I'd made this course a bit shorter – nine holes would have done."

On the green he turned to his fellow swimmers, smiled and announced proudly: "We made it guys." The remark was also aimed at the Bond brothers, who took on board the much wider significance of the four words – Jack Nicklaus and Martin and Hermon Bond had done what they set out to do, create a championship course for the future and gone through many ups and downs, disagreements and arguments to arrive at this historic moment.

Even some of the ducks, who had earlier scampered for cover, emerged as if to pay homage to the very best of golfers who, the ducks hoped – and prayed - would never dare fire a shot into the 18th which might score a direct hit on a member of their Anatidae waterfowl family.

The sky was still cluttered with clouds, queuing up to make their individual contribution to the "wetland" below. But Martin and Hermon Bond who, it was claimed, spent £250,000 on the big day, and all the members of the Bond family were on a different cloud - Cloud Nine. Hermon and Martin thought: "Well, we started this 16 years ago and now it's all come together. We've realised our ultimate dream."

And the brothers were proud of the players: "They all did it in great spirit, because it was tough going." And the invitation-only crowd of 1,000 spectators and the marshals had kept going too. A bit of Cornish rain wasn't going to deprive them of the chance to worship at the wet feet of golf's elite. The players were welcomed home by The Royal Marines Boys' Band, who marched up and down and down and up. They were not deterred by the elements and played their hearts out. The golfers and the crowd applauded and Faldo joined in the marching, splashing about in water up to his ankles, using, appropriately, an umbrella to play the part of the drum major. America's answer to Peter Alliss,

ABC sportscaster Jack Whitaker, on his first visit to Cornwall, remarked: "Mad dogs, Englishmen and golf enthusiasts come out in the rain."

Nicklaus had designed a tough course. That day the weather made it twice as tough. Nicklaus scored a 13 over par 85, Sandy Lyle went round in 84 and both Tom Watson, the five-times Open champion and Nick Faldo, the Open Champion, both finished on 78. The match was played in a fourball better-ball medal format, so Lyle and Faldo, with 75 – three over par for the 7,054 yard course – beat Nicklaus and Tom Watson by one stroke. So bad were the conditions that only five birdies were made, two by Faldo at the 7th and 16th and one each to Watson, at the 15th, Lyle at the 16th and Nicklaus at the last, with a magnificent putt of 30 feet. Faldo was level par for the first 11 holes, but that was when the rain and the wind reached their most severe.

Nicklaus admitted: "It's a day we're all going to be talking about for a long time. I'm just amazed that we've played. I have played in worse conditions but never for such a sustained period. It was awful. I don't know how the other guys held on to their clubs because I certainly couldn't. It got comical. What you saw out there was Lyle and Faldo beating Watson by one shot. I hardly contributed at all. I played atrociously but it's been a fun day. My back didn't hurt because I was numb all over. It's a tough course, too tough for me. It is five years since Hermon and Martin Bond asked me to build a golf course for them here. Now we've got a course to be proud of."

Nick Faldo, who finally got his shower, recognised and embraced the significance of the match: "It was a truly historic day, made all the more memorable by the conditions."

Sandy Lyle enjoyed the atmosphere: "I wasn't very happy with my own game, but I was very impressed by the course. There is no doubt, it is very good."

Tom Watson enjoyed the atrocious conditions: "I relish the challenge. This is when the golf course gets back at you."

Alan Bond, a professional caddy on the PGA Golf Tour for more than 30 years, caddied for Watson. For Alan, the elder son of Hermon and Rachel Bond, the highlight of all the memorable occasions at St Mellion was the official opening of the Nicklaus course and the trophy match: "The four players were legends. To have them open the course is, for me, the one thing that sticks out from everything.

"As everyone remembers, the weather and the rain were absolutely horrendous. Many years later Watson listed the ten worst weather conditions he'd ever played in. He mentioned Carnoustie and St Andrews and, also, in there amongst them, is the official opening day at St Mellion. So, he remembered that day as well."

Alan also remembered it vividly – and it wasn't all plain-sailing with Watson: "On the 10th hole, he hooked his drive a way up on the hill. It was a pretty good lie but the ball was way below his feet. The pin was at the back of the green and he asked me if he should take a two iron or a three iron. I'd never worked for the guy before and, it was like, he'd be lucky to get it out anywhere. I was thinking he's not going to reach so I said two iron. He hit this two iron, a laser, right at the pin and one hop, over the back of the green. He wasn't happy at all but I was thinking well, I just picked your bag up two hours ago. I think he fluffed his chip and made a double so I wasn't his favourite flavour at the time.

"Even though it was an exhibition match, all four players took it all very seriously. If you're a competitor of that stature, you don't just turn it on and turn it off. It's not just - let's get through this because the weather's appalling. They wanted to win. So it was nice to see the 'drive' that they had to win."

Chapter 49

THE WIDER PICTURE

Sunday, July 10, 1988 was scheduled, television-coverage wise, to be a big sporting day nationally, but almost everything else was rained off. So, the trophy event at St Mellion got much more extensive television coverage than originally scheduled, even into Europe, and even with the dripping cameras dropping out one by one.

John Shrewsbury produced all BBC TV's golf coverage, but this was the ultimate challenge: "It rained and rained and rained. Did it ever rain. Because it was only one match, we could get around the course but it meant hedge-hopping cameras, sending cameramen ahead of other cameramen to pick up the holes further on. We were live on BBC2 but the rain was so incessant the cables started to let water in and the cameramen couldn't see anything. The cameras started dropping out one by one.

"We still had enough cameras going at the 11th when Nicklaus shanked his tee shot right out on the right. Jack was almost looking at us as if to say 'Can I do it again?' – but we were live."

Conditions worsened by the minute. Thankfully, John and his team kept going, to the delight of Grandstand viewers, but it was touch-and-go if what was left of the equipment would last long enough to see the players hole out at the 18th and walk off.

"At the end, on the 18th hole, we had just one camera that was still operating," said John. "It was on the big hoist and because it was on the hoist it was protected from the rain because it was looking down all the time instead of looking up. So we managed to get the last putt on the final green.

"We really had no idea what was going to happen that day. Brand new golf course. Didn't know if we'd get the signals out all the way round but we'd gone for broke and tried our best and it all worked."

Richard Brown was tournament administrator for the B&H at St Mellion from 1990 to 1995 but, like millions of others, he remembered clearly the first St Mellion Trophy match: "There was no sport on television other than the St Mellion golf because of the rain all over the country. All the John Player cricket was cancelled. Everything scheduled for television, apart from St Mellion, was a washout. Probably everybody in the country was watching the golf at St Mellion, millions and millions of people, and they've talked about it ever since."

The official viewing figure was put at four million. Derrick Pillage, who was in charge of promotion and public relations for Benson & Hedges for some years and also helped organise the St Mellion Trophy event, thought that was a very conservative estimate: "I think the recorded viewer figure was more like eight million. But if you take the people who came in and out, watched a bit here and there, it was more like double that figure at least. And it was good television."

It was indeed, and the significance of the event was far-reaching. The local Member of Parliament at the time, Robert Hicks: "On the day it didn't quite register with me, but when I got back to Westminster on the Monday evening, over the following 72 hours I couldn't count the number of colleagues who came up to me and said they'd seen our new golf course on television. The story of the Bond brothers and what they achieved is absolutely incredible and, to me, it's epitomised by this single event, with national television coverage. Amazing. For me, this was the greatest, single occasion of all my memories of St Mellion."

The extensive coverage more than compensated for the bitter disappointment of the total lack of national television time nine years earlier when the coverage of the 1979 Benson & Hedges at St Mellion was cancelled on the eve of the event because of a strike at ITV.

Chapter 50

THE BIG STONE - AND THE BAD BUGGY

For this very special occasion St Mellion's director of golf David Webb had been to the tailors to invest in a new blazer and pair of trousers. After all, he wanted to look his very best in his role as master of ceremonies for the official opening of the Nicklaus Course. Shame about the rain, but the unveiling by Jack Nicklaus of the commemorative granite stone, on the way to the first tee, went well. A two-tonne chunk of Dartmoor granite, six feet tall and draped in the Stars and Stripes and the Union Flag. The inscription on the stone reads: "St Mellion International Championship Golf Course. The first in Great Britain designed by Jack Nicklaus and opened by him 10th July 1988. Built by the owners MARTIN AND HERMON BOND."

There were loads of people gathered around the first tee, probably about 500. The event was about to go live on BBC2. BBC director Alastair Scott announced that they were just minutes away from going live. David Webb, a very precise and proper gentleman, was in position, in his new blazer and trousers, alongside the four players on the right-hand side of the tee, looking in the direction of the village church, ready to introduce the players. Next thing, he was on his back on the ground, under the front wheels of a golf buggy carrying a BBC cameraman, equipment and a driver. Hermon Bond's wife Rachel was also trapped. David tried desperately to elbow his way out, but he was stuck in the mud and the buggy kept going, climbing up his back. The driver couldn't get it to stop. People were trying to push the buggy off him. They finally did.

"It was bad enough me being floored in front of four or five hundred people around the tee. Imagine the panic if the buggy had driven in to one of the players just four days before the Open Championship at Royal Lytham and St Annes," said David.

In fact Tom Watson had a very lucky escape. He came within inches of serious injury when the buggy careered out of control and slid down a bank on the tee. Watson leapt to safety: "Fortunately I could see what was happening and I wasn't going to let it run me over."

Rachel Bond had her back to the buggy when, suddenly, her right leg was trapped under the front of the vehicle. She was being pushed along by those trying to get the buggy off David Webb. She was shouting: "Mind my leg." Good job she had waterproofs on. She wasn't cut but she badly hurt the muscles in the lower half of her leg.

Derrick Pillage, also a friend of the Bonds and a highly-respected golf historian, saw the incident: "Rachel never batted an eyelid. Nicklaus saw what happened and walked back to Rachel and asked her: 'Are you alright?'."

Rachel said: "I thought I was going to walk it off but I got down to the first green and found that I couldn't walk. I had to come in and watch it on the television. I was disappointed because I was all geared up to walk the course."

At the prize-giving ceremony in the evening, poor Rachel, instead of sitting up all prim and proper, she was lying back in her chair with her right leg stretched out in front of her, bravely hiding the pain.

The irony of the buggy incident wasn't lost on David Webb: "A great start to the day for me! But, of course, the show had to go on, there was a job to be done, and, after cleaning myself off, I announced the players and the match was on its way."

His final task of the day was to officiate at the prize-giving. After that, his wife drove him into Plymouth's Freedom Fields Hospital, just in case. David considered himself lucky to escape with just a badly bruised ankle.

Had the accelerator got stuck, was there a short in the system because of the rain? The conclusion was the buggy's brakes failed because water had penetrated to the extent that it might as well have not had any brakes at all.

Despite David Webb's ordeal, the day was one of the most memorable of his life. The Bond brothers had asked him to introduce Jack Nicklaus to perform the commemorative stone unveiling ceremony. David had dedicated many years to the Bonds and their dream. This was for him a great honour and privilege. But he was nervous, to be standing there next to the greatest golfer in the history of the game. It was, to use an adjective which the United Kingdom has adopted from the United States, an "awesome" occasion. David almost had to pinch himself for confirmation that this still wasn't "the dream". This was the reality. It certainly took his breath away.

The ceremony over, the crowd moved on to the first tee for the start of the St Mellion Trophy match. Again, David Webb did the honours and announced the arrival of the players on the tee. And, significantly, as he named each player, he listed the "majors" they'd won around the world. And here, the four were, at St Mellion in Cornwall.

Much later in the day the presentation of the trophy took place indoors. Around 300 people gathered in the upstairs lounge of the clubhouse. Once again David Webb was master of ceremonies and introduced the players. He often thought back to that occasion: "All in all, a day to remember. It was an incredible day, a day I shall never, ever forget, and just a great privilege to be involved.

"I played a very, very small part. This day was all about Mr and Mrs Martin Bond, Mr and Mrs Hermon Bond and their families – and their dream coming true."

FOOTNOTE 1: Estimates of the total, final cost of the Nicklaus course vary widely. Figures of £3 million and £4 million have been quoted. It's thought, by some, that a more realistic figure would be double that - £8 million.

FOOTNOTE 2: There was also a lot of speculation, talk and rumour about the purse these world class players must have demanded for this round of very high-profile golf. Derrick Pillage insisted on putting the record straight from his perspective: "I was managing Sandy Lyle at the time and I know no money ever changed hands. Jack asked the other three to play and they just did it for Jack."

FOOTNOTE 3: The St Mellion Trophy match was repeated in 1989 with the same two teams. The weather was glorious – too hot in fact, but no one dare complain after the Apocalyptic conditions in 1988. The British pair retained the trophy.

Chapter 51

LEGLESS BRIAN MAYO AND THE 1988 ST MELLION TROPHY MATCH

Golf-mad Welshman Brian Mayo lost his legs because of his obsession with the cleanliness – of his golf balls.

He was so meticulous and pernickety that when his ball landed on the green and was marked in any way he would, before he putted, clean it by licking it. This habit became something of a ritual.

Tragically, on one occasion, after he licked his ball he became ill and fell into a coma. The ball was contaminated by weed killer spread on the green. Brian contracted a rare fungal meningitis and lost both his legs.

While he was in hospital he read a book on World War II flying ace Group Captain Douglas Bader who refused to give up golf when he lost his legs. Brian, a fanatical golfer with a handicap of eight, was determined to do the same. Within a few weeks of leaving hospital he was back on the course at his own club which he had helped create, Bryn Meadows Golf and Country Hotel in the Rhymney Valley in South East Wales.

Brian actually met Douglas Bader to get some tips on how not to fall over when he hit the ball. He wasn't going to let his physical handicap increase his golf handicap. With his artificial legs, he got his handicap down to seven!

Martin Watson, managing director at St Mellion and a close friend of Brian, said: "He was very proud of the fact that his handicap was one better with no legs. I remember him sitting at the bar, with his false legs off, and someone saying to him what an achievement it was to get his handicap even lower.

"Brian replied with a huge smile: 'If I'd known that was going to happen, I'd have had my legs off years ago'."

Martin, who had worked with Brian at Bryn Meadows, visited him during his time in hospital. When St Mellion was organising the 1988 Trophy match, management were told they could invite a certain number of people to attend. As Brian was an absolute Nicklaus nutcase, Martin Watson invited him. The only golf buggies allowed out on the course were for BBC cameramen and staff, with the exception of Martin, for two reasons. One reason was to deliver refreshments for the players, like drinks and bananas to various points on the course. The other was to act as chauffeur for Brian Mayo.

Martin said being with Brian was hilarious – and could be precarious: "On the golf course Brian would strike the ball – and fall over. It didn't happen all the time but it made playing golf with him an experience not to be forgotten. The solution on many occasions was to stand behind him and try to catch him after he hit the ball.

"His artificial legs had suction pads on them and when we were going up the stairs in the clubhouse the noise they made sounded like Brian was constantly farting. So I wasn't too keen on walking behind him but I had to, in case he would fall back.

"I was following him up the stairs and, because of the way he had to negotiate the stairs, he literally looked like he was pissed. And to make things look even more like he had several too many, he had a big grin on his face, he was always smiling. People came out of the lounge bar and looked at Brian. I said: 'Oh it's alright, my mate's legless'. Brian nearly fell over laughing."

Brian Mayo founded the British Amputee Golf Association and organised the British Amputee Championship, an annual event for players from all over the world. He contracted meningitis again and died on holiday in Florida in January 1999. He was 62.

Chapter 52

WHISKY AND WATER – A YEAR APART

Top American golfer Tom Watson flew into Plymouth Airport for the official opening of the Nicklaus course at St Mellion in 1988. Watson was met by St Mellion's managing director Martin Watson and they chatted on their way from the airport to the hotel. Martin Watson checked him in at reception, helped him with his bags and took him to his room.

In the evening there was a special dinner in the Lynher Suite upstairs in the clubhouse. The first of the four players to arrive at the reception which was 7.30 for 8.00 was Nick Faldo – at 6.55pm.

"I've always had the greatest respect for Nick Faldo," said Martin Watson. "With me and with my staff he was always polite, a gentleman. We stood and had an interesting talk about wines because he used to buy wine investments with some of his money.

"He had acquired a great knowledge of wines. He told me that when you're sitting on a plane flying to America it can be boring. On one crossing he picked up an in-flight magazine and read an article on wine and that's how he got into buying wine."

The last person to walk into the room, when most other people were getting ready to sit down to dinner, was Tom Watson. The only person he knew in the room apart from the other golfers was Martin Watson.

"I spoke to him at the bar and asked him would he like a drink. He replied: 'Martin, give me three fingers of Scotch'. I gave him the three fingers of Scotch in a glass, which is a fair measure of Scotch. He downed that and never had another drink. That's all he had all night."

For the second St Mellion Trophy match in 1989 Jack Nicklaus and Tom Watson brought their wives with them – Barbara and Linda. Martin Watson picked up Tom and Linda at the airport. They'd been to Ballybunion in Ireland and were at St Mellion before going on to the Open at Troon in Scotland. The couple stayed in one of the lodges in the timeshare village.

"Tom spotted the washing machine and I showed them how it worked," said Martin. "Later he phoned me in a bit of a panic to say the washing machine was leaking. I went down there and the whole of the downstairs of the timeshare was flooded. He was all very apologetic although it turned out it was nothing to do with him, it was a burst pipe."

Later, Martin had to wear another hat as provider of refreshments for the four players in the trophy match. He arrived at the 7th: "The cameras were going and Tom Watson called me over on to the tee and said: 'Martin, Martin, how's the timeshare?'. I said: 'It's alright, I think we can rescue it'. Jack Nicklaus was going: 'What's that all about?'."

When Martin said goodbye to Tom and Linda at the airport he asked Tom would it be any good putting a bet on him for the Open.

Watson turned, smiled at him and said: "Put your money on me." It was the 118th Open and history was about to be made. Mark Calcavecchia won his first major championship in a four-hole playoff over Greg Norman and Wayne Grady who tied for second place. This was the first time in the Open's history that a four-hole playoff was staged immediately after the final round. Previously, there had been an 18-hole playoff the following day. Calcavecchia picked up £80,000 and Norman and Grady shared the second and third prize of £55,000 each. Oh, and just for the record, Tom Watson came fourth and pocketed £40,000. The other Watson, Martin, won some money as well!

Chapter 53

THE LADY AND THE BEAR

He is regarded by many as the greatest golfer ever to be blessed to walk the fairways of the world's most famous courses. She is regarded by many as the greatest female golfer, perhaps the greatest golfer of all time and on a par with any man who set out to conquer any 18 holes anywhere.

We all know the exceptional achievements of the Golden Bear, Jack Nicklaus. Some may not be so familiar with the remarkable trail blazed by Joyce Wethered. She dominated the ladies' game in the 1920s. Her glamour and beauty were matched only by her smooth swing and perfect balance. In a different era, Jack Nicklaus's golden hair and piercing blue eyes were matched only by his determination to win and his hard and precise hitting of the ball. Joyce was a long hitter as well. How she and her colleagues ever managed to swing a club dressed in the golfing attire of the day – long skirts and often clumsy, heavy jackets – is a miracle.

Joyce was British Ladies Amateur Champion four times – 1922, 1924, 1925 and 1929 – and the English Ladies Championship for five consecutive years from 1920 to 1924. Eight times in the 1920s and 1930s she lifted the Worplesdon Mixed Foursome and was a regular in the British and English Ladies teams.

In 1932 Joyce played in the first Curtis Cup match between the United States and Great Britain and Ireland. The US won with 5.5 points to GB and Ireland's 3.5. But it was Joyce who stole the show and the headlines. She was matched against her American counterpart, Glenna Collett Vare – America's top female player. They met only three times in competitive combat. Joyce won this encounter in impressive fashion – six in front with four to play!

Of course, many books have been filled with the gargantuan achievements of the legendary Jack Nicklaus. They can be summed up in just three words – "Twenty Major Championships." Six times US Masters, four times US Open, five times PGA, three times British Open and two times United States Amateur Open.

Joyce retired from competitive play in 1930. In 1937 she married Sir John Heathcoat-Amory and became Lady Heathcoat-Amory. They lived in Devon. Her husband was the 3rd Baronet of the Heathcoat-Amory Baronets. Just as important to him as his hereditary honour was his love of cricket and he excelled at that. He was a very good batsmen and an accomplished bowler.

In 1975 Joyce entered the World Golf Hall of Fame. She lived at Knightshayes Court, a wonderful Victorian house at Tiverton, later owned by the National Trust. She continued to watch golf and the greats of the game and in 1989 she contacted St Mellion after hearing about a repeat of the St Mellion Trophy match. She had often expressed an interest in meeting the Golden Bear and asked if it would be possible. After all, she wasn't that far away from St Mellion, even for an 87-year-old!

The owners of St Mellion, Martin and Hermon Bond, decided it was time to make it happen. Nicklaus was contacted in America and agreed they should meet. So these two greats of golf finally met. On the day, the BBC allowed Joyce to follow the four players – Nicklaus, Watson, Faldo and Lyle - down the 18th fairway in a buggy and arranged for an interview afterwards.

It was David Webb, St Mellion's secretary, who was tasked to make it all come together. David, who always referred to the brothers as "Mr Martin" and "Mr Hermon", said Mr Hermon told him about a week before the trophy match that it would be a nice idea to invite Lady Heathcoat-Amory to come down to meet Jack Nicklaus.

"Joyce, Lady Heathcoat-Amory, was the greatest lady golfer of her generation and Jack Nicklaus was, of course, the greatest golfer in the history of the game. So I could not but agree with Mr Hermon's suggestion and he asked me to contact her to see if she would be able to come down," said David.

"That I did - and her son brought her down by car on what was a beautiful Sunday. It was bright sunshine and blue skies and Lady Heathcoat-Amory was a guest with the Bonds in the proprietors' suite. When the match finished Jack Nicklaus popped up to the proprietors' suite to meet Joyce. It was a meeting of two amazing golfers and a great success."

Photographer Gordon Bellman took some pictures of the historic meeting and later gave them to the Bonds. They suggested that Lady Heathcoat-Amory would like some copies and asked David Webb to contact her.

"I was quite happy and prepared to send them through to her in the post but, no no, she insisted in inviting me up to Knightshayes Court to deliver the photographs. I arrived there one afternoon and we had a lovely conversation in her rooms, talking about 'the day' at St Mellion which had only been a week or so previously.

"I got the strong impression that she thoroughly enjoyed meeting Jack Nicklaus and it was certainly a highlight for her, as it was for Jack and the Bond brothers," David said.

FOOTNOTE: Joyce, Lady Heathcoat-Amory, retired from the game with an incredible record. She was also so focused on her game that on her way to winning one of her English championships, at Sheringham in Norfolk, she lined up and holed a vital putt just as a noisy train trundled by. She was asked why it hadn't put her off and she replied, somewhat bemused: "What train?" To this day, golfers can be heard to say, "what train?" when they sink a putt despite some unexpected noise or distraction.

Lady Heathcoat-Amory died on the 18th of November 1997, the day after her 96th birthday. An exhibition of her memorabilia was mounted at Knightshayes Court.

Bobby Jones, the superb American champion golfer, was a great admirer of Joyce Wethered. At her peak, he once described her as "the finest golfer, man or woman, with the finest swing I have ever seen."

Chapter 54

THE HIGHS AND LOWS OF BRINGING SPORT INTO OUR FRONT ROOMS

The deputy head walked into a classroom in one of the five new comprehensive schools in Greater London. He was looking for a young pupil called John who was good at English but not much else. The deputy head walked up to John's desk and said in a very patronising voice: "I see your chosen career is to be a football reporter."

"Yes sir," John replied.

The deputy head: "Don't you think that's rather fanciful?"

John insisted: "No sir, that's what I want to do."

The deputy head: "It's so difficult to become a sports writer. I know English is your best subject but you have to be really very, very good to get a job in a newspaper. Why don't you go into banking, become a bank official?"

John protested: "But sir, I don't want to work in a bank."

The deputy head turned his back and walked out. John didn't ignore the deputy head's advice. In fact he used it to make him more determined than ever to achieve his dream – and more. Young John was John Shrewsbury who went on to become one of the most experienced and revered sports producers and directors on the small screen. If John had followed the career path suggested by his deputy head, the nation, if not the world, would have been deprived of his uncanny, natural but nurtured ability to bring to television some of the most memorable and historic moments of sport. He ended up being the one who was there to ensure those precious morsels were captured for ever. In one way he was actually making the history. He was part of it, he was making it happen by making the broadcasts and films which have become part of our heritage. And, along the way, he worked with some of the most famous names in several sports.

At the age of 15 John went straight from school into Fleet Street as an office boy working for Hulton Press which published Picture Post and children's comics like 'The Eagle'.

"I was 'Dan Dare's' office boy, the office boy on 'The Eagle'. It was the only way I could get a job in Fleet Street," said John.

The editor Clifford Makens was an ex-sports reporter who went on to become the sports editor of 'The Observer'. He got John a variety of jobs, one of which was with Hayters, the biggest sports agency in the south of England, doing reports for all the provincial newspapers around the country.

"I used to go and phone 'copy' through for the reporters and eventually wrote my own stuff. When Tottenham played Blackburn I would go along to Tottenham and five papers in the north of England would want a report on the match. The reporter would write five reports and I used to phone them through. But, after a while, when the reporter got to know you a bit better and you'd been around a bit, he would write a skeleton of the report and you would fill in the bits and the pieces as you were phoning the 'copy' or report over. It was great stuff and a really good learning curve."

John then got a job with an agent for big-name footballers like

Johnny Haynes and Jimmy Greaves and cricketers like Fred Trueman, Colin Cowdrey and Ted Dexter.

"Denis Compton was his partner. He was probably the most iconic man I have ever met in my life. I had eight years working with Denis and by that time we were producing cricket matches for Rothmans which were on a Sunday afternoon.

"BBC 2 had then gone into colour and was looking for a sport on a Sunday afternoon that started and ended in a day. Our cricket matches which lasted four hours sounded like a good idea.

"My job was to organise the grounds, the matches and the players. So, by the time I was 24, I knew every cricketer in Britain. I used to ring up Brian Close and tell him I needed an opening bat, a wicket keeper and a slow bowler in three weeks time at Worcester on a Sunday. They didn't play county cricket on a Sunday in those days.

"So Closey would bring along Geoff Boycott, Ray Wilson and others and we would make up the International Cavaliers team to play against the counties, the beneficiary, which used to take all the money. It became a lot of money because people used to come and watch the games.

"Gary Sobers was at that time qualifying for Nottinghamshire so he was free to play for us. So he, or Denis Compton or Colin Cowdrey captained our team."

The team went to Lords for the Middlesex beneficiary. The Lords officials co-operated with the arrangements but told John not to expect anybody to turn up.

"They sold out of programmes by twelve o'clock and the match didn't start until two! We had eight test match captains in the Cavaliers team and 20,000 people turned up to watch. The officials couldn't believe it," said John. The John Player League was to follow.

Because John had been working closely with the BBC for four years organising the cricket matches, in 1968 the corporation offered him a contract as an assistant producer specialising in cricket. He joined the BBC on May 13th that year, which was also his first wedding anniversary. He was a mere boy in the team but, just over two weeks' later he was working in video tape on the night of that year's European Cup Final, learning the ropes.

It was the 13th European Cup Final staged at Wembley between Manchester United and Benfica. Eight minutes into the second half, Bobby Charlton opened the scoring with a rare headed goal. The lead lasted 22 minutes before Jaime Graca scored for Benfica. It was 1–1 at the end of normal time.

Three minutes into extra time George Best performed his magic. He picked up the ball 25 yards out and worked his way into the penalty area before dribbling round the Benfica goalkeeper to roll the ball into an empty net. Then Brian Kidd celebrated his 19th birthday with goal number three just a minute later. Charlton made it 4-1 to make United the first English team to win the European Cup.

It was ten years since the Munich air disaster of 1958 in which United lost eight players, ten years during which Matt Busby repaid his thanks and gratitude for his own survival by building a team capable of reaching the heights of the game's glory.

For John Shrewsbury it was a glorious night for football. He went on to become a producer for 'Match of the Day' and covered matches for 30 years from 1972 until 2001. There were cricket events and athletics for 10 years with the likes of Seb Coe, Steve Ovett, Daley Thompson and Brendan Foster. There was tennis at Wimbledon with Bjorn Borg starring. John did six years with David Coleman on 'Sportsnight'. He produced outside broadcasts for football, athletics and golf. He directed 15 cup finals for the BBC and was involved in five world cups and seven

Olympic Games. He was the very first producer of the coverage of the London Marathon 1981.

"The hairs on the back of my neck stand up when I think about that because we broke new ground there. Nobody had ever done it before. Running 26 miles through London and the suburbs! How many cameras do we need? How many outside broadcast units do we need? Where can we put them? How do you get television pictures back over 26 miles, please?

"I mean, if you've got a bunch of cameras in a football ground, they stay there and the action stays there. Cricket pitch the same, everything. But runners, they run, 26 miles and you've got to find a way of seeing them every step of the way. It was a huge technical and production challenge. You can't drive up The Mall on a Sunday because it's against the local bylaw? So, how do we get our lead vehicle driving up The Mall? It was like going over Niagara Falls in a barrel because we had 7,000 runners. Back then 7,000 was a huge number. It was my job and I did it and I set the template for that in the first year."

He went on to do another five. "To do the Marathon was probably the highlight of my career...I think."

In 1985 the BBC's golf producer went back to his homeland of New Zealand and John took over the post in 1986. Two years later he came to St Mellion to produce coverage of the infamous, weather-wise, St Mellion Trophy event to mark the official opening of the Jack Nicklaus course. John worked for the BBC for 30 years and although he officially retired in 2000 he was retained to train the new team of young broadcasters to do the job properly and as he would expect it to be done. But he was then given a new role with the corporation as an ambassador or, as he would say, "a hand-shaker, flag waver and the pourer of oil on troubled waters" at The Masters in Augusta and the Open. If there were any issues that needed resolving, John Shrewsbury was the diplomat dispatched to "smooth things over".

Also, after he retired he went freelance and covered football for ITV: "It's nice to think that I directed football on national television in my 70th year. It was Sheffield Wednesday against Stoke."

For John this was a return to a ground which held some very sad memories. He was the producer/director for 'Match of the Day' at Hillsborough for the FA Cup semi-final on April 15, 1989 when 96 people died.

"I went into our broadcast van at midday to do a piece for 'Football Focus' and came out at midnight, because we had to service all the news bulletins through the rest of the day. I just knew that the one thing I couldn't do was show somebody dying. I had to convey what was going on and occasionally show close ups of people who had been saved. But you can't show somebody dying. Their parents may be sitting at home watching it on television. We had to be very careful and responsible about how we made the 'cuts'."

John had seen another major disaster four years earlier, on May 29, 1985, at the Heysel Stadium in Brussels. He was sitting next to Bobby Charlton. Thirty-nine people died an hour before kick-off. Barry Davies was the commentator and Bobby Charlton was the summariser.

"That was frightening. In a way it was even worse than Hillsborough because there was a lot of violence. Hillsborough wasn't violent, just a calamitous incident really. To be present at one of those tragedies would have been bad enough, but to be present at both....terrible."

John summed up his amazing career like this: "I've seen some tough sides of sport but I was very lucky. I've worked with the best guys, the tops, in my time which has been great. Working at the highest level you can in your particular field is as good as it gets. Hundreds of memories. A kaleidoscope of memories."

Chapter 55

ROOM SERVICE – IN WELLIES

It was time for the restaurant to be awarded stars by the AA. The organisation's inspector dined in the restaurant in the evening and everything went well. The next morning he asked for full English breakfast room service, but the staff were up to their eyes in it catering for guests who'd turned up in the restaurant for breakfast.

It was time for joint proprietor Hermon Bond to try out his skills as a waiter. He got the breakfast tray and walked over to the hotel to provide room service to the AA man.

Hermon knocked on the door, the man from the AA opened it and Hermon, in his wellies, proudly announced: "Alright boy, got your breakfast."

St Mellion got the stars it wanted!

This story is told by Di Pile who was restaurant manageress. She said the Bonds created employment which was tremendous. They opened up a lot of opportunities for a lot of people: "It was a family run business which, I think, was the most important thing. There were always people who would say they didn't want what the Bonds created and there were always people who would complain but, overall, it brought a lot to the area, especially during the Benson & Hedges and the spin-off that created."

When Hermon died, Di said it was a great honour for some of the original 'Bond Girls' as they were called to help at the gathering after the funeral: "We went up to Hermon's house and did the catering with Rachel, Hermon's wife. The Bond Girls who were there included Penny Baxter, Rowenna Brooking and Sue Tolley."

Di added that the whole essence of St Mellion was a togetherness and the strong work ethic: "We were just good friends and good mates. I consider myself extremely lucky to have worked there because it was a really good time in my life and I loved it, absolutely loved it. It was the fun time of my life, the social time of my life and one of the happiest."

Chapter 56

CACK-HANDED HERMON

Hermon Bond was what's called a cack-handed golfer - he played with his left hand below his right hand. He was a strong driver of the ball and invariably a very straight driver.

But John Rowe, who enjoyed playing golf with Hermon, said: "He had a habit of hitting the ball and saying: 'Where did it go?' I used to say: 'Oh, straight down the middle Hermon'. I feel sure that's all he wanted to hear because on one occasion when he asked me I replied: 'Never saw it Hermon' and he said: 'Oh it's alright, it's straight down the middle'.

Cornishman John Rowe, a retired police officer, joined Looe Bin Down Golf Club in 1970 and that's when he first met Hermon and Jim Bond who were both members. At one time he was club secretary in the seventies and eighties and Hermon invited him to be secretary again when the Bonds bought Looe.

He said the three Bond brothers were well-known: "It used to be said you could walk from Looe to St Mellion on Bond land because all three brothers, Jim, Martin and Hermon, had farmland across quite a bit of South East Cornwall."

John became secretary to the Cornwall Golf Union and was responsible for arranging fixtures for county teams: "If I phoned up Hermon and asked if we could have a match at St Mellion he'd always say 'yes'. I always felt it was a personal favour to me because county matches were invariably played on a Sunday. That meant that whichever course was being played had to donate or give away 15 starting times to the county which is a considerable expense, plus four or five starting times on the Saturday for the practice. So it was quite generous of any club to host a county match."

Hermon invited John up to St Mellion for a game on the Nicklaus course and there were two strands to Hermon's bet – John wouldn't go round in under 90 and he'd lose half-a-dozen balls.

"Hermon said we'd have a quid on it. I managed to do both. I got round in under 90 and with the same ball I started with. But the thing I regret is, I never got my pound.

"Whenever you played golf with Hermon you might just have a few pence on the result, but Hermon would fight as much for 10p a hole as if it was £100 a hole."

John Rowe said Cornwall has a couple of very good golf courses at St Enodoc and Trevose which are nationally known, but St Mellion, with the additional publicity they generated with the Nicklaus course, certainly put Cornwall and the South West on the international map golf-wise: "It has been a successful course, too difficult for some people, but it's certainly an achievement and that was no doubt down to the foresight and tenacity of the Bonds to get it through."

Chapter 57

THIS IS HEAVEN ON EARTH

It takes an awful lot to impress John Shrewsbury. After all, as the producer of golf for BBC TV, he'd been all over the country covering the game and he'd worked on the Benson & Hedges at Fulford.

But John wasn't known as John "Shrewd" Shrewsbury for nothing. He spotted something. He detected that the professionals had "outgrown" the Fulford course.

"There were a couple of holes on the finishing circuit, par fives, which they could hit with a drive and an eight iron," he said.

That might have been good golf, but it wasn't, necessarily, in John's professional opinion, good television – boring perhaps for the viewer.

So John was looking for another, much more challenging venue for the B&H. He talked to the European Tour's George O'Grady and Ken Scofield about it. They said there was a new course down in Cornwall, designed by Jack Nicklaus, that they were looking at. They said it could be a matchplay course but they thought it could be a regular tournament course. They asked John if he wanted to come along with them to take a look at it - and he agreed.

John takes up the story: "I'd never been to Cornwall in my life. But we went one day to St Mellion, the three of us with a couple of our people. We met the Bond brothers, Martin and Hermon, John Yeo, who was the professional then, and a couple of others.

"I took one look at this place and I thought 'I can't believe this'. It was amazing. It was Heaven on earth. It was magical. It was Camelot.

"We walked down the 10th hole to the stream - and then I saw the 11th hole. My mind is thinking 'pictures' straight away. Then we walked across to the 12th tee and I looked down that fantastic avenue of trees. I could see that the place was made for television."

The group walked the entire course and John was convinced it would make a great venue.

Martin and Hermon, almost in unison, asked: "D'you think it's a matchplay course?" John replied that he thought it was a golf course you could do anything with you wanted.

John and his colleagues went away to think about what they had seen and promised to come back to the Bonds later. In the meantime, Hermon astutely invited John to come down and play a round. The day John chose, it poured with rain! But it stopped raining before they teed off.

Walking down the first, John said to Hermon: "Crikey, there's a lot of standing water, I'm surprised the course is open."

Hermon replied, in his fullest Cornish accent: "Well boy, if I say it's open, it's open."

For John Shrewsbury that was a significant moment. It was, for him, the first indication of what Hermon Bond – and his brother

Martin - were all about. They were the bosses. They were St Mellion.

John reported back to George O'Grady and Ken Scofield. He told them St Mellion would work. George and Ken talked to the tour representatives and it was suggested an event was held at St Mellion to test the course and facilities.

So the St Mellion Trophy event was held in 1988, with Nick Faldo and Sandy Lyle taking on Jack Nicklaus and Tom Watson to officially open the Nicklaus Course. The 1988 contest is legendary, because of the weather, but it allowed John, despite the challenges posed by the conditions, to tell the European Tour: "St Mellion is terrific."

And so, it was decided the Benson & Hedges should move to St Mellion, partly due to the contribution, input and support of John Shrewsbury, who, from day one, fell in love with the place and the people.

The St Mellion Trophy event was held again in 1989 and televised again – in perfect weather conditions with brilliant sunshine. John, his director Alistair Scott, Nick Faldo, Sandy Lyle and their caddies flew down in a private plane from Gleneagles, where they had been at the Bell's Scottish Open, on the Saturday night for the event on the Sunday.

Then, the following year, in 1990, the B&H returned to St Mellion.

John was enthused: "After the St Mellion Trophy events we were off and running. The Benson & Hedges was one of the highlights of the golfing year for us because the venue was so spectacular and the whole atmosphere of the place was wonderful.

"We used to have the barbecues in the evening in the old barn and all the players used to come – Seve, Olazabal, Woosey - and even help with the cooking."

Northern Ireland golfer Ronan Rafferty, who wasn't a great supporter of the course initially, would be the "wine waiter". Quite a few people declined replenishing their glass from him because of his critical comments about the course.

But, John said, everyone used to muck in: "It was a fabulous atmosphere and it was unique. I was covering golf tournaments all over the country in those days and there was nothing like it. The pro-am beforehand was fantastic, with a great atmosphere at that as well, then the tournament itself with the barbecues in the evening, it was just something different.

"The Bond brothers just presided over it all. They took everything in their stride. Nobody was feted, everybody was treated the same, everyone was given great consideration and anything they wanted they could have. It was just a fabulous place to be. It was always fun to go to, always good fun. So much so that we used to probably do three recces at St Mellion instead of normally one or two. We liked to go down at least three times."

John was happy for the B&H to stay at St Mellion because, over the years, the BBC staff had refined their camera positions and knew exactly where they would get the most picturesque shots. So, it was a personal blow to him when the decision was taken to move the B&H from St Mellion to The Oxfordshire.

"The Oxfordshire was just a flat field, the last place we wanted to go, but of course money talked at that time with the tour and so on and that's their business and so in the end they made the decision to leave.

"That was a great sadness because I knew that Hermon in particular would have liked another couple of years of the B&H at St Mellion."

So, perhaps, it's not surprising that, for John Shrewsbury, his most significant moment at St Mellion was the first Benson & Hedges International Open on the Nicklaus Course in 1990.

“That will stick in my mind for ever, because it was new, because the B&H was coming to a new venue and what would come out of it? Would the public come? Would they turn up and would it be a success? Would the atmosphere be right or would it be flat?

“As it turned out, it was all that we’d hoped it would be. A marvellous venue and a terrific event. And we always got a good winner at St Mellion, we always had a worthy winner. Olazabal won it, Seve won it. Top, top people because you had to be on top of your game to play the Nicklaus course. It was no push-over.

“We got some wonderful, spectacular pictures from it. The 11th was always the signature hole.”

Chapter 58

YOU ARE ST MELLION.

Martin and Hermon Bond didn't hesitate in telling people if it hadn't been for Len Owen none of what evolved at St Mellion would have been possible. Len would tell the same people it had nothing to do with him – it was all down to the Bonds.

In 1970 Len Owen took on the role of Benson & Hedges special events manager. He ended up bringing the 1979 B&H International Open to St Mellion, thanks to the City of York celebrating its 1900th anniversary in 1971. It was in AD71 that the Romans founded the City of Eboracum (it became the City of York many, many centuries later!).

The organisers of the celebrations wanted to include a golf tournament at Fulford Golf Course. They needed someone with the expertise to run the event. Len had a series of meetings with councillors and officials and Benson & Hedges put some money into it to make it a big occasion.

The tournament was called the Benson & Hedges Festival of Golf. It was won by Tony Jacklin who, six years later, came to St Mellion for an exhibition match to celebrate the creation of the original course.

The Fulford tournament became an annual event. The pros liked the course, players like Ken Brown, Bernhard Langer, Mark

James and Howard Clark all supported the event. They didn't say it was an Augusta or anything near it, but they loved the greens.

After the first five years at Fulford the event was re-christened the B&H International Open and continued to be played there.

But, in 1979, it came to St Mellion, for just one year before returning to Fulford. Len Owen confessed the move to St Mellion wasn't the wisest decision of his career: "I decided to take a change of venue. It wasn't the best thing I've ever done in my life, to be truthful, because the St Mellion course wasn't really ready for a tournament."

The event was difficult to set up and run and it was widely accepted, even by the Bond brothers, that the old course was too young and hadn't settled. Although it was designed by J Hamilton Stutt, it wasn't designed for European Tour events or the standard required for them.

"The Bonds were disappointed but very gentlemanly about the loss of the tournament and we remained friends. I'd never said that we would be there for more than one year," said Len.

Back at Fulford the B&H continued to be played there annually. But within a few years Martin and Hermon Bond had got Jack Nicklaus to agree to design a course for them.

Len recalled: "The tournament had become one of the top three in England, probably in Europe, for prize money and so on. I realised that eventually we were going to have to move somewhere and a Nicklaus course in a whole new area of the country appealed to us, so we went wholeheartedly for it."

Len Owen spent a lot of time overseeing the creation of the infrastructure that was needed at St Mellion – electricity, gas, water. So, while the Nicklaus course was being constructed, he was on hand to advise what went where. He was there at least half a dozen times when Nicklaus made personal visits to monitor the progress of his course. There was a high level of co-operation among all those involved, which made the final result the best it could be.

Len loved working with the Bonds. His experience at Fulford was that if he wanted anything done, there would have to be a committee meeting about it, which could delay things, sometimes up until literally a day or two before the tournament was starting. St Mellion was another world.

"The difference with Martin and Hermon was, as they were always telling you: 'We're the proprietors, so leave it to us'. I asked about shaving the tops of the huge banks at St Mellion so the tents, marquees and hospitality units for the tented village could be on a flat surface. I thought it would take weeks to sort out. But it was done within two or three days. The brothers often used to laugh about it: 'Done before you wake up in the morning'. It wasn't quite that fast, but it was pretty quick.

"Without that work being done we couldn't have had a successful tented village there – and I was pleased with the result."

Len did just the one tournament at St Mellion, the 1990 Open which was won by Jose Maria Olazabal, said his "goodbyes" and retired at the age of 60. He handed over the reins to Jim Elkins but kept in touch with the brothers and would see them at future B&H Tournaments at St Mellion.

"The tented village grew over the years. The amphitheatre that was created round the 18th green was just brilliant and I think television liked that. There were a dozen hospitality units all around the green and the grandstands were growing higher and higher. I've never seen anything any better than that scene for that occasion."

The layout round the 18th set the template for other tournaments. The "horseshoe" of hospitality venues and grandstands was copied at Wentworth, the Open and in Europe.

FOOTNOTE: The brothers always fought shy of publicity. Hermon would run a mile at the thought of speaking into a microphone. Both he and Martin would try, wherever possible, to avoid getting on the stage for tournament presentations and prize-givings.

Len Owen would tell them: "You've got to be on stage. You ARE St Mellion, whether you like it or not. You're the men who went to get Jack Nicklaus – and by golly, you got him."

But the Bonds did what they were most comfortable with. They would go on stage reluctantly - but left the public speaking to others.

"I never heard either of them say a single word into a microphone," said Len.

Chapter 59

The BENSON & HEDGES YEARS 1990 to 1995

The eagerly awaited return of the B&H International Open to St Mellion in 1990 was the first of six great years of Tournament golf for the host club.

Every year produced thrilling results as the difficulty of the course combined with the variable early Spring conditions began to take a toll on the field. Only the very best players prevailed in these trying circumstances, much to the delight of the large enthusiastic crowds.

The winners were:

1990 - Jose Maria Olazabal – Score 279 by one stroke from Ian Woosnam

1991 - Bernhard Langer – Score 286 by two strokes from Vijay Singh

1992 - Peter Senior – Score 287 in a playoff with Tony Johnstone

1993 - Paul Broadhurst – Score 276 by one stroke from Mark James and J M Olazabal

1994 - Seve Ballesteros - Score 281 by three strokes from Nick Faldo

1995 - Peter O'Malley – Score 280 by one stroke from Mark James and Constantino Rocca

Certain victories were more memorable than others but each was hard fought and well deserved, often in testing conditions.

Many spectators long for the day when once again they can cheer their favourites to victory as in those memorable days of the early nineties.

The highlight for many a player at the B&H Open was the famous barbecues and end of tournament party - this is how they came about.

Martin Watson, the then general manager, lived in the house adjacent to the 14th hole on the "old" course.

The building next door was unoccupied for most of the year so it was used by Richard Brown from Benson & Hedges for about eight weeks when he was setting things up for the International Open. He'd move into the timeshare lodge for the duration of the tournament itself.

One evening a couple of days before the tournament the Benson & Hedges people were there and some of the golfers had arrived. There was no social event arranged for them so Martin Watson told Richard Brown and Jim Elkins, also from B&H, to come round to his place for a barbecue.

"I started arranging a barbecue for a few people and asked Martin and Hermon if they'd like to come and they said they'd love to. They asked me who was doing it and who was getting all the food and so on. I said I was and Hermon said: 'Don't be so stupid boy. We'll get the bloody chefs down. Come with me and we'll bloody sort it out'.

"I can remember going to the cellar with him and filling boxes with drink. He kept telling me to get a bottle of Gin, a bottle of

Scotch, wine and a bottle of this and that and put it in the boxes.

"I told my wife Sally we were having a barbecue and when I said maybe 20 or 30 were coming she was wondering how we were going to do it. With that, a van arrived with a couple of chefs, a barbecue and chairs. They set it up in the back garden and then the food arrived and it was job done."

Every year since the B&H returned to St Mellion in 1990, barbecues were held every evening on site, down in the old barn. They were a unique feature of the week. A chance for players, their families and officials to relax and unwind. Everybody who was anybody was there.

Seve Ballesteros was there with his wife Carmen, their three-year-old son Javier Baldomero and his baby brother Miguel. Carmen was expecting their third child. Seve was downstairs and the B&H's Jim Elkins was wandering around, hardly eating, just making sure that everything was going ok.

Seve came up to Jim and said very quietly: "Yim (his pronunciation of Jim) my boys like ice cream."

Jim politely told him: "Seve, it's getting late, it's getting dark outside, we are in a barn in the middle of a golf course, where am I meant to get ice cream from at this time of the night?"

Seve pleaded: "Do try Yim, my boys do like ice cream."

So Jim got on the radio to William "Will" Raynham. Will was a junior assistant manager and he was upstairs in the barn. Jim explained the situation to Will. They debated what colour the ice cream should be. Jim said any colour would do, as long as it was ice cream!

Will decided to accept the challenge. He got in a golf buggy, with no lights of course, drove up one of the fairways, arrived at the clubhouse and made his way to the kitchens. His search for ice cream proved successful, but now he had to get the stuff down to the barn. Will found a large, flat oval container and scooped the ice cream on to it. Then he set off in the buggy, steering with one hand and balancing the container on the palm of his other hand above his head, like a waiter carrying a tray of glasses. The ice cream arrived intact.

Jim Elkins was impressed: "Will came back in the buggy over mounds and round corners in what was by then complete and utter darkness. The container was full of every colour of ice cream you could imagine, whether it was green, yellow, pink, blue, every colour, little rows of them."

Will handed the container to Jim who put it on the side, tapped Seve on the shoulder and said: "Seve, your boys like ice cream. What sort of ice cream do they like?" The disbelief on his face and his smile were followed by a couple of polite expletives and the words: "Yim, you my friend."

For Jim Elkins it was little moments like this that made the whole thing stretch way beyond the tournament itself because: "You can't bottle that sort of memory."

The barbecues were the idea of Len Owen who was B&H special events director for the 1990 tournament at St Mellion following the impromptu pre -tournament one hosted by Martin Watson.

All the big names were in the timeshare lodges, some with their wives and families, and Len asked them would they come along with their families if he put on barbecues in the evenings. They promised they would, and they did.

"It was a wonderful, wonderful week of perpetual sunshine for that event, perpetual barbecues and all the top players who were staying on the site came to the barbecues - and the officials too," said Len, who was about to retire.

"It was just how I wanted to finish my years with the B&H. It was a wonderful way to go out. Jose Maria Olazabal, who I didn't think spoke all that much English, came into the barn after he won the tournament, came over to me, put his arms around me and said: 'You are the best tournament director'."

The Pro -Am that preceded every B&H Open proved to be very popular with celebrities and sports stars alike. Here is what a few of them said:

Ronnie Corbett, whose golf bag was almost as tall as him, if he took his golf cap off: "It's wonderful, majestic, a magnificent course. Very difficult to play if you're my height and can't see over the horizon. It's a credit to the enterprise of the Bond brothers and the skill of Jack Nicklaus."

Michael Parkinson: "It's in wonderful nick and once it's completely matured it's going to be absolutely superb. I'd like to see the great players play it to show us how it should be done."

Jimmy Tarbuck: "It's a wonderful set up and when you get good weather it's one of the best places in the world. I'm sure the locals and the holidaymakers will appreciate it. I mean, it's one hell of a course."

Jethro: "I play golf for pleasure not punishment."

Colin Montgomery: "It's the only course we play on tour where 72 means 72."

Rod Hull: "A joy to play. The next time I come I will try to find the course itself."

Chapter 60

WALKING THROUGH PARADISE

"St Mellion is unique" according to Jim Elkins, the B&H special events director who oversaw the tournaments on the Nicklaus course from 1991 to 1995: "Certainly in the days of the Benson & Hedges, not only the venue but also the proprietors Martin and Hermon and the people around them created that uniqueness.

"The Nicklaus golf course is certainly still unique, but I think it was more than that in those days. The Bonds just had this massive, great big family and those sort of situations are never going to be repeated.

"Now-a-days, new golf courses are being built, multi-nationals get involved, massive hotels go up and big leisure complexes and God knows what. They're filled with corporate and everything else, but they're not anything like St Mellion was from concept through to fruition. Nothing like it. If you tried to do it that way now, you wouldn't succeed – simple as that."

In the eyes of the Bond brothers the tournament had to be the best that could be staged and put on from everybody's point of view - the spectators, television, golfers, everyone. The co-operation from the Bonds was exceptional.

"A good example of that was the help we got with closing the 18th hole of the old course for two months to build the tented golf village," said Jim. "We never, ever heard a complaint from a member, and I knew a lot of members, particularly all the captains and the committees, about a hole being taken from 'their' golf course.

"It was the only course that was open to them for quite a long period of time because the Nicklaus course was closed to members for something like 23 days before the tournament for its preparation. Actually, there wasn't 18 holes of golf for the members to play for quite a long period of time every year and yet, their pride in their golf course being used for a major event far exceeded the inconvenience that they might have.

"That's a classic analogy of what St Mellion was all about. Not only the Bonds agreeing that that should be the case, but all the members, without exception, were more than happy to be inconvenienced for that period of time because they were very, very proud of what they were part of."

The lasting memory held by Mitchell Platts, the director of corporate affairs and public relations for the European Tour, was that the Bonds were fantastic hosts: "Together as brothers they set down the marker for St Mellion in the way they went about their hospitality. Not only did the players enjoy coming to St Mellion and playing and staying, but also the media and Pro-Am guests.

"Right from the start they embraced everybody and that was, perhaps, their number one asset because everybody wanted to return to St Mellion.

"If the Bonds didn't have the vision in the beginning to turn farmland into an outstanding golf course and attract the world's greatest golfers to play at St Mellion, you would not have what is here today.

"Equally, if Crown Golf had not come in and seen what the

future was for St Mellion and created what they have with the wonderful hotel and a golf course that everyone would want to play, then we wouldn't have the future that we've got.

"The Bond brothers had this great flair about them and a desire to actually bring big time golf to this part of the country and to their own farmland. Of course they went about it with exactly the right people and together I think they have created a masterpiece that has grown and grown and grown."

Mitchell Platts agreed with the view of Jeff Chapman, the owner and chairman of the Bennelong Group which owns Crown Golf, that St Mellion was accessible to millions of people in the UK: "Jeff said St Mellion was only a tank-full of petrol away and I think that's the way the Bond brothers looked at it and it was true then. It's no different now to the way Bennelong and Crown Golf look at it."

FOOTNOTE: 1991 was the first year Jim Elkins was in total charge of the Benson & Hedges International Open at St Mellion as the new special events director. Jim was keen to spend time just chatting with Hermon away from the madding crowd and he found the best way to achieve this was to go walking with Hermon down to the 12th hole and along the woods to the right-hand side: "To get quality time with Hermon, you had to do that and he was always happy to do that. He'd put his wellies on and off he'd march. You could spend two or three hours and get a lot of business, in inverted commas, done just walking through Martin and Hermon's 'Paradise'."

Chapter 61

GO WITH THE FLOW

Sue McLaughlin's first day at work in St Mellion was on main reception on the eve of the first day of the return of the Benson & Hedges in 1990.

"I was on the late shift from three o'clock until eleven o'clock with Vi Burleigh who was senior receptionist," said Sue. "We were stood there checking people in for the tournament and who should be checking in but Severiano Ballesteros. Seve was the most handsome man I've ever seen. It was fantastic. Later on Nick Faldo checked in. Very tall, very good looking."

Sue had always wanted to work at St Mellion, she loved the place, its people and the atmosphere so much. So, when the opportunity arose, she left her job in the Civil Service, took a £4,000 cut in annual salary and joined the team at St Mellion.

She said those initial first few days in the job were very memorable: "I was on the early shift on the morning of the first day of the tournament and they were all coming in for their breakfast. Bernhard Langer was stood there with his banana. Every morning he came in for breakfast with his banana and his can of special energy drink.

"In those days we had an autograph book on the desk and there were lots of players who willingly signed the book, people like Sam Torrance.

"That was a very active week and because I was a new girl I was a bit of a gopher as well and I was up and down to the timeshare lodges on the golf buggies. Lord Brocket of Brocket Hall was in one of the lodges. I had to go down with a parcel one day and I rang the doorbell. He came to the door in his very nice smoking dressing gown and his leather mules. That was Lord Brocket. There were lots of dignitaries around."

Sue was there for all six of the Benson & Hedges tournaments. The rest of the time she was running the sports desk. When Ken Hunt took over as general manager in 1993 she was appointed timeshare manager: "It's brought me into contact with people from all around the world and the one thousand timeshare owners became quite personal friends as well."

There were 19 timeshare lodges with 50 weeks – a total of 976 weeks of timeshare. There were also 12 hotel lodges available to rent. The first six timeshare lodges were built by Henry Boot of Sheffield who sold the weeks. Then Wimpey came in and more were built by sub-contractor John Kemble, a local builder.

"In the mid- eighties timeshare was in its infancy and St Mellion was one of the forerunners and the Bonds could see the potential. It was high profile timeshare and it was all marketed and sold through the main national newspapers," said Sue.

"People bought the timeshare because when they came back the next year it was exactly the same and they wondered how we kept them so good. They're a home from home for many people."

Sue added that both Martin and Hermon were charismatic: "Even though there were no airs, no graces to them there was something about the aura about them and about St Mellion. I think that was their doing because, right from the early days, they employed local people that loved their job.

"It was a family business and staff looked on St Mellion as their second home. The brothers treated all the club members and guests accordingly.

"The Bonds have left behind a marvellous facility. Years ago this place was buzzing with Americans, Chinese, Japanese, always coach loads of people coming in. It was extremely well known on the map, it was world famous. A very, very good place to work and a lovely place.

"I just remember the Bond era – lots of events, big buzz, Benson & Hedges, the tented village, all the hospitality, the food, very professional. And, of course, friendships, friends, everyone was one big family, and the personal attention to everything by the Bonds and their direct line managers.

"Having seen all the changes, I've gone with the flow which was one of Hermon's favourite expressions: 'Go with the flow dear' and he used to always say 'Keep your head down maid, keep your head down'. That summaries Hermon: 'Go with the flow'."

Chapter 62

MRS BAXTER, A PENNY FOR YOUR THOUGHTS – 40 YEARS ON!

There wasn't a member of the Brooking family living in the village of St Mellion who didn't work at the golf and country club. Mrs Brooking, Rowenna, known as Rowie, started her career in St Mellion cooking in the Buttery. Then she became a waitress and then she used to work through the night to "lay up" tables for dinners and weddings.

Mr Brooking, Don, was the maintenance man, the odd job man who could turn his hand to any task. One of their daughters Michelle worked as a receptionist on the old sports desk for a few years.

Another daughter Penny still works at St Mellion, more than 40 years after she started as a part-time, weekend waitress. Don's brother's daughter Carol Brooking was also a waitress. Her daughter Donna Weeks then worked in the conference and banqueting side of the business. And Penny's son Daniel helped out on the conference and banqueting side.

Perhaps Penny Baxter – she married a professional footballer Derek Baxter – became the best-known member of the Brooking family at St Mellion. She started as a part-time waitress for St Mellion's first Christmas in December 1976 and, in this 30th anniversary year of the official opening of the Nicklaus course, she is function and events co-ordinator.

"Lots of local people did that first Christmas," Penny recalled. "There were lots of young people who helped the Bonds out at Christmas time - and mum and dad were working here already."

The Bonds had "pinched" her parents from other places they were working to come and join the team, or what was, the family of St Mellion Golf and Country Club. And the brothers knew the Brooking family. Penny went to school with Hermon's boys Alan and Graham - they would catch the school bus together to go to Callington.

The wages came in little brown envelopes handed out by "Uncle Dick" Mitchell who used to be the Bonds' accountant. After that first Christmas, Penny became a regular waitress. They were doing Sunday lunches and the diners would meet first in the upstairs lounge for drinks, so Penny was a drinks waitress. She was still at school, so it was still only a job to earn some pocket money.

Colin Mitchell was the general manager when a full-time position became available as a receptionist on the sports desk for the leisure side of the complex, the swimming pool and tennis, squash and badminton courts. He felt Penny would be suitable for the position and approached her parents, but completing her education was also important. It was decided that Colin would contact Callington Comprehensive School to see if she could take the job but also go back to finish her studies and exams. And that was agreed.

Penny did go back to school and did get the qualifications she needed to be a secretary but, by then, she'd realised she didn't want to be stuck behind a desk in an office.

"I found that I enjoyed having close contact with the general public. A couple of years later a position became available on the main hotel reception desk, which I applied for and got."

Penny was one of a select group of staff chosen to promote the 1978 PGA Cup Match between Great Britain and Ireland and the United States of America. They went all round the South West of England dressed in promotional T shirts and distributing leaflets, posters and information to golf clubs and shops. In Torquay they ended up on the Radio One Road Show.

"I can actually say that I couldn't have done a better thing than working here because I've met so many people who I would never ever meet at any other time or under any other circumstances. It was just right across the board, people who would pop up unexpectedly to play golf, like Prince Andrew and Hugh Grant."

Penny was on main reception for the first Benson & Hedges International Open at St Mellion in 1979. She dealt with all the ticket sales for the tournament: "I took home boxes of application forms, tickets and envelopes and worked into the wee small hours to get the tickets ready to go out the following morning. There were thousands and thousands of them.

"Seve Ballesteros was great. No airs and graces about him, very charming, very shy, very quiet. Bernhard Langer was the other guy who was a real gentleman, always so polite."

Penny went on to become the head receptionist and then in April 1988 she came off reception to take on the role which she has played for decades, although it changed over those years. Basically, she did everything and worked very closely with David Webb – bookings for golf days, weddings, Christmas and conferences. As that side of the business grew, another member of staff took on club members' events and Christmas and then weddings, so Penny could concentrate on other things – conferences, banqueting and meetings. She also organised members' events, the matches for the men, the ladies and the fossils.

Penny said: "Throughout all the Bond years I enjoyed it loads, tremendously. It was a great place to be, it brought opportunities to so many people and I'm glad that I was able to take part in those opportunities. It was an exciting time and an amusing time and I loved it."

Chapter 63

A BOND INVITATION

One day in early 1992 David Webb, the club secretary, rang Thelma McEvoy from St Mellion and said: "Mr Martin and Mr Hermon have asked me to ask you if you'd consider being Lady Captain."

A surprised but delighted Thelma accepted immediately. Later she said: "That's how it was done in those days. It wasn't a decision made by a ladies committee, it was Martin and Hermon's decision. I had no idea whatsoever why they picked me but I considered it to be a great honour."

All Men and Lady Captains were chosen this way as the brothers were adamant that the privilege of captaincy would only be conferred upon the worthiest individuals.

Captains were, like all the team, expected to work. The Tournament and the lead up to it were always busy but exciting times for the captains as they were involved at every step along the way.

Thelma McEvoy only ever played golf with Hermon Bond once, in 1993, the year she was lady captain. The two played against members of staff which was an annual tradition.

"Hermon always really decided on the day what his handicap

would be. If it was blowing or raining, it would be several shots higher," said Thelma. "Both of us played extremely well and Hermon kept saying: 'That's 'ansome maid'."

Apart from being involved as Captain in matches with all the Cornwall clubs in the league and friendly matches with clubs in Devon as well as Cornwall and the social side, there was the hard work during the Benson & Hedges International Open – after being entertained to lunch and afternoon tea in the marquee by the 18th on the Friday.

"The Lady Captain had to organise all the ladies to do the scoring on the last two days. You got a phone call on the Friday night to say that probably 65 or 66 pros had made the cut and qualified for the last 36 holes. You then had to find a lady to go with each pair to keep the score.

"You had a clipboard with a sheet on it and you had to record whether they drove on to the fairway or into the rough, how many shots it took them to get to the green, whether they went into a bunker and how many putts they had.

"At the end of each hole you had to report the details to a scorer who was sat at the end of the green with a walkie-talkie to send the stats, or statistics, back to base. We got paid £15 a day which we thought was a lot of money then. It was good."

But the real icing on the cake was to get to walk in with the golfers and the lady captain normally went out with the last pair so, in theory, she would come in with the winner.

"That's what happened to me in 1993 when Paul Broadhurst won. Two years later, in 1995, the 25th B&H and its last year at St Mellion, I also brought the winner in. I was going round with Peter O'Malley and, although he wasn't in the last group, he won," said Thelma.

The ladies loved mingling with the world's top golfers: "Frank Nobilo the New Zealander was lovely and Sandy Lyle. And, as for Ernie Els, he was absolutely gorgeous. All the girls wanted to score his match."

Thelma said St Mellion was a very special place: "Throughout Cornwall and Devon it has always been head and shoulders above everybody else because of the Nicklaus course.

"When we had ladies open days or guest days the prize fund and the food were wonderful. The Bonds always came up trumps for the ladies. People would cut your arm off to invite them. It was the place to come. We used to have two open days a year and you'd have 120 ladies each time. If you didn't book early in the year you didn't get in. It was amazing. Martin and Hermon have left a wonderful legacy for Cornwall, something unique."

FOOTNOTE: Thelma McEvoy bumped into television commentator Peter Alliss one breakfast-time and they had a chat about the wet weather. She told him confidently: "Well, it will stop raining in a minute." Peter replied: "Can I quote you?"

"I don't know if he did quote me, but when he was commentating at the US Masters he mentioned the Cornish farmers the Bonds and the Nicklaus course in Cornwall. He said maybe they were watching the television coverage. He made the comment because Hermon and Rachel Bond's elder son Alan was caddying for one of the players, Martin Laird."

Chapter 64

THE B&H SHOULD HAVE BEEN LATER IN THE YEAR

Eleven years on and with the prestige of the new Nicklaus Course, the B&H was back in 1990. The Bonds never really lost touch with the people from B&H since the 1979 event.

After the course successfully staged the 1987 Weetabix British Ladies Open Championship, Len Owen and Derek Pillage from B&H came to take a look and play the course. They could see a future for the B&H back at St Mellion.

All the services and infrastructure had been put in for a tented village on the Old Course – electric, water, drainage – all they had to do was plug or tap in to the system. Instead of "make do" as back in 1979, everything was done in a proper manner. Everything was ready.

And, the course was getting better every year, although there was always an issue over the date of the B&H. Many thought it was too early. One year it was in late April and there was frost on the greens. Not the sort of thing the greenkeepers wanted to deal with, but they did. Golf commentator Peter Alliss even wrote a letter suggesting it would be nice if the date was changed to the summer time because it could be inhospitably cold late April, early May. If it was a bit later, it would be warmer, the trees and shrubs would be out – and the attendance could have been swollen by holidaymakers.

It was a miracle Jose Maria Olazabal could actually hit a ball when he played in the pro-am. He'd just come back from winning the Masters in Augusta. It was a bit of a shock to the system, coming from temperatures of about 80 degrees Fahrenheit to just above freezing. He had a woolly hat pulled down over his ears and was wrapped up really warm.

Martin Bond felt: "It was unfair to us, to the television, to the players, to everybody. What annoyed us was that the European Tour went back onto the Continent for another month. Well, they could have stayed back there for a month and then come here."

Nevertheless, around 40,000 people would flock to St Mellion for the tournament. That, in itself, was a remarkable achievement. Martin Bond put it this way: "The Royal Cornwall Show got 100,000 after 100 years, we got 40,000 after the Nicklaus course had been open only three years, so it wasn't bad."

Hermon said it continued to be a learning curve. They'd identify things each year to make the event even better the following year. The brothers used to take a buggy or a truck and tour the cars parks, counting the cars, and they found that quite encouraging. And, also, it was clear many people had travelled from outside the county.

Chapter 65

STARTING FROM SCRATCH

"It's easier to say in words, as it so often is in life, that you're going to do that, or you're going to go there and do something. But when you get a brand new venue like St Mellion which had never seen a European Tour event, you literally have to start from scratch" – words of wisdom from Richard Brown, tournament administrator for the Benson & Hedges at St Mellion from 1990 to 1995.

"You have to think of traffic and where you're going to park the different sections like the public, corporate hospitality, competitors, caddies, members etc. Then you've got to work out where you're going to check them for tickets, where you're going to take the money, how they're going to come into the course.

"Then you have to plan all the other things like accommodation, First Aid, the supply of electricity and water, how you're going to deal with liquid waste as well as ordinary waste, everything. You literally have to start from scratch and then try and piece everything together and go through every single section from A to Z."

The spectator village had to be away from the natural flow of people. That did cause problems in the first year because the two nines of the Nicklaus course were separated.

"We put too many catering outlets and things like that in between the 9th green and the 10th. They did an enormous amount of business but the village didn't do that much business because people in actual fact didn't have to go to the village. They could get what they wanted to eat on the way down to the 10th and the toilets were there as well," said Richard. "So the second year we did away with a lot of the food and refreshments by the 10th and put it all into the village which became well used."

Richard added that although there were problems the great thing with the Bonds was that they wanted to make it work, they wanted to make it happen and, as long as any requests were sensible, they were only too happy to carry them out, particularly in regard to water and electrics and so on.

Richard was at St Mellion for the 1989 St Mellion Trophy exhibition match, so he had a pretty good idea how he was going to rope and stake the course to control the spectators: "It was a fantastic spectator course because virtually most of the time people were above the players and they could watch the ball at flying height rather than from ground level."

But Richard Brown had to deal with an odd situation involving the 7th, 8th and 9th holes. Spectators came up on the top of the hill at the 7th and could be directed along to the back of the 8th green. But there was no way of getting them out from the back of the 8th green without getting in the way of the 9th tee.

"We went out there with Martin Bond and said we really needed a path going round the top of the 8th green so we can lead people up the left of the 9th. Literally within 24 hours the bulldozer was out there making the path and it was dealt with.

"That was the kind of thing the Bonds did. If you wanted something and they saw the sense in it and the reason why, then they did it. They were brilliant. They just wanted to make it a success, which it was."

Much of the physical work associated with the staging of the event was carried out by Martin's two sons Jon and Chris Bond. These guys worked tirelessly and cheerfully to ensure that the client, B&H, were completely satisfied.

Richard felt the Bonds' success led to, what he called "an enormous amount of Cornish jealousy": "If they wanted to do things after the success of St Mellion, they almost had to use false names and use other people to do transactions because people were just so jealous of them."

Representatives from Benson & Hedges and the BBC who came to St Mellion for the tournaments would play golf with Hermon and Martin. It was a unique experience!

"There was no way you could concentrate because they were always trying gamesmanship wherever they could," said Richard Brown. "You quickly realised that Hermon had his own set of rules, rather than the R&A rules. Most of us understood 'placing the ball' to be that you could wipe and place the ball within six inches on the fairway, but not so with Hermon. His understanding was that he could place the ball anywhere.

"One day we played the 3rd, with the big cliff on the right. Surprisingly enough, we found Hermon's ball half way down the cliff. He went down this cliff with a wood and we couldn't understand how he was ever going to play the ball from the cliff up on to the fairway with a wood. Until we watched him pick up the ball, put it on the biggest tuft of grass he could find and hit it up.

"We challenged him: 'Hermon, you can't place in the rough!' But his answer was: 'Oh boy, I can do what I like'. That was typical Hermon, typical."

Richard gave another example of Martin and Hermon's gamesmanship: "You'd be on the green, faced with a four or five feet putt. You'd have Martin standing behind you and Hermon standing in front of you and they'd start chatting. Martin would say: 'Hermon, don't you think we ought to give him this putt?' Hermon would say: 'No I don't think we ought to give him this putt. I think we should see it'.

"Of course half the time they won the battle and you did miss the putt. But you took it all on the chin in the end and they enjoyed it and we enjoyed it. It was all just a bit of fun."

Hermon's favourite answer when he was asked about his handicap was: "It's 18, plus VAT."

Chapter 66

ONSITE CATERING

Former deputy general manager Mark Lovell recalls the B&H years with affection. For him the annual Benson & Hedges tournaments were the highlight of his long career at the venue.

The club's 200 staff were involved and the entire catering block of Plymouth College of Further Education closed for the duration of the tournament so the students could work in the clubhouse or in the corporate entertainment side of things out by the 18th green. Between 200 and 300 students were bussed in to St Mellion. About 80 would work in the clubhouse and another 200 in the hospitality marquees and the tented village.

"It was a very important part of the students' year because they liked the link with the event and they loved it because it was a prestigious event. We used to make contacts with good students who would later become staff at the club," said Mark.

A special bar was put on for the proprietors' suite which was used to entertain guests from the tournament, players and friends of the Bonds. There were four or five girls running a crèche in the clubhouse for children of staff members and players.

Also, there was a doctor in the hotel and at the back of the hotel there was a physiotherapy bus for the golfers. The Tamar Suite was given over to feeding the Press and the Press marquee was next to that. The restaurant was used to entertain some of St Mellion's main customers. Companies took over the Bond Suite and the Nicklaus Suite for private entertaining. Upstairs, the Lynher Suite was used for entertainment.

"The whole thing was an amazing operation and Martin Watson was a legend in terms of the planning of the events. And it was great for the members who got involved driving courtesy cars and as marshals. And, of course, the police were involved and they enjoyed it. The list was never ending. It involved so many people. It was an amazing time."

Mark added that one estimate was that the week was worth somewhere in the region of £5 to £6 million to the local economy with the supply or food, the provision of accommodation and everything else. Every single room in every single B&B everywhere was occupied: "And, who's to say how many people saw the golf on the television and, as a result, came to St Mellion or the surrounding area to stay. That's unquantifiable."

Chapter 67

A NEW COURSE RECORD – BUT NOT FOR LONG

The 1995 Benson and Hedges International Open was a very special occasion. It was the 25th anniversary of the tournament and, as it turned out, the seventh and last time it was staged at St Mellion.

Costantino Rocca shot 64 to claim a new course record - and the celebrations began. But, 20 to 30 minutes later, Carl Mason finished with a 63, nine under par.

Mason had ended up on the 18th in totally the wrong position. Top right, just on the fringe with the pin back left. He had to get down in two from there to tie the course record.

Jim Elkins, the B&H special events director, was in the hospitality suite at the back of the 18th green: "Carl knew he was on for a fantastic round although I don't think if he necessarily knew at that moment in time that he was on for the course record.

"I went down and managed to wriggle through the crowd and stand on one side of the green as he played the shot of his life. It was an absolutely impossible shot to have to play. Right across the green. I thought if he can get within four or five feet of breaking the record. But what happens? The ball went in the hole.

"You can imagine, there's me – at nine o'clock to the green, him at three o'clock to the green, some 40 to 50 feet to putt. He looked up, saw me, and I looked up, saw him and we both shrugged our shoulder as if to say 'what's all that about'."

Costantino Rocca earlier course record meant he shared the runner-up spot with Mark James. The winner was Peter O'Malley to whom the big winners cheque made a huge difference, or so he told the crowd at the prize giving ceremony.

The 1991 B&H was the first year Jim Elkins was fully in charge of the tournament having taken over from Len Owen who had retired. Bernhard Langer was five over par after two holes in his first round. Sometime during the day Jim went to the bookies and put some money on him. He came in with a 77 so he actually parred the rest of the course and went on to win the tournament.

"The odds that first morning we pretty good, let's just put it that way," Jim said. "Five over after two holes. The worst start I think he or any of the superstars ever made. Again, it was just one of those things. It happened. And what a great ambassador Bernhard Langer was not only for golf, but for the tournament as well. He previously had made the decision to play a ball from up a tree at Fulford in the 1981 B&H Open. "When people think of the Benson & Hedges they also think of Bernhard Langer as well as the venues. There was always something memorable about him and our tournament. He loved it and always made sure he played it, even when he moved to the United States."

Chapter 68

THE BOND EMPIRE GROWS

The Bonds were expanding and nothing, but nothing was going to get in their way – not even a closed gate at Bodmin Golf and Country Club.

The original idea for a golf course near Bodmin came from a local businessman Jenti Madhvani in the late seventies. Very early on in the scheme he went to see the Bond brothers and sought their help and advice on the best way forward. They agreed to help him in any way they could and gave him lots of different pointers, based on what they'd done and achieved themselves. The course was built and the Bonds were among the guests for its official opening.

Unfortunately Mr Madhvani didn't have the financial resources to go through with the project. The golf course opened in May 1991 on a 150-acre site and the club had 150 playing members. Mr Madhvani also had planning permission for 30 luxury detached homes and a small hotel. But the club collapsed with debts of over £3 million and went into receivership.

The Bonds heard the club was in difficulties and had gone bust. So, one day when they were in the area, they decided to pop in. But the gate was shut. So they got over the gate, went in and the receivers were there with Mr Madhvani and his wife. Later they put in an offer and bought the club.

That was 1993. Three years earlier the Bonds had bought Looe Bin Down Golf Club, which was also in receivership. The course was designed by six-times Open champion Harry Vardon in 1933, just four years before he died.

One day Hermon's younger son Graham got a call to go to the Looe club to meet his father and uncle, not knowing what to expect.

They simply said to Graham: "There you are, get on with it." In typical Bond brother fashion, that was their way of appointing Graham manager at Looe. Hermon bluntly told his son: "You can run this place, but don't spend any money."

So Graham was determined to go out of his way to obey his father's wishes: "I did what I was told to do, not spend any money. I would go back to St Mellion in the evenings and nick any stationery or folders I needed from dad and uncle's office and take them down to Looe!"

The Looe club is in a beautiful location. The clubhouse and the elevated 18th tee look out over the coastline to Looe Island, also known as St George's Island. But the previous owner Ken Wood had converted the front part of the clubhouse into a private flat. One of the first things Graham did was to get rid of that and bring the area back into use by the members. So Graham did spend a bit of money, but it was an essential piece of work and dad and Uncle Martin were happy.

When the Bonds bought the Bodmin club it had just half-a-dozen staff. The course was designed by John Hamilton Stutt, the architect for the Old Course at St Mellion. The purchase included sites for houses at the club but the plots weren't selling because of the economic climate.

The club was renamed Lanhydrock and Graham was also made manager there. The clubhouse opened in 1994, with almost 30 full and part-time staff. The Bonds sold the building sites to local and national developers. Graham and his wife Clare were made joint directors of Lanhydrock and it was decided to implement the planning permission for the hotel. It made sense, because of the central location in the county, to provide a good quality hotel, with 20 twin bedrooms and 24 luxury double bedrooms. It opened in 2006. There are also conference facilities and it's now called Lanhydrock Hotel and Golf Club.

And, of course, just like St Mellion, not a penny of grant aid funded the development. The cost of the hotel and refurbishment of the clubhouse and its facilities? – almost £3 million. It was money well spent and the investment also created many new jobs.

Chapter 69

FROM ODD-JOB BOY TO DEPUTY GENERAL MANAGER

Mark Lovell joined the staff at St Mellion in August 1982 as a very innocent 17-year-old. His first task was to clean up the back yard. When he left in November 2004, after the Bonds had sold to American Golf, he was deputy general manager. Mark's career at St Mellion is a classic example of how the Bond brothers encouraged and nurtured staff who they believed had potential. Mark certainly had plenty of that.

He began on the government-funded Youth Opportunities Programme, working Monday to Friday as, basically, an odd-job boy, earning £25 a week: "I was putting quite a lot of effort into what I was doing. I will always remember after a couple of weeks the general manager David Webb coming out of his office one Friday afternoon and calling me over. He said: 'I've been watching you and seeing what you've been doing'. Then he went to petty cash and gave me an extra tenner for what I was doing. That was a lot of money. It was fantastic and I felt I was very fortunate to have started at a time when I had so many good people around me, people who appreciated me, as well as being the people I worked for and did a lot for."

Mark met Martin and Hermon Bond very quickly: "To meet the proprietors within two or three days of starting was quite something. Now, sometimes, you wouldn't meet the owners of a business for months, if ever at all."

Mark was lucky enough to see Jack Nicklaus when he made his first visit to St Mellion to be shown the land for his golf course: "I remember thinking this was arguably the best golfer the world had ever seen coming to the place where I had started work. It was a bit bizarre. You can imagine, age 17, and Jack Nicklaus suddenly appears. Nobody really knew he was coming. To see someone like that at my age was just an amazing thing.

"The Bonds treated him the same as anyone else, a little bit of respect obviously because of who he was, but just very open and very, very straightforward."

Mark spent a year as an odd-job boy. Then he spent two years studying catering at Camborne College, but still working weekends at St Mellion. He also got time off college to be at St Mellion for major golf events. Then, in the summer of 1985 he was offered the position of junior assistant manager and went on to become day house manager and then specialised in events, conferences and banqueting.

Over the years, Mark got to know Martin and Hermon well: "As fond as I was of Hermon, you would have to say he was quite abrasive, very forthright, very to the point, but incredibly likeable. He had done so well by being quite shrewd, being quite blunt and being such a team as he was together with his brother. They worked their way through many, many difficult situations, through good and bad."

Mark added that Martin was much gentler, more thoughtful: "He was the great thinker. The shrewder one, but it some ways he could be actually worse than Hermon if things got tough. He could be as clinical and cutting, if not more so than Hermon.

"But, they were the same with everybody, pretty much. If

something was out of order, you knew about it and they could be really quite stinging and critical if that was the case. But if you worked for them and looked after them, they looked after you.

"Part of their success was playing on the image of being thick Cornish yokel farmers. They would reel people in, make them feel that they, the brothers, were a bit dumb and then nail them. They could be lethal."

But they were also caring: "On one occasion Martin took me aside and asked me how my house was going. I had literally put every penny into a new house. I was on my own at the time so I did the whole thing myself. I'll never forget Martin's words to me: 'Do me a favour, if ever you get into any difficulty let me know and I'll make sure I look after you'.

"To me, to be given that kind of support at a very vulnerable time when you're making your first purchase was amazing. I don't think you get much of that any more these days.

"But Martin and Hermon also had to make many, many tough decisions. They were not afraid to make a decision. They may have thought over it for a long time, but they were tough when they had to be."

Mark said the Bonds' achievements went way beyond golf courses and leisure facilities: "You think of how many brides and grooms had wonderful times there and experienced a wonderful place, all the golf societies who stayed and played there, the functions, the council civic dinners. There are just so many things that have happened there. The staff who worked there over the years. St Mellion touched the lives of many thousands of people in different ways over the Bond years.

"My time at St Mellion was fantastic because I grew up with a lot of what was going on, whether it was the Timeshare Village, the Nicklaus course being built, the leisure complex. I saw the whole thing grow and evolve. Everything at St Mellion was massively positive."

Mark, who married St Mellion's golf co-ordinator Fiona Walker, left in November 2004 to work at the Rifle Volunteer at St Anne's Chapel in South East Cornwall. In August 2005 he and Fiona got a call from former St Mellion general manager Ken Hunt who, along with his wife Ruth who had been marketing director at St Mellion, then had the Combe House Hotel near Honiton in Devon. Mark became general manager at Combe House and Fiona was office manager.

FOOTNOTE: Mark Lovell met many famous snooker players at St Mellion: "Steve Davis had his own kind-of 'space invaders' machine put up in his bedroom or in the corridor outside. Terry Griffiths would complain that the balls were too cold, they were too moist, they didn't make the right contact. Then he'd make a 135 clearance! Ray Reardon was a gentleman. He played well. He did it right. He was old school, good old school."

Chapter 70

CHANGES

There were many changes at the club in the months following the 1993 B&H tournament with Martin Watson moving to pastures new and the role of general manager being taken by hotelier Ken Hunt, assisted by his wife Ruth as marketing director.

This move was not universally popular, as pleasant as Ken and Ruth were, they were not quickly accepted by the membership. Another group of people who were unhappy about the change were the team from B&H who had grown used to the "old" way of doing things and did not take quickly to the Hunts.

Their lack of golf knowledge also created some reservation in the eyes of many but this was overcome quickly with the appointment of Paddy Flavin as Director of Golf and Leisure, as he had a proven track record of delivering results in a commercial golf environment.

Two episodes which demonstrate that the Hunts were not restricted by traditional golf thinking are recalled by many with a mixture of horror and amusement.

The first was an idea by Ruth to capture and sedate some of the famous St Mellion 18th green ducks and fit them with toy helmets. Then they would be photographed for a newspaper article with the headline "The Ducks take cover from errant

Golfers!" When you consider that the golfers in question were some of the very best in the world it does not take a great imagination to realise that this did not go down at all well with the B&H publicity machine.

The second incident was when Ruth invited the Channel 4 Big Breakfast Show with Keith Chegwin to St Mellion on the eve of the 1994 B&H Open. The nature of this show and its host was that something whacky was bound to occur. Sure enough it did! It took the form of a game of GOLF/POLO in golf buggies with real golf clubs and beach balls! European Tour player Glenn Ralph was elected to play with Paddy driving him, against Chegwin's team. Again eyebrows were raised, but it was on national television and that was good publicity for St Mellion

The Golf Operations team was revamped under the leadership of Paddy and some significant appointments were made, many of whom are still at the club.

Golf Manager David Moon and Course Manager Mike Bush are two such individuals and both have made significant contributions to the ongoing success of the club. And Mark Lovell was particularly grateful to Paddy for employing Fiona Walker as golf co-ordinator as he later married her! Fiona was a very good golfer who formerly worked for Lord Forte but was keen to pursue a career in golf management which she achieved with distinction.

Robert Brewer, now secretary manager at Royal Wimbledon Golf Club, was recruited to replace Roy Battishall as course manager when Roy retired. Robert went on to rise rapidly through the ranks of American Golf as a general manager with what is now Crown Golf.

Chapter 71

THE HUNT YEARS – THE BONDS CONTINUE TO INVEST

Appointed to replace Martin Watson who had moved on, Ken and Ruth Hunt took up the baton in earnest in 1994. Based on their years of experience as hoteliers the Hunts drafted a plan for repositioning St Mellion, starting with undertaking a major revamp of the food and beverage offering and an upgrade to the leisure side of the business.

To this end, many of the dining areas were redecorated to reflect a more trendy approach to the whole dining experience. A new executive head chef Ian Crook was appointed and work started in earnest to upgrade the food and beverage operation.

Ken and Ruth were also keen to upgrade the experience for leisure users and with architect Alan Leather's help plans were drawn up for a major £2.7 million refurbishment of this element of the business. The plans included another swimming pool for the serious swimmer, a fully-equipped modern gym and a spa area - in fact largely what is now known as the Aero Club.

This ambitious project was undertaken in early 1996 with the added challenge of keeping the existing facility open at the same time. Long serving leisure manager Clare Byles and her team certainly had their work cut out during the period of the contract which was executed by Kembles.

It was to be Paddy Flavin's last task at St Mellion for some 10 years until his return as a consultant to Crown Golf. There were frequent trips from his new employment at Woodbury Park Hotel and Golf Club near Exeter to fulfil his promise to the Bond brothers that he would get the Leisure Club job off the ground with Alan Leather.

Another strategic initiative that the new management team implemented was the "twinning" of St Mellion with La Baule in Brittany and the PGA West Course in Palm Beach, Florida. Both of these associations were designed to raise the international profile of St Mellion and to provide members with some value-added bonuses through access to these prestigious resorts. The matches between the French and English Clubs were jolly affairs indeed!

Strong relationships were also formed with Brittany Ferries at this point to the mutual benefit of both parties.

Having lost the B&H Open, Ken and Ruth Hunt set about staging other large scale events to keep the name of the club to the forefront of peoples' minds. In particular, they organised and ran open air concerts featuring Kenny Ball and his Jazzmen and the Soprano in Red Lesley Garrett. These were being held on Friday and Saturday, August 15 & 16, 1996 to mark the 20th anniversary of St Mellion Golf and Country Club.

All the stops were being pulled out. David Webb put together a special exhibition of photographs and memorabilia. Friday night would see Kenny Ball and his musicians perform and on Saturday night the 18th fairway would be transformed into a giant theatre for Lesley's performance.

But Saturday, August 16, 1996 was to prove a big challenge for Mark Lovell because, back in March that year, a couple had booked St Mellion for their wedding reception on that same day. The bride-to-be had lost her father, so it was left to mother and daughter to organise the big day, without dad. But the Bond brothers told Mark, the conference and banqueting manager: "We're definitely going to go with the concert dates. You'll have to deal with the wedding issue. You're the man for the job."

Mark knew the "the happy couple" wouldn't be very happy. He had to tell them that they could still get married that day but they would be competing with something else, there would be another event going on at the same time: "I had the onerous task of inviting the mother and daughter in to tell them that on the same day as the wedding there would be an open air concert. It was quite tense. You can image that their life almost fell apart around them.

"It was my job to try to recover the situation. I had a couple of weeks of anger and frustration. Then the groom got involved and started phoning me and telling me what he thought of me because we had changed the goal posts.

"We had moved the goal posts and you can imagine the couple thinking that the nicest day of their lives was going to be taken over or high-jacked by thousands of people walking through their wedding."

But Mark Lovell turned the whole thing around to make it a wedding never to be forgotten – for all the right reasons.

"Everything had been shut down in readiness for the concert but we arranged it so that the wedding party and guests, about 60 people, virtually had private use of the hotel. The car park was turned into a private car park, but we arranged for all their guests to have free passes for their cars to get into the private parking.

"They had drinks in the bar and photographs were taken. There were no interruptions because there weren't that many other people around.

"Then they had their meal in the Lynher Suite which, in those days, had no air conditioning so the windows needed to be open.

"We arranged for a jazz band to play during the reception because we knew Lesley Garrett would be 300 or 400 yards away 'giving it stick' rehearsing during the afternoon. And, low and behold, just as the wedding speeches were about to be made, she finished her rehearsal. So, I got away with that.

"They did the speeches, uninterrupted, so, so far, it was going really, really well. The difficult bit was always going to be when the concert guests started to arrive. They were funnelled in down round the back of the hotel to the auditorium.

"We got round that. We asked all the wedding party and guests to bring their wellie boots, coats and brollies with them, just in case. Those were to be left downstairs in the Tamar Suite, which was theirs to use because there was nothing else going on in the clubhouse.

"We escorted the guests down to the Tamar Suite and, because it was a beautiful summer's evening, they didn't need their coats, brollies or wellies.

"I then walked them across to their own private marquee, which the Bonds paid for, so they could watch the first half of the concert, for free. One lady was bad on her legs and had difficulty walking, so we took her over to the marquee and back in a golf buggy. There was a little bar for them in the marquee. Then I was a Pied Piper and led them all the way back to the Tamar Suite in the dark. We closed all the windows and doors and there was a wedding buffet and disco.

"At the end of the night the fireworks went up and they had a free firework display as well. It was deemed to be one of the finest firework displays anybody had ever seen. Then Lesley Garrett came in and the couple had their photograph taken with her.

"It was a lovely day for them and a happy ending for everyone. I was worried and kept thinking that something was going to go wrong. But nothing did. It turned into one of the best days of their lives and of course all their guests were talking about it. It was a fantastic, glorious day and night."

Ken Hunt was a tireless worker who was absolutely passionate about raising the standards of service and quality. He believed fervently in training young people and allowing them to flourish in a happy working environment.

After some initial resistance he gradually started to win some of the doubters over and he was always charming and fun to be around, so most of the staff responded well to him. He re-defined many peoples roles within the business but he always managed to do this with some sensitivity. There were a lot of Martin Watson supporters who would always harp back to the "old days" and, for them, Ken would always remain an outsider.

He was supported by his wife Ruth who managed somehow to juggle raising two small children with the demanding role of sales and marketing director. Their business exchanges were often volatile but there was no doubting the strength of their love for each other.

They had met in London at Strand Hotel, where Ken was a young assistant general manager, on Ruth's first day as a trainee. She said that within a minute of meeting him she had made her mind up that this was the man she was to marry!

However, her plans for an early wedding had to be shelved as Ken left the hotel within weeks to embark on an adventure as part of a scientific expedition to Antarctica. But they married soon after his return. They emigrated to Australia where, for many years, they successfully ran an hotel in the Hunter Valley.

During their time at St Mellion, Ken and Ruth brought a different approach but yet, in its own way, it was still very much St Mellion. Like the Bonds, the Hunts were kind, considerate and caring people.

Mark Lovell praised Ken, who was general manager for three years before the sale to American Golf: "That was a difficult time. St Mellion had lost the Benson & Hedges in 1995. Ken did get the place bubbling up a little bit, but we all know that when you're going to sell a business you're not going to spend loads of money on it at that point."

Chapter 72

VERY THICK SKINNED – YOU HAD TO BE

All local authority planning officers have to be thick skinned. They have to make recommendations to councillors on planning applications, based on policies. They are under a lot of pressure. There was a thought that if you were a planning chief dealing with Martin and Hermon Bond you needed several layers of very thick skin.

During local government re-organisation in the early seventies Cornishman Jack Harcombe became Caradon District Council's first chief planning officer, just in time to deal with the initial plans for a golf course and clubhouse at St Mellion.

Of the three top planning officials in the council most closely involved with the growth of the Bond empire, Jack was the one who, by far, had the easiest ride. Jack went to see Hermon and Martin on the farmland at St Mellion: "I thought from my initial look at it that it would perhaps be a good thing. The council was actively promoting economic activity in Caradon and we were anxious to create new work, new jobs and better employment prospects and this proposal seemed to offer all that. I also thought it would be in quite a strategic location on the edge of Plymouth and could fulfil a very useful function."

There was a certain amount of opposition. Jack took a group of councillors out to view the site one Saturday morning. The members of the planning committee were taken on a tour of the land on a tractor-drawn trailer. The only major planning drawback that he could see was that the Bonds wanted to gain access to the clubhouse and golf course through St Mellion village itself, which was totally unacceptable.

"I suggested quite strongly that if they wanted to get planning consent they'd got to think more carefully about the access, it was absolutely essential," added Jack. "As it was, the application didn't take very long to go through the planning process, but only after they accepted that they needed to invest a lot more by providing a new access. Once there was co-operation on that and they were able to meet the county surveyor's requirements it was fairly plain sailing."

If Hermon and Martin were trying to save money by not providing a separate access – and, knowing the Bonds, they probably were, then Jack Harcombe regarded that as "standard developer resistance".

"Developers don't want to provide more than they feel they can get away with. I could understand a new access was a major investment but it became a major part of the application."

Jack said his initial hunch that the proposal would perhaps be a good thing for the area proved right: "What's been created at St Mellion is a vital part of the economy of South East Cornwall. It put the area on the map. Just the Benson & Hedges International Open there in 1979 brought it into national significance."

Jack Harcombe left in 1984. Another Cornishman David Brown was then chief planning officer for four years. His stance from day one was: "I would not do anybody any favours. I gave up membership of everything I was involved in when I became chief planning officer because I wasn't going to be persuaded by anything or anybody. Also, I wouldn't socialise with planning applicants or the councillors because you then weakened your own position."

David Brown had two things in common with Martin and Hermon Bond, he was Cornish and he'd lived on a farm. And he had a third thing in common with Hermon – a bad back. It was so painful he did some of his work lying on the floor in his office beside his desk. But there was no common ground when the Bonds announced they wanted permission for 125 up-market detached houses to finance the Nicklaus course.

"I told them: 'I shall object to one, let alone 125'. They said: 'Well you do your bit boy. We've had them (the councillors) out here for whisky, two at a time in front of the fire, we know what way the vote's going to go'."

David Brown added that local and national policies were that there should be no houses in the country unless fully justified on agricultural or other special grounds: "But when the application came up for discussion, on the same agenda was an application by someone else for one bungalow on the edge of St Mellion village on a side road leading to the golf course. I felt that was justified so I recommended refusal of the 125 and approval for the one. The committee members reversed both my recommendations.

"We needed the golf course, a feature like that, in the poor economy of Cornwall, but all of a sudden to decide that a number of houses were needed to pay for it, I felt from my bones right from the start that they needed to find finance from somewhere else. I still believe I'm right because the major tournament people could pull out at any time, no matter who designed the course.

"When the councillors made that decision I did think to myself: 'What the hell am I doing here? I'm paid to do a job but I can't do my job properly because they're not taking any notice of me on the most important things'."

David summed up his reaction to the Bonds: "I never found them in the slightest bit formidable. I found them both very friendly. Hermon and I had the same problem – bad backs. I used to ask how he was and he used to ask how I was. In a way we had a bond immediately. I came from a farming background and I didn't blame any farmer for trying to make money other than through farming because our farm was very, very hard work for little reward. They say that in that area of Cornwall, half inch down is granite.

"I felt the development of St Mellion was of considerable benefit and I admired the Bonds for what they'd done and I was pleased to have been able to have something to do with it.

"I wished to encourage them to do anything in that line, but not if we had to pay for it by going against policies again and again to their benefit when you were having local people who couldn't even get one house, especially as the St Mellion golf course houses weren't exactly in the range of local people."

David added that he had no antagonism towards the Bonds. What he regretted was that some of the councillors were so blatantly easy to sway: "Councillors gave permission to somebody who kept 12 goats in his back garden so he wanted a bungalow out in the country to look after them. He built this bloody great mansion and then got rid of the goats. Then there was the chap who had two ferrets so he had to have a bungalow out in the country. So first it was 12 goats, then two ferrets, what comes next - a parrot, a budgerigar?

"I laughed about these things at the time. That was how I could get through the committee meetings and I could introduce humour to it. But, towards the end, with my bad back, I started to lose my sense of humour."

In a way St Mellion was echoed later on when David Brown was approached by naval officers to say that the Royal Navy's Tamar

Club in Hong Kong was being sold and the navy had something like £21 million to spend and it was either going to be the South West or it was going to be Scotland.

"I said I'd got the very site that I'd like them to go to. It would stop Saltash growing northwards as it might do and spoil the beauty of the area. And the Navy would be providing the area with a considerable asset. I took them to meet the owners of the land and the end result was the China Fleet Golf and Country Club.

"I felt that the Bonds had done the same thing. They produced something that Cornwall should have which was a bit up-quality, a bit of investment with jobs and so on."

David Brown decided to take early retirement because of his back problems. He was 51.

Next up in the planning hot seat at Caradon was Yorkshireman Alan Hartridge. He said the brothers were always very courteous throughout all the discussions he had with them.

"I don't know what they were saying behind my back or what they may have been calling me. I think probably after I left the room they'd say I was a bloody something or other. To a certain extent they regarded me as 'one of the enemy'.

"Once Hermon did say something to me about a Yorkshireman. It wasn't offensive to me and he said it in such a way, about him being blunt speaking and me being as well, I took it as a compliment.

"Martin was more like a calming influence when I was trying to explain planning laws and why they should apply to everybody. I think he understood a little bit more about the situation and what the planning principles were about. Hermon always thought it was just bureaucracy and they should be the exception, why couldn't I understand that they were simple pig farmers trying to do the best for Cornwall.

"Generally speaking, Hermon would say something and then Martin would put it in more diplomatic speak."

Alan said the height of the Bonds' achievements was the Benson & Hedges and other major events: "Going around and looking we, the officers, could see, and it twigged with all the councillors – look at all these people, spending money in the area, staying in the area and it's something to be proud of.

"If fact it was something that Caradon could be proud of. We had our annual dinners there, conferences were organised. St Mellion was sort of a flagship for the area but it did come at a price – the housing in Dunstan Lane. That ribbon of development and its location is nothing to be proud of because it's divorced from the community."

Alan Hartridge's overall view of the Bonds and St Mellion was this: "It was investment that was sorely needed in the area and it has been a source of pride to many in South East Cornwall that we've had that facility. Although the landscape of the golf course might be a little bit 'Florida' on a Cornish landscape, to be able to attract the Benson & Hedges and major tournaments like that has brought a lot of benefit to South East Cornwall.

"That scale of development wasn't a bad thing and it probably brought more good to the area than harm and it did inject some investment into the area and some pride into the area at a time when the economy of Cornwall needed the investment.

"Martin and Hermon were larger than life and knew how to deal with people. For pig farmers to be able to attract people like Jack Nicklaus and get that investment must have been quite something and they were smart enough to know that they needed to have high quality facilities and to know that if you mention the word 'employment' to councillors, they'll go for it. That's why they were millionaires and I'm not.

"The legacy that the Bond brothers left at St Mellion is a jewel in the crown of South East Cornwall with a potential to attract major events which would be of benefit to the area. Beyond doubt, it's a nationally-recognised recreational facility and it has the potential for attracting more major events."

Chapter 73

A MILLION WAS NOT ENOUGH

But, the carrot of a nice, cool, round one million pounds the Bond brothers dangled in front of the noses of the organisers of the Ryder Cup was never going to be enough to bring the event to St Mellion.

When the tournament was on at the Belfry, Martin and Hermon went to meet Sandy Jones to see if St Mellion could be considered. Jones was the chief executive of the Professional Golfers' Association and headed the Ryder Cup selection committee along with Ken Schofield from the European Tour. They had both been to St Mellion for the Benson and Hedges after it returned there in 1990 to be staged on the Nicklaus course.

The brothers promised widespread improvements, a bigger hotel and better access arrangements, but that was as far as the proposal got.

"One million pounds was a lot of money at the time but, afterwards, we realised they had much bigger ideas than that," said Martin. "They certainly saw much bigger money than that."

Chapter 74

UN CORTE POR ENCIMA DEL RESTO

Severiano Ballesteros will always be regarded as one of the greatest golfers the world has ever known. His major wins as a professional totalled more than 90.

But the Spaniard wasn't playing particularly good golf when he came to St Mellion in 1994 for the 24th Benson & Hedges International Open. He had severe back problems. He had been in the doldrums for almost two years.

After the pro-am before the tournament the joint owner of St Mellion Hermon Bond said to Seve: "Hey boy, I bet you £100 you won't make the cut."

Seve just smiled – as only Seve could smile – and said nothing.

Of course, it was not one of Hermon's most astute bets. Seve won the tournament. He finished seven under par after rounds of 69, 70, 72 and 70, to beat Nick Faldo by three strokes. It was an amazing achievement for him on the arduous Nicklaus course.

We don't know if Hermon honoured the bet when Seve made the cut after the first two days, but Hermon was a man of honour, so he most certainly did pay up, in some way or another. And, of course, Hermon's bet was just another bit of mischief because he and Martin were very keen to see Seve make the cut, because the golfer would prove a massive crowd-puller for the final two days of the tournament.

The presentation was about to take place at the 18th green. The table was there with the trophy on it and Martin and Hermon Bond were among those waiting to greet the triumphant Ballesteros.

During the ceremony Seve was interviewed by the Scottish TV sports presenter Dougie Donnelly who said to him: "Well Seve, this must be a relief to you after all your problems." (A reference to his back pain and recent lack of form)

Seve replied: "Problem? I have no problem. The people in Bosnia have problem. This only golf."

But then the charismatic Spaniard lightened the mood by directing his sparkling eyes at Hermon Bond, conjuring up the widest grin he could with his sparkling white teeth and saying in his broken English: "Well Hermon, I make the cut."

The crowd erupted. For those who witnessed it, it was a spine-tingling moment. There followed genuine handshakes and manly cuddles. A truly great sporting and golfing moment.

Severiano Ballesteros got his hands on the trophy on May 8, 1994. He died, of brain cancer, aged 54, on May 7, 2011, just one day short of the 17th anniversary of his triumph at St Mellion.

He was un corte por encima del resto - a cut above the rest. He was humble about it, but a private letter written to Martin and Hermon after his victory shows how much it meant to him: "It gave both my family and me a lot of happiness to have won this year's Benson & Hedges International Open and I am very happy that my victory has contributed to the success of the tournament's organisation and the big exposure given to your club. My wife and I appreciate very much all the kindness we received at St Mellion. Warm regards." The letter was typewritten, Seve signed it in his own hand.

Seve's win stands out as one of the real highlights of the Benson & Hedges tournament at St Mellion. The Nicklaus course was not a Seve Ballesteros-type course because he didn't hit the ball straight and true with every shot. Jim Elkins, the Benson & Hedges special events director, said: "That's how the guy was and that's why everybody loved him so much."

As the tournament reached its climax there was no clear leader and any one of 15 players could have won it on the last day.

Jim Elkins: "On the last day Seve parred the first 15 holes and on the 16th, a par 5 with a dog leg round the corner, he ended up after two shots in an impossible position on the left hand side, on a 45 degree gradient with a green with bunkers surrounding it and, at the back of the green, a steep slope down into the woods.

"I thought there was only one shot he was going to play and that was into the bunkers for three, blast it out and single putt to get his par and off he'd go.

"No, not Seve, he went for the green and he played the most impossible shot you have ever seen. He found the green and two-putted for a par, so he'd parred the first 16 holes.

"He then birdied 17 and 18 to win the tournament and the emotion from 15,000 around that final green was something that, if you could bottle it, you could sell it for a fortune."

Jim Elkins said he and Seve spoke about that particular day many, many times and it was just one of those memories that anyone there will never forget.

(Contracts were signed with certain players to attract big names to the big events. For that particular tournament the contracts were based purely on the individual player's performance, not on them actually turning up. Jim Elkins signed the contract with Ballesteros on behalf of the B&H)

"It cost us a lot more money but, by golly, we got our money's worth out of it. There was an incentive to make the cut and then more incentives for top ten and top five, including winning, and there was a sliding scale. Seve scooped the jackpot and got the gold trophy. It was just a magical, magical moment for everybody I think," said Jim.

Ballesteros remains the all-time favourite golfer of Graham Bond, the younger son of Hermon and Rachel Bond. For Graham, Seve's victory was the highlight to top all the highlights which shine out from the great years at the club.

"Seve made golf 'great' in Britain and Europe. He was the one, with all due respects to Faldo, Woosnam and all those sort of guys. He was charismatic. He wasn't just knocking it down the middle – boring golf. He'd get into all sorts of trouble and be able to get out of it. And he had such a rapport with the public and spectators. He wasn't surrounded by security guards. Those were the days when you could go and talk to people like him.

"Seve was such a breath of fresh air, with his Ryder Cup spirit. He is the number one European golfer of all time, without a question," said Graham.

Someone else remembers Ballesteros at the 1994 B&H, not just for his win but also for what happened before, during the practice round. The maestro was on the back tee at the par 3 11th with only half a dozen people watching.

One of those was David Moon, St Mellion's joint head-pro at the time: "I'm just standing to the side of him. He picked up a club and just 'flushed' through the ball. Just a pure golf strike.

The ball goes on its way. The flag was front and central, slightly to the left. The ball pitches eight feet from the flag with a bit of spin and straight into the hole. Just one of those great moments I will never forget. Rumour has it, that was his first big-time hole in one. He is such an icon and his name and St Mellion go together."

Chapter 75

THE ROYAL CHIP AND BALL

It was the final day of the 24th Benson & Hedges International Open at St Mellion in May 1994. Anyone who was privileged enough to be there to see the lovely, modest, talented Severiano Ballesteros win the trophy still remembers it. The victory was, indeed, memorable and inspiring. Those who couldn't be there to witness the momentous event included the very keenest of Royal golfers who, at the time, was all at sea. The Duke of York was a Lieutenant Commander in the Royal Navy and commanding the Hunt Class Minehunter HMS Cottesmore. Prince Andrew was somewhere in the English Channel, heading towards Plymouth. He had been enthusiastically watching the B&H on the tele.

After play had finished late on the Sunday afternoon, at the end of a busy, hectic, successful Benson and Hedges, Martin and Hermon Bond were relieved it was all over. The pressure was off. Time for a post mortem on the event and then....relaxation. At least that's what they thought. People like the club's director of corporate golf David Webb were in reflective mood, pleased because the formalities of the prize-giving had gone smoothly. As tradition had it, the brothers put on a barbecue in the old barn for the staff who had worked so hard, during the previous four or five days in particular, to entertain them as a "thank you", along with the players and tournament officials.

At about six o'clock David Webb was in his office preparing to go from the clubhouse to the barn – most of his colleagues were already down there with some of the players. But he received a telephone call from reception to say two gentlemen from the police wanted to speak to him. He knew he hadn't committed any crime, some obscure misdemeanour, so assumed it was representatives of the Plymouth Police Golf Society wanting to talk to him about a possible golf society booking.

He asked reception to show the two men up. "I quickly realised I was wrong, it wasn't the local police golf society because, standing in front of me, were two gentlemen in very, very smart suits," David said. "One of them passed his card to me and said they were Royal protection officers with Prince Andrew. They said the prince had been watching the tournament on television as he'd been sailing into Plymouth over the last couple of days on his ship and he would very much like to have a game of golf here the next day, Monday, if that would be possible."

David told the two officers to leave it with him as he would be seeing Mr Martin and Mr Hermon (he always referred to them in that way) at the barbecue. And off he went to the barn and spoke to Mr Martin first.

Martin shouted across the crowded barn: "Hermon, we've got a game of golf tomorrow."

The exact words uttered by Hermon when he was told who the guest golfer was have, perhaps fortuitously, never been officially documented. But it's generally accepted by those present at the time that Hermon said something like: "Let the boyo come around. We'll give him a good thrashing." We all know his language was much more "colourful" than that!

The brothers were well pleased. A Royal visit. Who'd have thought it. David Webb got back to the Royal protection officers and Prince Andrew was invited to come to St Mellion the next day. The Bonds were to take on the Prince, who needed a partner. John Shrewsbury was at St Mellion in his role as the executive director of BBC Sport. He was also a personal friend of the Bond brothers and he'd played golf before with Prince Andrew. So, he was the ideal choice.

The course was eerily quiet on the Monday in the wake of the tournament. The clearing up operations were underway. It was a lovely day. The Royal party would park in the Bond brothers' two reserved spaces close to the clubhouse entrance and the prince, who would be bringing his own golf clubs with him, would be met by David Webb and escorted up to the proprietors' suite. This was to be an unofficial, private visit, but everyone was told to be on their best behaviour - and that included Hermon. After all, the Prince Andrew Albert Christian Edward, Earl of Inverness, Baron Killyleagh , was born second in line to the throne, although he dropped down the pecking order a bit as the years went by. And he had been the grand young Duke of York for almost eight years when he came to St Mellion to play his royal round.

Those about to meet Prince Andrew had been repeatedly told to refer to him initially as "Sir". But, as the duke was on an informal, unofficial visit, he may well say: "Call me Andrew." A hot buffet was awaiting the prince for him to enjoy in the proprietors' suite before his round of golf. But he was running late and the hot buffet was turning into a cold buffet. The Bond brothers and others assembled to meet the prince started nibbling away while they waited patiently for the royal arrival. Then Hermon needed to go to the toilet. It was classic bad timing. While he was spending a penny, the Prince came into the room and was introduced to everyone else. Then Hermon burst in, rushed over to Prince Andrew, beaming from ear to ear, shook his hand vigorously, forced a plate under the duke's nose and spluttered out the words: "Hello, I'm Hermon Bond, have a chip!"

There was a moment's silence. It seemed like an eternity for those privileged few in the room. Then Andrew smiled – and laughed – and took a cold chip.

Roger Bush, a personal friend of the Bonds and a business associate, was there and recalled: "Hermon's rather unconventional greeting for a prince of the realm broke the ice, which was absolutely wonderful. It also told the prince a lot about Hermon and a lot about Martin. He was in the company of 'real people'."

After the introductions and a quick cuppa, the prince changed his shoes in the car park. As they headed for the first tee, Hermon asked the prince if there was any chance of a picture of them together. But the duke didn't want a photo taken in that location and suggested somewhere quiet. Hermon knew exactly the place, the 5th. He asked David Webb to organise a photographer. David thought: "Short notice, but nothing is impossible." He saw the players up to the first tee, saw them off and then contacted Callington Studios. On the first hole the duke got a par four and at the par five 2nd he got a four, a birdie. Hermon told the prince: "Hey boy, we'll have to see proof of your handicap if you keep playing like this."

John Shrewsbury said Hermon, who always liked to win, no matter who the opponent, was getting agitated: "Hermon's two down already and not very happy. We got to the third hole and the prince said: 'Is this a par four as well?' Hermon said: 'It is, and if you get a four here you ain't coming back no more.' The duke laughed, we all laughed."

Martin Bond remembered it as if it was yesterday: "The prince was a very good golfer. He didn't hit the fairway at all but he would still make a par or better."

The photographer arrived at the clubhouse and David Webb took him out on a buggy to the 5th green. He took a very nice group photograph of the four players and then disappeared.

Jim Elkins, who was special events director for B&H, rode a buggy down to the par 5 7th: "I'd gone out just to see how it was going. It was going fine and they seemed happy so I decided I'd meet up with them after nine holes and just have a little chat. When I got to the 9th green I heard a conversation between Prince Andrew and Hermon from either side of the green. Hermon said something like: 'Oi Andy, it's two foot outside right'. I thought: 'This is going fine. No problem. All the 'sirs' curtsies and bows have all gone out the window, this is a proper game of golf."

On the twelfth, one of the four, not the Prince, had a bad shot and the ball was lost. Prince Andrew said: "I know where that is. I've got 20-20 vision." He went right to it in the rough. Martin introduced the prince to some of the green keeping staff and his sons, Jon and Chris, who were taking away the ropes and stakes used to control the crowds during the tournament.

Prince Andrew and John Shrewsbury won the match two-and-one. They'd played for a single golf ball. As John and the duke rode away from the 18th on a golf buggy, they had this chat:

Andrew: "Well, that's alright, we've won a ball each, hopefully, maybe half-a-ball each."

John: "That's very nice sir but there's one thing, when the ball or balls are presented, can you just say to Hermon you hope they didn't come from Trago Mills."

Andrew: "What's Trago Mills?"

John: "It's a local out-of-town discount store."

Andrew: "Oh great."

Hermon, who had been out of earshot of this conversation, reluctantly told the winners: "Alright, we'll give you the ball inside."

Andrew, bang on cue: "Hermon, I hope it didn't come from Trago Mills."

Hermon went: "How the hell do you know Trago Mills?"

John Shrewsbury said this was the sweetest of moments with Prince Andrew, getting one over on one of the biggest practical jokers of all time, Hermon Bond.

After the game, Prince Andrew didn't leave until 8pm. He went back to the proprietors' suite and had a drink and a snack. Martin had been due to take his wife Angela out for dinner but had to ring her and say he was going to be late – By Royal Appointment! The prince mingled with quite a few people including other members of the Bond family and Richard Brown, the B&H tournament administrator, and his wife Annette. Then the photographer re-appeared with the pictures.

Jim Elkins said: "We thought it would be a quick cuppa and sandwich and that would be it. After half an hour he'd be looking at his watch and wanting to go and get back on his ship. It didn't quite work out like that. I ended up on a two-seater settee with Prince Andrew and it was incredible, absolutely incredible. He was so open about everything but, come about eight o'clock, I was bruised all down my left-hand side because every time there was a joke or innuendo or something from anybody I would get a thump in the ribs from the Duke of York. It was one of those memorable occasions. Something you could never buy, you could never dream it was going to happen, but it happened. Lovely guy, besotted by golf. He had probably six or seven hours education by a couple of Cornishmen which I'm sure he won't forget."

Martin summed up his recollections of the day: "A very nice young man he was, there was no doubt about that. He was great, great company, a good golfer and we really enjoyed it. He was tremendous. What was the nicest thing of all, his security people said they didn't think they'd ever seen him as relaxed, which I thought was good."

For David Webb, it was an unexpected privilege to meet Prince Andrew, but, for the Bonds it was a very significant day to have Prince Andrew at their golf course, at their club. Especially after Seve had won the tournament and there'd been tremendous publicity in the national and local golfing Press. It was a very enjoyable game of golf for the four players, but it was also a big day for St Mellion and, indeed, the Bond brothers.

A couple of weeks after the Royal round, a letter dated the 19th of May arrived from Sunninghill Park in Berkshire. It was from Prince Andrew: "Dear Martin and Hermon, I'm writing to thank you both for the opportunity of playing the course at St Mellion. Such a high quality course in such excellent condition is quite a challenge. I thoroughly enjoyed my visit to the club and have many happy memories of a wonderful day's golf. I much appreciated the warm hospitality which was extended to me."

Then Prince Andrew wrote in his own hand: "I also hope that someday you will be able to retrieve your ball! Yours sincerely Andrew."

Martin and Hermon remembered: "We played for a single golf ball because Royalty don't carry money. We thought we may have got a ball out of it to say the least, but we lost."

FOOTNOTE 1: There were other "Royal visits" to St Mellion over the years. Prince Charles, Duke of Cornwall, was there on numerous occasions on Duchy business and a couple of times, socially, to see the Bonds. The sniffer dogs would come in the day before and royal protection detectives would tell everyone to keep the visit a secret. Hermon always found that a challenge.

FOOTNOTE 2: Prior to these convivial meetings there was one occasion on which the Bonds refused an invite to lunch in the Duchy of Cornwall London offices but, instead, invited Prince

Charles to pop in to St Mellion for a sandwich sometime when he was down this way. The phone rang during one of the traditional Monday lunches the brothers had with their lawyer Edward Andreae-Jones, or AJ. He answered it. It was the secretary of the Duchy of Cornwall in London inviting Martin and Hermon to have a formal lunch at the Duchy offices in London.

"But Hermon and Martin did not want to go. At that particular time, they saw no merit in it. I kept getting these messages from the Duchy repeating the invite. In the end I had to speak to the personal assistant to the secretary of the Duchy of Cornwall," said AJ.

"I said: 'You've got to realise two things – we have a great respect for the Duke of Cornwall, the Prince of Wales, but there is an impenetrable barrier between us, the River Tamar, which we seldom cross. But Martin and Hermon have said if the prince is down this way and would like to come and share a sandwich, he's welcome to'. A note was made of it and, two or three months later, bless him, he did."

FOOTNOTE 3: St Mellion had another Royal connection through its racing horses and the famous St Mellion Fairway who came fourth in the 1998 Grand National. Fairway also ran in the 1999 National and there's a Press cutting in one of the scrapbooks of Rachel Bond, Hermon Bond's wife, before the race: "Royal hopes rest with last year's fourth St Mellion Fairway. Prince Edward's fiancée Sophie Rhys-Jones drew the Martin Pipe-trained 10-year-old in a sweepstake organised by jewellers Boodle and Dunthorne. She works for the Liverpool company, which supplies Aintree's trophies, as a public relations consultant, but will miss the big race because of a prior engagement." Fairway finished but didn't win Sophie any money.

FOOTNOTE 4: After that memorable royal round John Shrewsbury saw the Duke occasionally on the golf circuit. More often than not, Prince Andrew talked to John about his day at St Mellion.

Chapter 76

LEN OWEN MEETS SEVE

Seve Ballesteros always used to call Len Owen from the Benson & Hedges "Lane" and he would often say: "Lane, you know you are the one everybody trust, you are the one everybody look up to."

Len had first met Seve through his brother and fellow golf pro Manuel Ballesteros, who Len only knew to say "hello" to. Manuel's English was good but Seve couldn't speak a word of it when he first came to Fulford for the Benson & Hedges in the early seventies.

Manuel asked Len to go to the practice ground with him. Len watched a young man, probably no more than 18, hitting ball after ball perfectly.

Len said to Manuel: "This lad's very good. Who is he?"

Manuel replied: 'He my brother'."

Len thinks there was a purpose in what Manuel did: "Manuel didn't trust anybody, but he trusted me and I think he told Seve that if he had any real problems he could trust me, and he always did."

Len Owen was always grateful to Manuel for having the trust in him to the extent that he was comfortable about that trust being extended to include Seve. It was an invaluable friendship.

So, when Len went to America to talk to players, who were there for tournaments, about being in the next B&H, obviously one of the people he wanted to see was Seve. Seve would always insist they went out to dinner together, always somewhere which did authentic Spanish food.

"It was a joyful experience to have dinner with Seve. He was full of funny stories and Ryder Cup stories. He made me laugh. He would always insist that I had a bottle of wine and he would have just a little drop from it because he would be playing in a tournament the next morning. About 9.15 or so he'd say: 'I go now. Thank you for your company'."

Chapter 77

SEVE AND HIS RUSTY OLD BANGER

John Simpson, who was Nick Faldo's former manager, was very friendly with Seve and went across to Santander in Northern Spain to see him. Seve, who was by this time a superstar, turned up at the airport to pick him up in the most battered old piece of rusty motor car John had ever seen in his life.

John asked him: "Seve, why are you driving that heap of junk?"

Seve replied: "Why, you no like it?"

John: "You should have a better car than this. You're a big man everywhere, but especially here in Santander."

Seve: "Well, you get me one."

So, when John Simpson returned to the UK he ordered Seve a brand new Range Rover and it was duly delivered. Seve did drive it, but when he next picked up John at the airport, he turned up in the same rusty old piece of rubbish.

John, somewhat irritated, asked him: "Seve, why are you still driving this thing?"

Seve: "Range Rover too expensive on petrol."

Chapter 78

SEVE OUT OF BOUNDS

Hermon Bond was no Barbara Woodhouse. But he did train his Black Labrador Bruce to find and fetch lost golf balls, anybody's lost balls. Then he'd try to sell them as "seconds" but the staff in the pro's shop thought that wasn't a good advertisement for a high-class golf complex. Golf balls with dog teeth marks on them didn't go down well!

However, Hermon always was a very good salesman and he made his "seconds" his very own lucrative side-line, independent of the pro's shop. Bruce was so tuned in to finding the balls they might as well have been scented he was so good at seeking out his "prey". In fact Bruce was so good at his job that Hermon had a dustbin full of balls at home, ready for marketing.

No location on either of the golf courses was beyond Bruce's radar – that was until the Ballesteros moment on the 13th of the Nicklaus course. It was a pro-am and Seve was playing with Hermon. The par 4 13th is very narrow and there's a lot of greenery on the steep slopes on both sides of the fairway.

Seve hit his drive a long way but well up to the right. Hermon stands back and proclaims: "Bloody hell Seve, not even Brucie goes up there!"

Hermon's wife Rachel didn't particularly like dogs so she wasn't best pleased when her son Graham and his wife Clare gave Hermon Bruce. They had bought Bruce from Clare's uncle who bred and trained him. Bruce was given to Hermon to encourage him to take exercise and go out walking after he had a major operation on his back. So Rachel, reluctantly, accepted Bruce because he did manage to get Hermon out of his doldrums after the surgery. Bruce made him walk.

"Bruce grew up with our children and became a big dog. He was fantastic, a show-type dog," said Clare, who always referred to Rachel and Hermon as mum and dad. "But Hermon died before Bruce and that was a big thing. He used to say: 'I don't know what I'll do if anything ever happens to Bruce'.

"In a way, thank God Hermon went first. Mum kept Bruce who lasted another 15, 18 months. He was 15 years old and had done really well and we all cried when he had to be put down. He was the last bit of Dad," said Clare.

Clare and Graham waited 18 months before they bought a dog of their own and they knew they had to get Rachel on their side to occasionally look after the new dog.

Clare: "Mum was very partial to Severiano Ballesteros because she'd met him of course. And she had a lovely picture of herself with him. I knew if I got the dog's name right and trained the dog so he was well behaved it would be fine. So we got a Black Labrador and called him 'Seve' and Mum accepted him. He went to grannies with the children and had his own kennel and everything. Hermon would have loved him, but Seve wasn't interested in picking up golf balls, he was more of a swimmer."

Graham and Clare own Lanhydrock Hotel and Golf Club, so Seve went on the website on one of the directors' spots. Dog-loving customers loved it and when people checked in they were more interested in meeting Seve than anyone else.

There were – and are - lots of “chalks and cheeses” in the Bond family, according to Clare. Martin and Hermon were chalk and cheese, Graham and his brother Alan were chalk and cheese and Graham and Clare are chalk and cheese too.

Clare made a bit of a reputation for herself during the B&H years. She gave Hermon and Rachel Bond their first grandchild around the same time that Jack and Barbara Nicklaus had their first grandchild. Clare had Oliver just after the Benson & Hedges International Open at St Mellion in 1992 and then Christian was born shortly before the 1994 B&H.

“I was always fat and producing around the tournament time. It was the Benson & Hedges baby boom period,” she said.

Clare said throughout the years the brothers were always still themselves: “I think maybe outsiders might have seen something different. Maybe they saw the flashy cars and the better clothes and the improvement in lifestyle.

“But at home, they had the off-cuts of the carpets that were going down in the lounge at St Mellion and you’d go in Dad’s (Hermon’s) office at home and there’d be a chair that was whipped from over at the golf club. They appreciated everything. They weren’t ‘flash’ at all.”

Hermon taught Oliver and Christian to play golf. He’d tell them: “Just whack it boy, just whack it”.

Clare said Hermon was also very good and kind to her sister-in-law in America Kay, Alan’s wife.

Clare found Martin to be very firm, quite hard, a little impatient but fair and very warm as an uncle. He would always be there: “Hermon had great vision. He was brave. He was a people person, what a salesman. So warm, big hands and tactile, always give you a hug.

"Dad milked the 'Cornish yokel farmer' character and Graham used to cringe. I don't think Dad ever lost that common touch.

"It wasn't all good. There's a lot of stress goes with a family business. It's not all it's cracked up to be. If you care, which Hermon did, and he took on board all of the club members' comments, it can get to you and it got to him."

Clare said Christian learned to play poker on holiday in France: "Hermon would be thrilled with that. He will never be gone. Every time I hear the 'w' word, and I don't mean 'womble' I think of him. It's his word, isn't it."

Chapter 79

AN INTRODUCTION TO SEVE

Hermon Bond introduced his friend Peter Hunter to Seve Ballesteros in the passageway down near the pro's shop in the same way he always introduced Peter to people and Peter regarded it as a great honour.

Hermon said: "Seve, Seve, come here. I want you to meet a very great friend of the family." Peter told Seve it was a great honour to meet him.

Then Hermon looked right into Seve's eyes and said: "D'you know Seve — you speak better bloody English than he does."

Seve didn't speak very good English at that time, but he loved the joke.

Chapter 80

TARGET GOLF – WITH A DIFFERENCE

Hermon Bond would insist his golfing handicap was "ex-directory". He loved to play for money, not vast sums of the stuff, but, for him, it made the game even more competitive. And he won the purse quite regularly! He would play with the bank manager Bill Warman, a charming chap and quite a good golfer, and Peter Hunter, a roofing contractor who was a great friend of the Bonds.

And he enjoyed golf lessons. Hermon would often ring from the house, his mansion on the hill, and ask the joint head-pro David Moon to give him a lesson. A minute or two later Hermon was down at the club, beeping his horn impatiently, and telling David to get a move on. Off they drove, up to the range.

"The lessons were great fun because whilst he was a tidy player he was so set in his ways," said David. "He was the boss after all and I used to tell him how good he was and make him feel good about his golf swing. That was not a lie because to be fair to him he was very difficult to beat as he was so competitive. Unorthodox but effective."

When it came to Martin Bond's lessons, they were a bit different. He was very much driven to improve his golf. He used to have alignment problems. He could never aim straight, always down the right hand side. He was forever working on that aspect of his game.

One day, both brothers were having a lesson at the top of the driving range along with Richard Brown, a friend of the brothers who was tournament administrator for the B&H for all the years it was at St Mellion.

David Moon said: “We were hitting some shots down and we ran out of balls. So, we walked down the range, I thought, to pick up some balls. However, Hermon turned the situation into a wager with Martin, as he used to do with anything that could be turned into a wager.

“I think they only bet ten pence, which is the daft thing. The bet was - could Hermon hit his Range Rover with a shot back up the range to where the vehicle was parked. If he hit the target, the damage caused would have cost hundreds, but that seemed to be irrelevant.

“Hermon had eight or nine shots. Fortunately, he didn’t hit his car once. That was probably a blessing, but he probably was not trying that hard, he just loved shocking people.

“It was a great privilege for me to be able to coach both of them. Hermon was a big man in every way. Such a presence. I’ve never met a man with such a presence, before or since him, he just had this great aura about him.”

Chapter 81

STICKS AND STONES MAY BREAK YOUR CLUBS, BUT TROPHIES CAN NEVER HARM YOU!

Mark McNulty was a Zimbabwean professional golfer who later in life took out Irish citizenship. What a combination. But perhaps it was the Irish in him that prompted him to "take the Mickey" out of Martin and Hermon Bond.

Architect Alan Leather, who was involved in some of the Bond brothers' most significant projects, told this story: "In the early days, because the Nicklaus course was carved into the hillsides, you got a lot of stones in the fairways and it took a long time for that to be cleaned out and the course to bed in.

"I used to always play in the Pro-Ams of the Benson & Hedges tournament. Two things stand out in my mind about the prize-giving. The first one was Seve Ballesteros telling a rude joke in broken English. It would have been a funny joke, but Seve trying to tell it was even funnier.

"The second one was that Mark McNulty, who is a gentleman in the game, and wouldn't say boo to a goose he is such a gentleman, broke his seven iron on a stone in the middle of the 12th fairway when he was making his approach shot to the green in the pro-am.

"The head of the club literally snapped off at the bottom of the shaft. During the afternoon he had the head of the club mounted on a wooden plate and an engraved brass plaque made. Just before the presentations he asked for the proceedings to be stopped while he made a special presentation to Hermon and Martin.

"He presented this broken club to them and you could just see Hermon having this huge conflict in his brain as to whether magnanimously accept it in the joking manner in which it was offered or to lose his rag because someone was criticising his course. That summed up Hermon to me because in a way he was quite sensitive.

"He didn't take criticism and he wasn't ever quite sure whether what you said to him was a joke or criticism. Mark McNulty that day succeeded in almost making Hermon speechless. He and Martin just graciously accepted the 'trophy' but it was very, very funny."

Chapter 82

THE BALL CHALLENGE

Hermon Bond challenged Alan Leather to a game of golf on the Nicklaus course, more to make up the four needed for the round than any other reason. Alan, who was playing off single figures at the time, was subjected to the usual banter, like: "Here boy, you're s'pposed to be good."

Hermon never played for nothing. He had to be playing for something, be it a fiver or some golf balls. On this occasion he said to Alan: "I'll have a tube of balls on it boy." Alan said: "Fine, ok Hermon. I don't bet on golf but yeah, fine, ok."

Alan proceeded to have "one of those rounds." He was one under par after five holes and Hermon was getting a bit uptight. Alan went on to win the game quite easily. Hermon grunted and said reluctantly: "I'll go and pay up then." He went to the pro's shop and returned with a tube of balls for Alan and he accepted them.

"It wasn't until I got home and opened them up that I discovered they were a particular make of ball, things that nobody in their right mind would play with. So, he always, always had the last word, but he was quite a character."

When Alan Leather's firm did the design for the Roserrow Golf and Country Club at Polzeath in Cornwall he put on an exhibition of the proposals in the firm's pavilion at the Benson & Hedges at St Mellion. The company was in the throes of seeking planning permission for the course and housing design and was keen to attract support.

"Martin and Hermon came in and looked at the display. Martin studied it intently and said: 'It's looking good Alan, hope you're successful'.

"Hermon said with a grunt: 'Never did anything that good for us boy'. He was a bit like my dad, a man of faint praise and, as a result, wonderful."

Alan summed the brothers up like this: "Martin was a very genuine, kind man and I had enormous respect for him. I think he was a very reluctant entrepreneur, that's my assessment. In a way I think Martin would have been very happy to be left to farming. I think he got carried along by Hermon's enthusiasm. But Martin was a very genuine man. He was one of those people who would do anything for anybody. He was a very quiet man in the nice sense. He wasn't pushy, he wasn't in your face. I had a lot of time for Martin and his judgement. I was very fond of him.

"Hermon was extremely difficult but by God I liked him. You either loved Hermon or you hated him. There was no half measure but I think he was the same. He either took to you or he didn't and I missed him severely for a long while because he was one of those larger than life characters that you only meet occasionally in your life. There aren't enough characters in this world and occasionally you come across the Hermons of this world. For as long as I live I will never forget him. He's left an indelible mark on me, whether that's for good or ill I don't really know.

"I don't think there's any doubt that Martin and Hermon left a legacy that South East Cornwall should treasure. There are many of us who were involved in the tournaments in different ways and we'll always remember that that's been part of our lives.

"The good thing about Hermon and Martin was that no matter how small a part you played they made you aware that you had played a part.

"I think South East Cornwall should be pleased that the Bonds were part of South East Cornwall for that period of time and they achieved a lot. They put South East Cornwall on the map and I guarantee you those images of St Mellion on BBC television on a weekend afternoon when they were covering the B&H had a real positive effect on tourism in the area."

Chapter 83

DON'T BOTHER, LET THEM GO – WE'RE OUT

The Benson & Hedges had returned to St Mellion in 1990 after an absence of 11 years, back at its old home where it all started in 1971, Fulford Golf Club. The St Mellion arrangement was open-ended, renewed on an annual bases. The event stayed on the Nicklaus course for six tournaments until 1995, the 25th International Open.

After the 1995 tournament the top men of the PGA and the B&H sat down with the Bonds who asked them to keep the event at St Mellion. Ken Scofield, the head of the European Tour was there and Nigel Northridge from B&H. But money talks, and the sponsors were being offered a very lucrative deal by the Oxfordshire Golf Club, £350,000 for one year.

Ken Scofield could get more money up front with the change of venue. And Nigel Northridge wanted to be sure of BBC Television coverage, an essential ingredient as far as B&H was concerned. But the BBC wanted to stay at St Mellion because the course came across so well on the television. The Oxfordshire landscape was pretty bland.

Hermon Bond was prepared to put money up to get the tournament to stay and asked: "How much to you want?" But his brother Martin thought that was a waste of time and said as much at the meeting with Ken Scofield and Nigel Northridge:

"You aren't staying, no matter what, are you? Hermon you're wasting your time offering them money. Don't bother, let them go, forget it, they're going, finished, we're out.

"The question we need to ask is if we pay money, say £250,000, how many more people will have heard of us at the end of next year and is that worth that kind of investment?"

Hermon chipped in: "We are grateful for the exposure we've had over the years. Now, what do you boys want for lunch?" That was the end of it.

Martin said later: "I knew whatever was said, the decision had already been made. We were at the end of our time as far as they were concerned. They wanted a change, which was fine. Throwing money at them wouldn't have done any good whatsoever. In a way we were letting ourselves down by pleading with them to stay. That was no good."

Hermon was very upset and very disappointed because of all he and his brother had done to help with the tournament. And it had been important for the club. Television coverage on both sides of the Atlantic gave St Mellion huge publicity. Hermon used to count the number of times "St Mellion" was mentioned on the radio and television. But, he just loved having the event there. Hermon was much more emotional about it than his brother. He literally lived it, it was his life.

Hermon's son Graham thought Martin had read the situation perfectly: "Uncle was right. There was no point chasing it because once you start doing that they'll just have you over a barrel."

The B&H years at St Mellion were great years. It was a real thrill for the brothers to see the number of people who came to watch the golf – estimated at between 40,000 and 50,000 over the five days. The Bonds felt, and this wasn't sour grapes on their part, that when the tournament moved to the Oxfordshire, it didn't come over on television very well.

"The television pictures from St Mellion were phenomenal because of the difficult terrain – the hills, the valleys and the trees. It was lovely," said Martin. "But The Oxfordshire was very bleak, a lovely course but bleak, no trees, nothing."

Hermon and his wife Rachel went up for the first B&H there in 1996. It was all still very new, a bit like St Mellion for its first B&H in 1979. Hermon still couldn't accept the tournament going there. There weren't the crowds, the course was flat with a few trees, it had no character. It was his opinion that, now he'd seen it at The Oxfordshire, he wouldn't want to go a second time. Hermon said: "A lot of the players like it nice and flat so they can bring in better scores. Wasn't like that at St Mellion!"

Chapter 84

FAMILY MATTERS

Seeing mum and dad and their kids all coming to St Mellion together was what it was all about. Using the different facilities, enjoying themselves, having something to eat together and all going home as a family. That was very gratifying for Martin and Hermon Bond, because they had always intended St Mellion to be a family club and remain so, no matter what was happening on the golfing side.

"This was why we set it up, this was why it was built at the outset, to be different from other golf clubs so that families could come. There was no point being the same as other clubs," said Hermon.

Martin added: "We wanted families to come along and enjoy themselves, and they did. It's not a big thing, but to us it meant a hell of a lot. Of course there were lots of golfing highlights over the years but to see the family aspect of the club brought us a lot of pleasure and satisfaction."

Men and women golfers at St Mellion were equal. They all paid the same fees and they could play whenever they wanted. A famous Liverpool footballer and his wife arrived at the club and his wife asked if it was ladies day that day because ladies were playing. Martin told her they played golf any time. It was nice to tell her how "non-sexist" St Mellion was because around Liverpool women weren't allowed into some of the golf clubs!

The Bonds remained positive through thick and thin. One reason they maintained that attitude was because they felt they had a responsibility to their staff. "We had people working for us, we had to be positive. Some you lead, some you 'kick' and others you just encourage," said Martin. "You've got to be positive, whatever the situation."

Chapter 85

THE SALE OF ST MELLION

It was November 1996. Everything on the fairways was rosy - St Mellion was fine and Graham Bond, Hermon's younger son, was running the clubs at Looe and Lanhydrock.

Martin Bond and his wife Angela were at home at Trerule Farm, Trerulefoot, getting ready to go to the Looe Club's annual dinner at the Hannafore Point Hotel in West Looe. Without any indication or warning, Martin had a heart attack and was rushed to hospital. He was allowed home after a few days. But he had a second heart attack and needed a quadruple bypass. The heart operation was done in London in February 1997 and that same May Martin had a knee replacement.

"I had to say to myself 'Hang on, it's time I eased off a bit'," said Martin. His brother Hermon's problem was his back and it had been for many, many years. Hermon had an operation and things got better. He was able to play golf again.

After Martin had his operation, the brothers jointly reached the conclusion Martin had already come to. Reluctantly, to a certain extent, they dropped down a gear or two. And, in the middle of 1997 the Bond Brothers who, for more than 20 years had given their hearts and souls to, first create the unthinkable, and then expand the dream, put St Mellion up for sale.

But Hermon was still conflicted about the sale, the loss of the tournament and what he saw as the unfulfilled projects including the plan for a top hotel he had often envisioned. He would meet Paddy Flavin, who had moved to run Woodbury Park near Exeter, at Ashburton and talk these matters over and get them straight in his head. In truth all Paddy had to do was listen as Hermon knew in his heart of hearts that it was the right thing to do. Two of these sessions took place and then suddenly Hermon seemed reconciled to the decision to move forward.

It went on the market. Two companies were interested. By 1998 it was sold to American Golf. Looe Golf Club was also sold. So many rumours, guesses and estimates of the selling price have been bandied about over the years. The figure was, at the time confidential, and remains so today, although one expert described it as "a very high premium price."

Severing ties with St Mellion hit Hermon hardest. It was his baby, his home overlooked it, he saw it every day. But, he decided: "I can't go on for ever and I felt we couldn't progress any further with the expansion of St Mellion. And I'd had enough of planning confrontations and battles."

It was, indeed, the end of an era. Martin said: "We thought the time had come. I was 64, Hermon was 62. Our health and families came before everything else. We were still farming quite a lot of land. We had Lanhydrock, Graham was looking after that, so we had somewhere to play golf. So we were ok.

"I think it was time to move on, something told us. There was no tinge of sadness as far as I was concerned. It's just another phase, like selling the pigs back in 1978 to help finance the club. You move on."

Hermon's wife Rachel said: "All this really started in 1959 when the Bonds rented Dunstan Farm at St Mellion. When I got married first it was taking meals up to the men harvesting. Then, when the golf came along, it was just a roller-coaster really. We moved on to the next project and then the next project. We just moved on. It was a challenge and we did it. That's all. You don't think you're the big 'I am'."

Martin summed it up: "I think we'd done our bit. As a family, we'd created a lot of work for people which had been a policy of ours for all the time I can remember."

Their accountant Peter Riley thought they made the right decision: "The time had come. They'd had a huge planning battle to get nowhere with Caradon District Council. I think it partly comes back to Hermon's character. He would say: 'If you're not going to support us then sod you'. I think there was quite a strong element in Hermon that said he'd had enough, he'd battled long and hard and if they weren't prepared to support him then why should he bang his head on the brick wall any further. I think the timing was right for a variety of reasons."

Mark Lovell, who worked at St Mellion for many years, believed one of the reasons for the sale was the stress of running a massive business with a multi-million pound annual turnover.

"The sale was sad, a tragedy. It was controversial because people wondered why and it was a low point because it was the end of a very significant era, the Bonds at St Mellion.

"But when they said they were going to sell up, I wasn't totally surprised. Here were two guys who'd worked their backsides off over the years. Hermon had suffered quite a lot of ill health with his bad back. Martin had heart attacks. And there were all the hard farming years before that and the overlap and extra workload of the farming operations running alongside the creation and development of St Mellion.

"They made a decision and they made the right decision. I think they got out at the right time."

Mark thought the brothers missed certain parts of it although he was sure there were other parts they didn't miss: "The business was a massive strain on them but they loved the people and they used to love the 'craic'. But it gets tiring in the end and although disappointed when things changed, it must have been a huge sigh of relief.

"And it must have been a confusing time for them. They must have felt really sorry to let it go after developing it and doing everything. But there must also have been a feeling of relief because, as they got older, it must have been a huge burden."

Clare Bond, the wife of Graham Bond, younger son of Hermon and Rachel, said: "Although it was time that Hermon should start slowing down and retiring, he particularly missed it because he lived on the site and it was a major part of his life."

The sale was put into the hands of property specialists for golf and leisure businesses Chesterton HMH. It said in its brochure that the sale of St Mellion International was a "retirement sale due to ill health." There was much more to it than that. The Bonds had already brought in Roger Harris, an accountant for many years in the South West, a partner in KPMG for 25 years and senior regional partner.

It was after he retired in 1996 that he was approached by the Bonds to come to St Mellion. Roger insisted his involvement was not to get St Mellion ready for sale. Roger, a keen golfer, a member at St Mellion and good friend of the brothers, said: "I was brought in by Martin and Hermon because the business had grown to such a stage that they felt they needed someone to provide some outside financial expertise. But I think, in the background, they probably had an inkling in their mind that the time was going to come that they might think about selling.

"With big businesses like St Mellion was at the time, you either need a very significant re-financing in one way or another or, possibly, you consider whether the time has come to sell. It concentrates the mind."

Roger Harris added that one of the crucial factors for the future of St Mellion was access to another major golf tournament: "We would have needed another tournament relatively quickly after the B&H if we were going to keep up the momentum that had been created in terms of the development of the club. The loss of the B&H meant that the club was going to suffer to some extent. Attracting another tournament was undoubtedly one of the issues for the brothers."

Roger had been made chief executive at St Mellion and it was after he'd been there for about six months that the favourite option which emerged was to sell: "The brothers thought very seriously about what they thought was the best future for themselves, which is perfectly reasonable, and St Mellion. That's what they did and that's why they made the decision to sell."

Roger Harris was an expert in corporate finance and various mergers, acquisitions and sales and he was a great believer in the strategy that once a decision was made to do something, you did it – and you did it quickly.

"If you drag something out there's a fair chance that it goes wrong and, normally after you've done a deal and you don't do it reasonably quickly, the only way the price is going to go is down. Martin and Hermon had agreed they were going to sell, we'd agreed that American Golf were the right candidates, we'd agreed the price of the golf courses, there was some debate as to the value of some additional land, but that was being resolved. There was no point in any delay," said Roger.

Another factor was that staff were getting nervous about their future employment, but the Bonds were determined to put in place as many safeguards for staff as were legally possible.

"Right through any negotiations with American Golf the employees and the club members were on every agenda. The staff would tell you that we went probably more than the extra mile to make sure the staff were safeguarded. That was important and it also led to a relatively quick sale," said Roger.

"As far as the members were concerned, you didn't want to be giving them the impression that either there's going to be a gap between the current owners selling and the new owners coming in or that something horrible could happen. You have to avoid uncertainty if at all possible. If you're going to make a sale and a change, you do it quickly.

"It was all done within two to three months and that didn't surprise me because the main thing we wanted to do was preserve the goodwill. The goodwill we were talking about was the employees and the members. So to protect that, those elements, you need to move quickly."

Roger Harris said American Golf paid a premium price for St Mellion: "It was very substantial. The figure is confidential, but it was a lot of money. At that time, other than the courses very close to London, it was probably one of the best prices achieved for a golfing complex in the UK. It was a very high premium price."

It was a gruelling time for the Bond brothers as they endeavoured to do the best they could for everyone involved at St Mellion. Roger Harris put it this way: "The money, the cash is one thing, but the fact that your baby has gone is another, isn't it?

"I think it affected Hermon more than Martin. I suspect that Martin was a little bit happier with his farming than the club but Hermon loved the club. Hermon was keen to be at the club and involved. He loved it and he lived it."

Roger, who had worked with many top business people over the years, put the Bonds on a par with any of them: "They had terrific perception but that was modified, if you like, in terms that they wanted to do something for the area.

"They had terrific energy and enthusiasm to carry through what they had started. They were both such strong characters that the people who they dealt with, including somebody like Jack Nicklaus, would have recognised what they saw as true icons of the golfing business world. There's not the slightest doubt that they will go down in history as two very significant Cornishmen in business and personal terms."

FOOTNOTE: There was the possibility of at least two local consortium making an offer for St Mellion. Roger Harris said: "I think if they could have moved quickly enough Hermon and Martin might have been interested. But there are problems in selling significant businesses to local consortia."

Chapter 86

THE ST MELLION WAY

St Mellion Way, one of the horses owned by Hermon and Martin Bond and their wives Rachel and Angela, was due to run at Taunton Racecourse on the 28th of December 2000. He was to be in a field of 12 for the Reindeer Novices Handicap Hurdle Race over two miles, three furlongs and 110 yards. The only thing was, St Mellion Way was a complete donkey. In his previous four outings for the Bonds the best he'd managed was fourth at Towcester in May that year and again fourth at Newton Abbot in June.

However, this outing would have a very special significance. Five days earlier, on Christmas Eve, Hermon Bond had died suddenly of a heart attack. With hundreds, indeed thousands, mourning the loss of Hermon and trying to come to terms with the shock of his death, the question was - should St Mellion Way run or not? Also, Rachel Bond had still to bury her husband of 41 years. And it was poignant too for her, because they'd got engaged at Christmas 1958.

St Mellion Way's trainer Venetia Williams liked Hermon immensely and was deeply upset by his death. She was the one to pose the delicate question to Rachel. Rachel didn't hesitate. "Let him run," she said. The jockey B J Cowley was told Hermon had passed away. It seems St Mellion Way knew as well. It was as if the horse felt in every sinew of his body that this race was different from the rest. And, was Hermon now looking down on him from the ultimate grandstand seat? St Mellion Way won!

Roger Bush, a close friend of the Bonds, was there for this totally surreal moment: "I will never forget it. I was in the grandstand around the paddocks. I don't know why but for some reason I walked into the middle of the course, stood there all alone on my own and cried my eyes out. I could cry now thinking about it.

"Rachel had told Venetia it was ok to run St Mellion Way and I went up to Taunton with Venetia. He was a donkey, he really was. But, and I can't explain it to this day, I knew he would win. He just went off in front, 20 lengths in front. Normally when they go off in front like that they just run out of puff, but I knew this horse wouldn't. Down the back straight he went. He just kept going and going. Nothing was going to stop him. It wasn't a three horse race and here was this donkey, which normally wouldn't have stood a chance, winning it.

"I spoke to the jockey as they were coming back in and said the horse wasn't 'blowing out a candle'. Normally they are puffing and panting. It was strange. I can remember seeing Venetia go up into the winner's enclosure and collecting the trophy on behalf of the absentee owners. I'm not a religious guy, but something unreal, something magical happened that day. Uncanny, extraordinary, bizarre, never seen anything like it in my life. It's as if St Mellion Way knew Hermon was gone and he was winning this for him. He never won a race after that."

Someone who was a religious person was the Bonds' solicitor Edward Andreae-Jones, or AJ to everyone. He insisted the win involved some divine intervention: "That was the good Lord smiling down. I know the Almighty had a role in that."

Trainer Venetia Williams said it was an extraordinary occasion, not the fact that the horse won, but the way that he won.

On the 6th of January 2001, a few days after Hermon's funeral, St Mellion Par did him proud at Haydock. He won the Brewster Novice Handicap Chase, although this was no surprise. St Mellion Par was a good horse who'd won before. The trainer was Philip Hobbs and the jockey R Widger.

If Hermon was watching from on high he would have appreciated the irony, but he would also have been boiling over with rage – because he hadn't been able to place any bets!

In May 1995 St Mellion hosted the Benson & Hedges International Open for the sixth successive year and it was also the 25th B&H. On the 9th of May St Mellion Green was running in the Jamboree Novice Hurdle Race at Wincanton. The trainer was Jim Old and the jockey Richard Dunwoody.

Roger Bush recalled: "St Mellion Green would just about pull a milk float if you asked him kindly. He wouldn't go very far with it, he was absolutely useless. But we were at a tournament dinner and I remember Hermon leaping off the top table and coming across to me: 'Bushy, Bushy, he's won, he's won'. St Mellion Green never won a race before or since."

Hermon had introduced his wife-to-be Rachel Best to betting at the Newton Abbot Races in 1957. She came home £8 up on the day and joked: "This is great, this is the future." Many years later, in 1990, spurred on by Hermon's love of horses and horse racing, he and Rachel and his brother Martin and his wife Angela decided it was time to go into ownership. Hermon had friends in Ireland who brought racing horses over, and he bought one. It was the first of many horses to have the prefix "St Mellion". They had a list of possible names – Bunker, Par, Green, Stream, Wood, Way, Fairway.

And it was St Mellion Fairway who was to give the Bonds their greatest success. He was 17 hands high and a good stand-by horse. A big, strong horse who liked wet weather. He was no good on dry ground. The wetter and muddier the better, because he was a plodder. He didn't have a fast finish, but he had the stamina to keep going. It was the 1998 Grand National at Aintree. Hermon and Rachel went up the night before.

"I pulled the curtains back in the morning and it was emptying down with rain," said Rachel. "I told Hermon: 'Gosh, 'tis in our favour'. The rain was pouring down, it really was. It was so wet." Before the race, the couple walked the course in the morning. The jumps were high and intimidating.

They're off – and the Bonds anxiously watched the large television screen. "Fairway", ridden by Andrew Thornton, just kept plodding on – and came in fourth – much to the despair of Cornish bookies, who lost thousands. Lots of people in Cornwall bet on "St Mellion Fairway" because they knew the Bonds. And, fourth place also attracted prize money for the owner. So you could say Hermon, being a betting man, won twice! They came home "in high glee". Hermon had a picture painted for Rachel of "Fairway" in the lead coming round the top corner in the race. It hangs in their home. "Fairway", with jockey Jimmy Frost, was back at The National in 1999. Not many finished that year, but "Plodder Fairway", even in conditions which didn't suit him, came in 9th out of a field of 32. Only 13 horses finished. Sadly, he had to be put down after developing colic.

Many young horses were bought from Ireland. Some were alright, some were not and were sold on. The first trainer was Jim Old in Wiltshire and then David Nicholson at Jackdaw Castle in the Cheltenham area, Philip Hobbs in North Devon, Paul Webber from the Cambridge area. Hermon always liked to put the horses with someone he liked. But David Nicholson was, perhaps, his favourite. Every time he and Rachel went to see how the horses were doing, David would be straight to the fridge in the kitchen for a bottle of chilled Champagne. They'd stand in the kitchen, sipping Champagne, (in Hermon and Rachel's case it was literally a sip) and talking about the individual horses.

Hermon enjoyed betting on horses but never parted with too much money on his own. He was less conservative when it came to placing a bet at the Cheltenham Races. It's said some betting folk are lucky, not many. But Hermon was one of them. If he had a good day at Cheltenham, Rachel would be in an extremely good mood. She knew a modest treat was coming up. On one occasion they stopped at a store on the way home. Rachel remembered: "I was just looking, not thinking, at those two-sided mirrors, the one's magnified on one side. I didn't have one and Hermon asked me which one I liked and off he went and bought it for me. It was about £40 or £50. So he must have had a good day at the races that day."

Roger Bush said Hermon, in particular, got immense pleasure out of the horses and horse racing. "He didn't drink, he didn't smoke, this was the way he relaxed. He absolutely loved it. Hermon and Martin were so lucky with their horses because the vast majority they bought won at least one race."

It was decided to sell the St Mellion horses in 2001 but at least the success of the golf complex, after which the horses were named, had allowed Hermon to indulge in his love of horses and horse racing.

Chapter 87

AMERICAN GOLF AND CROWN GOLF

There were great hopes that American Golf would come in off the back of what the Bonds had achieved at St Mellion and take the resort forward to greater things. After all, that's why Martin and Hermon had sold to American Golf. They were looking for a purchaser who would literally put the foot on the accelerator and make things happen, rather than simply let it drift along.

The brothers had been encouraged by the advice from the property agents Chesterton HMH, one of the three top leisure and golf experts in the country, that there were a number of leading leisure club operators who were likely to be interested.

Roger Harris had been brought in by the Bonds to advise them on their options for the future and the brothers had decided to sell: "We had a number of people who did show considerable interest but the one who became the hot favourite both with the agents and ourselves was American Golf.

"When we looked at them and their set up in the States it was quite staggering, there was no doubt about that. They had a lot of top-named golf clubs and their management expertise and their asset backing was fantastic."

The chairman of American Golf David Price, a Welshman, came over and flew up and down the fairways. When he landed he was incredibly enthusiastic about what they could do at St Mellion, both in terms of developing the complex and developing American Golf in the United Kingdom. They did seem the outstanding candidates to take St Mellion forward.

Roger added: "When you're selling a business, you're entitled to ask the purchaser what he's going to do and the outline plans they had for St Mellion were to develop it as their major UK establishment. American Golf had 21 golf clubs in the UK at the time, they were going to make St Mellion the top one and expand out to 50 in the UK within five years or something like that. It really was very, very ambitious indeed.

"They gave us the impression that they were going to take it forward at a rapid rate. They loved what was here and were looking at various possibilities for expansion including another executive golf course. They would have, and could have, carried out the plans that had been approved which included a five star hotel, housing and a golf academy.

"They did regard it as the jewel in their UK crown and as something they were going to develop as their UK headquarters."

So, Roger Harris and Martin and Hermon Bond were convinced that American Golf meant business at St Mellion. However, it was not to be.

Roger Harris explained why, in his expert opinion, it didn't happen: "American Golf had greatly overstretched themselves in the States and had to cut back quite violently and, of course, it left exposed their English investment-owned plans. That meant that they did not go forward at St Mellion as they originally planned.

"I do not believe they intended to buy it to do nothing and sell it on. I do believe that they intended to develop it as they had indicated. But they had forced on them by the US banks the need to cut back in the States and it is the old, old story of protectionism or whatever – if you get in trouble at home, you cut down overseas. That's what happened. American Golf did not let us down deliberately."

It was a huge disappointment to the Bonds, after they'd opted for American Golf as the best "custodians" of St Mellion. But it wasn't their fault.

Matters finally came to a head after the terrorist attack on the Twin Towers at the World Trade Center on September 11, 2001 and eventually the Crown Golf Group bought all 22 courses operated by American Golf in the UK.

Crown Golf recognised St Mellion as the "Flagship" in their then group of 27 clubs and were determined to restore its status to its former glory.

In late 2005 they set about investigating the possibilities for adding value to their asset while making a genuine effort to bring Tournament golf back to Cornwall and the wider western region of England. A strong team of industry experts was gathered in early January 2006 to plan a strategy for moving the project forward.

In the team was Paddy Flavin who, having sold his golf club Merrist Wood in Surrey to Crown, was commissioned to help gain the necessary approvals. Paddy said: "This was the ideal opportunity to bring to fruition all the plans that Hermon felt were unfulfilled. You don't often get the chance to set things straight in life and here I was being given the opportunity to help bring all the grand plans from the past into reality. I jumped at the offer."

It was felt that securing a European Tour event was vital if St Mellion was once again to become recognised as one of the best courses in the land. However, it was also recognised that without suitable accommodation on site it would be almost impossible to persuade the Tour to travel West.

It was decided to seek planning permission for a new 80-bedroom hotel, 265 houses and alteration of the existing golf course, including the practice facilities.

That task went to Alan Leather Associates, while Crown Golf negotiated with the European Tour with a view to hosting a full event in 2009.

The Tour asked if St Mellion could host the English Seniors Open for the European Senior Tour and it was agreed that this would be done in August 2006 and 2007 - but more of that later.

Alan Leather's architectural firm had completely revamped the clubhouse for American Golf. He said: "If we had not done what we did I don't think Crown Golf would have bought it. We did sufficient in terms of re-organising and re-furbishing the clubhouse to make it clear what could happen in the future. So American Golf did have a positive impact on St Mellion."

In March 2007, in addition to the 80-bedroom hotel, planning permission was granted for 265 houses on the site. The location of the plots meant that the "Old" course needed to be altered.

With input from Paddy Flavin and course manager Mike Bush, Alan personally designed the new holes for the old resort course, now known as the "Kernow" Course. Kernow means Cornwall in the old Gaelic language spoken for centuries in Cornwall/ Kernow.

Now, with Crown Golf in charge, St Mellion has been enhanced further with the 80-bedroom four star hotel, designed by Alan Leather and built by Midas Construction. The hotel offers several dining options as well as providing easy access to the golf shop and leisure facilities.

"It's a lovely feeling to see it, after all of the years and all of the heartache and all of the arguments. Quietly Hermon would be pleased, but he wouldn't tell you. I think he'd be secretly pleased but I think he would struggle to tell you so," said Alan.

Chapter 88

BRAVE BOND BALLS

"This facility was built on a very brave decision by the Bond brothers," said Stephen Lewis, the former chief executive of Crown Golf, the owners of St Mellion.

"Without question, they were ahead of their time. A lot of people in that situation would have gone down the traditional route of building a low-investment golf course, designed by some local person.

"They had a much broader vision than that, an ambition which was to make St Mellion an international destination. To do that you have to make some very bold and very costly decisions. That was to attract Jack Nicklaus, then probably the most famous course designer in the world, to come and create one of the jewels, certainly in our crown now. That takes a lot of 'balls' – to put it bluntly."

Stephen Lewis's family had, in the late seventies and eighties, developed what became known as the Gloucester Hotel and Country Club, and it was during that time that he met and got to know Martin and Hermon Bond.

"They were larger than life characters, living up to their powerful vision. They opened the Nicklaus course and they were in the process of establishing its reputation. We were running our own hotel and country club which had nothing like as good a quality golf course as St Mellion and it was extremely brave of them to pursue their dream.

"The legacy they have left behind is a brand, an awareness of St Mellion across the country. Whenever I talk about Crown Golf, and I could list several of their other courses, the one that always gets a 'Oh, yes, I've heard of that' reaction is St Mellion. So what they've given Crown is a talisman for the rest of the group of golf clubs on which they can hang the quality of service that they try to provide across all their clubs."

In 2007 Crown Golf spend £2.5 million on improvements to the Nicklaus course and the old course, most of it on the Nicklaus course.

"St Mellion is without question their flagship facility," said Stephen Lewis. "It's unique within the portfolio in that it is a full resort offering not just golf but also activities for all the family as well. Jack Nicklaus didn't do too many golf courses in the UK and in my time we were extremely proud that we were the owner of the one he did first."

Jeff Chapman, the ultimate owner of Crown Golf, had tremendous admiration for what the brothers achieved: "To have that mix of looking to diversify their farming business and thinking of golf and then thinking, not only of golf, but of international golf and of getting the best designer in the world and then being able to pull it off....

"They were very good at saying 'Well, we're just potato and pig farmers from Cornwall'. I can image Jack Nicklaus sitting in Ohio being contacted by these farmers from Cornwall and thinking 'What's going on?'. But there is something about their vision and the way they went about it - and just their commitment to doing it - that I think got everyone involved and to be able to then get Nicklaus here and build it is astonishing.

"Our part in it in trying to extend it a little bit and re-work a few of the bits and pieces that over time probably needed re-working is very minor compared to their part in actually building something from scratch.

"When you do that you really have no idea where it's going to end. You sort of have a hope that it's going to end up looking like something. But it's a real journey and for Martin and Hermon Bond to go and take that journey and fight all the battles and the wars along the way and build something like this is just outstanding. I can't appreciate how they could do it but I'm just full of admiration for the fact that they did."

Jeff added: "St Mellion came as part of a package but it was obviously the major club within that package and remains so. It is our flagship course and resort. All the other clubs are significant in their own communities and are all very good, but in none of them have we had international competitions and the history of international golf that we have here at St Mellion.

"We were very keen when we acquired it to be able to bring back international golf to Cornwall and to St Mellion and we've done that to a certain extent by putting on European Senior Tour events."

When Jeff made his first visit to St Mellion in May 2005 he immediately saw the tremendous potential it offered: "I realised it had a rich tradition of being a great club and I loved the Nicklaus signature course. I'm no great golfing aficionado but I just felt it was part of the countryside. It wasn't just something that had been plonked there. It had been worked around the topography and that, to me, was a real work of art. I appreciated that."

The Nicklaus course reminded him of the Legends Course on the Moonah Links on the Mornington Peninsula just outside Melbourne in Australia.

"It's also good to see a golf course that's architecturally structured in a way that it moves with the topography, rather than coming in with a whole team of bulldozers and ending up with back to back 'gun barrel' straight holes which are not particularly interesting. I'm sure Jack Nicklaus is extremely proud of what he's been able to produce here as one of his early designs. It's something that we're proud of as well."

In 2004 and 2005 St Mellion was still a great resort but Jeff Chapman was instantly taken with the idea of developing a plan to gradually improve the facilities.

"We wanted to enhance what was already at St Mellion, what had been put here magnificently by the Bond family. Seeing what the Bonds had done to develop it, it really didn't take a lot more to improve and extend some of the facilities, do a slight renovation of some of the golfing and leisure facilities, to be able to potentially put it back on to the world stage.

"For it to be recognised as of international standard and equal to any of the major resorts around the world is something of which the Cornish community and England ought to be very proud. St Mellion is something special, unique," he said.

FOOTNOTE: By the time Jeff Chapman came on the scene Hermon had passed away, however Jeff made a special effort to contact and meet Martin.

"I found him to be just a very charming person, easy to talk to, easy to get on with, not ostentatious at all. We hit it off very early. Martin and his wife Angela said they were coming to Australia so we invited them to come and see us. We went with them to the 2006 Boxing Day test match at the Melbourne Cricket Ground. Australia beat England by an innings and 99 runs!"

The current Chief Executive of Crown Golf is Stephen Towers, formerly Managing Director of St Mellion, said "In the coming years we hope to once again add St Mellion to the European Tour's annual itinerary. We have the course, the infrastructure and the desire". We await news with interest.

Chapter 89

THE ASHES – GOLF NOT CRICKET

Golfers – of all standards and abilities – stroll round the Kernow Course and the Nicklaus Course at St Mellion. Some days their play is better than others. Sometimes the weather is better than others.

But some days are perfect days. The sky is clear, the sun is warm, there's the slightest of breezes – and you're on the elevated tee at the 11th on the Nicklaus Course. This par three is glorious, even more so when you're playing your best golf ever and your tee shot hits the target and gently rolls across the green to rest just 18 inches from the pin.

You wander down the lane towards the green with your playing partner. The birds in the trees and bushes are the only "spectators". They're singing their hearts out – could it be in appreciation of such a good shot?

You're on the green, the pin is out. Take your time now. The ball rattles into the hole. That clattering sound is much sweeter when the 1.68-inch wide white ball enters that 4.25-inch wide and 4.5-inch deep white circle for a birdie two. Not a par, a bogey or worse!

You lean over, bend down, retrieve the little beauty, clasp it firmly in your fist and punch the cloudless sky. You wish some other humans had witnessed this magical moment, apart from your partner, who caught the water with their first shot and picked up after hooking their second tee shot way off to the left of the green. But, at least, the birds are still watching!

The only thing that would have bettered the feeling would have been a hole in one. Perhaps next time. But, for now, a two will do.

It's at moments like this that golfers briefly glide off into Utopia, a momentary state of suspended animation – they feel like they have died and gone to heaven. This is now much more than a meticulously manicured and tenderly trimmed golf green and hole. This land has now acquired the status of hallowed ground.

It's one reason why some people will never, ever be parted from the grass beneath their feet on these 36 holes of golf.

St Mellion's golf manager David Moon didn't make that particular birdie two. But he will have his ashes scattered here. And he isn't the first golfer and won't be the last – who treasures St Mellion as his or her second home, a home from home – whose ashes will come to rest on this green, green grass of home.

Sue Shrewsbury's ashes were scattered on the 12th of the Nicklaus course. Sue was the wife of John Shrewsbury, BBC Television's golf producer, who masterminded the coverage of the St Mellion Trophy matches in 1988 and 1989 and the Benson & Hedges International Opens which followed from 1990 onwards. The couple were close friends of the St Mellion owners Martin and Hermon Bond.

John Shrewsbury said: "Sue used to sit behind the 12th green and say: 'This is the most tranquil place I have ever been. This is peace and quiet and lovely and I would like my ashes scattered here.' I said to her: 'Well, I'm going first, so will you scatter my ashes here?'

"She went first so we fulfilled her wish. It was a sadness obviously, but a nice sadness in a funny kind of way. My family went down and we scattered Sue's ashes at three or four places around the 12th where she used to sit, and so, she's still there. We still have her presence."

The ashes of Harold Duke were scattered on the 5th hole of the Nicklaus course, by a camellia tree. He was a member and it was his wife Nora who was the club's first lady captain in 1977. St Mellion former ladies captain and ladies golf secretary Thelma McEvoy said: "The tree was named 'Harold' and every time the ladies played the hole they would 'talk to Harold'. And there was also a tradition that twice a year they would water Harold with beer to help him grow!"

Nora was re-united with Harold when her ashes were also scattered on the 5th. The ladies section paid for a memorial stone and Nora's daughter and family were there for the ceremony. The ashes of Grace Stevens, who was one of the founder members, are by the chestnut tree on the 11th of the Kernow course.

During the Bond era several members or their families, about a dozen, requested that their ashes be scattered on the two courses at St Mellion. It was David Moon's task to organise the occasions and he has made similar arrangements a number of times since the Bond days.

"It just shows you the love the members have of St Mellion. It's a place that they defend passionately. It's their place, St Mellion is their home," said David.

Martin Bond said: "People came to St Mellion as families and they'd enjoyed it so much they thought they'd like to leave their ashes on the course in different areas. We also gave permission for trees to be planted in memory of members, with a little base plate with details on it. But we were always careful about the numbers of seats and benches we allowed because you could be inundated and have rows of seats everywhere if you weren't careful."

Hermon said: "With ash scattering and tree planting, the families were pleased to do it and we were pleased to be able to let them do it. It was a tribute to them and, in a way, a tribute to us and St Mellion."

Martin added: "Quite touching really. If they'd enjoyed themselves and could remember something good, that was fine by us. And it's quite nice that members of their families came back again to see where the ashes were scattered, to look at the tree growing or to sit on the seat or bench."

A final word from David Moon on what he wants to happen when he's "played his last round": "I would love to grace the 11th on the Nicklaus course. It's the 'signature' hole of the course. To me it's a combination of the 12th and 16th at Augusta. Seve Ballesteros had a hole in one at the 11th, Nicklaus had his famous shank shot there, so much has happened down there.

"Wouldn't be a bad place to go, would it. Maybe they could scatter my ashes on the green 'cause it's probably the only chance I've got of hitting the green in one!"

Chapter 90

ST MELLION – KNOWN IN EVERY CORNER OF THE WORLD

It's always dangerous to claim that a certain place on planet earth is that well known that, wherever you go around the globe, someone will have heard of it. But it could be argued that in the case of St Mellion such a boast is a pretty safe bet.

Chartered architect Alan Leather is proof of that: "The thing about St Mellion is that it is a very special place. There is just something about the place when you walk round it that just captivates you."

Alan, who had a practice in Charlestown near St Austell, took over the architectural work at St Mellion from Peter Stubbs of Plymouth, who designed the original clubhouse and hotel. Alan enjoyed playing golf and relished taking part in Pro-Am Tournaments with a whole host of tour professionals, the likes of Sandy Lyle and Peter Baker, and quite a few celebrities.

"Those were good times. But that isn't it for me, it's the place. There's just something about the place that grabs hold of you and that 'special something' is shared by lots of other people worldwide," he enthused.

You might think Alan's far too much of a gushing romantic, viewing St Mellion as some kind of Utopia. But he illustrated his point - through an illustration! Alan painted, he modestly claimed "not very well", but he did loads of paintings of St Mellion and several of the holes.

"One hole I painted is the 11th on the Nicklaus course, the beautiful, atmospheric 202 yard, par 3 – looking back, the classic view across the green up to the tee and beyond to the village church.

"I did two sketches, sitting down there on the bench where the BBC used to have their television camera and then took a series of photographs. I painted it from a combination of the sketches and photos when I was in Florida," said Alan.

It took weeks to finish. It was a big oil painting, about three feet by two feet. Alan had it framed in a framing shop in the Mall in Sarasota in Florida. It was ready about five days before he collected it, so, in the meantime, the staff hung it on the wall. There was nothing on the painting, no writing, nothing to identify where it is.

"When I went to collect the painting, they told me dozens of people who came into the shop saw it and recognised it as St Mellion. And the staff told me they could have sold it dozens of times over. Alright, I know this was Florida, but it was just amazing to think that so many people instantly knew precisely what the painting was depicting - from a piece of art by an amateur.

"I never sold it. I hung it on the wall in our house in Florida. It is St Mellion. It captures St Mellion. It has that St Mellion tranquil feel. St Mellion had that image," said Alan.

Chris Bond, Martin and Angela Bond's second son, had a similar story from Down Under: "I remember we walked into the Melbourne Cricket Ground for a Boxing Day test match and there were probably 70,000 people there. Dad had his St Mellion

T-shirt on, 12,500 miles from home, and someone said to him: ‘Oh St Mellion, I know St Mellion, do you play golf there?’

“Dad just said: ‘Well actually I do’. He wouldn’t say he founded it and owned it with his brother, he’d never say that. But that just personified it for me. Unless you were on the moon, you couldn’t be any further away from home, but they knew St Mellion.”

Chapter 91

MORE DIVERSIFICATION

The Bonds of Trerulefoot were always looking to move forward. Despite the success of St Mellion, they were open-minded about other ways to progress and diversify - again. Martin Bond and his children – Jon, Chris and Alison - moved into fishing lakes, plant hire with operators or self-drive, excavations, civil engineering and timber.

The W H Bond business has several divisions – civil engineering, plant hire, timber and, of course, agriculture, and it also has wind and solar power operations on its land. It has 90 full time employees and between 25 and 30 sub-contractors.

Martin's gone, but Alison Bond, speaking on behalf of the three children, said: "We are lucky, we can all get on well. We have our moments. But, we've each got our own strengths so we complement each other."

Does that remind you of anyone?!

Chapter 92

THE WORLD IS NOT ENOUGH

It may be that the family of W H Bond is related to the Bonds of Erth Barton near Saltash who date back to 1400. W H Bond's ancestors can be traced back to about 1800. But that's it.

The Bonds of Erth Barton family crest carries the motto 'Orbis Non Sufficit'. It's quite apt. It means basically 'the world does not suffice' or 'the world is not enough'.

It is 007 James Bond's adopted family motto and the title of the 19th Bond movie 'The World is Not Enough'.

Perhaps it's an appropriate motto for the Bonds of St Mellion.

Chapter 93

ST MELLION, UNIQUE IN MANY WAYS, THANKS TO THE BRAVE BROTHERS

Jack Nicklaus steadfastly maintained that St Mellion would always hold a special place in his heart. There were several reasons for this, including the course being his first in the UK, the challenge its design and construction gave him and, perhaps just as important, the solid and strong friendship which grew between him and Martin and Hermon Bond.

Thirty years on, we can share with you what Jack wrote in private correspondence to the brothers and the wider Bond family: "You were unwavering in your desire to bring a special golf experience to St Mellion and I'm very pleased that you convinced me to get involved. Not only did we create a superb and unique golf course, we forged a nice friendship.

"I know many years have now passed since my company Nicklaus Design created St Mellion for you, but I still remember the challenge we were given to design a golf course on the side of a hill. We had no choice but to stair-step the holes into place. To this day, I don't think there is another course like it in the UK.

"Everyone at Nicklaus Design is proud of what we were able to create at St Mellion and I, personally, know that Martin and Hermon would be as pleased as I am that it continues to offer a first-class golf experience."

As the years have gone by and landmark anniversaries of the Nicklaus course have been reached, the Golden Bear has shared these thoughts in letters to the club members: "When I first walked the land with Martin and Hermon, I imagine very few thought this venue would one day host a significant European Tour event (the Benson & Hedges International Open) drawing such greats as Seve Ballesteros, Bernhard Langer and Jose Maria Olazabal, but Martin and Hermon did. And it's a great credit to them that they worked so hard to quickly establish a tournament tradition.

"Hole for hole, it is a great golf course and has always been a good, strong test of golf. As you know, St Mellion was my first golf course project in England and will always be very special to me. We created an exceptional and unique golfing experience at St Mellion and I hope that golfers will continue to enjoy it for generations to come."

A few days after the official opening of his course on the 10th of July 1988 Jack Nicklaus wrote this for the brochure commemorating the historic event: "When my staff first looked at the land it made them doubt whether we could fit in 18 holes of any kind, let alone 18 holes of championship calibre.

"I've always responded to a challenge, so this intrigued me. Then, when I got to meet the Bonds and visit the site, so did Martin and Hermon themselves – very down-to-earth people, but with a grand dream and the vision, tenacity and courage to make it come true.

"The more difficult the land, the costlier it is to build a fine golf course. The farther we went at St Mellion, the more frightening the expense became – including the purchase of extra land.

"There were some tough discussions, followed by some hard decisions for the Bonds to make. One reason the course turned out so well is that they made all the right ones!

"St Mellion will always have a special place in my heart – for what we were finally able to achieve, for the brave people behind it who became such good friends, and because it was my first 'across the pond'."

As the anniversaries come and go, Jack Nicklaus has always sent his apologies for not being there in person, but saying he was certainly there in spirit, and he would add this: "I hope you enjoy gathering with old friends to reminisce about the past and celebrate the future of St Mellion."

APPENDIX

DID YOU KNOW THAT....

Two hundred and fifty 25-feet tall Ash trees were planted on the course from the Bonds own plantation in 1976. One man was kept busy watering them all the time, but it was so dry only seven survived.

....

"A lot of our success was not being afraid to ask people who we thought, and we could see, were switched on. You've got to have good advisers and a lot of our success was due to good advice": Martin and Hermon Bond.

....

The Bond brothers were very conscious of the costs of the original clubhouse and the amount of borrowing it was going to involve. So, costs were cut to the bone. The grey brick walls were left bare on the inside – they weren't plastered. That saved a fortune. Hermon and Martin got the builders to tear down some of the walls and re-build them because they weren't happy with the pointing and the finish. It had to be exactly right or it would look awful.

....

The organisers of the first Benson & Hedges at St Mellion in 1979 were very concerned that there seemed to be a very slow flow of spectators' cars into the car parks. It was dribs and drabs – and they were getting worried. The reason? Every car was stopped at the entrance by Hermon Bond who was selling raffle tickets – for charity.

....

Maurice Bembridge won the 1979 B&H. He spent the entire tournament complaining about the course and the entire prize-giving saying how wonderful it was.

....

During his speech at the presentation ceremony Maurice Bembridge innocently quipped: "Well, there's a Martin and Hermon Bond, all we need now is a James Bond." The brothers interrupted: "We've got one of them too, step forward our brother Jim."

....

Bernhard Langer took his religious beliefs very seriously. He would hold his own "services" and prayer meetings for any players who wanted to take time out to reflect on non-golfing matters.

....

Some people supported the development of St Mellion because they regarded the ducks, particularly the ones which inhabited the pond beside the 18th green, as an example of the owners' desire to protect wildlife.

....

Martin and Hermon Bond would regularly burn their paperwork, particularly in the early years. It wasn't quite every night that smoke rose in the sky, but it was quite often. The brothers knew what their plans were and how they were going to go about them, but they didn't want anybody else finding out. These bonfires became known as "the Bondfires."

....

Golf commentator Peter Alliss filled many a "gap" by referring to the ducks at the 18th. Sometimes they had to be "shooed off" the green to avoid them making an untimely exist from the tournament - due to a direct hit! Wonderful talking point. Good television. Hermon Bond thought some people remembered the ducks more than the golf.

....

In the early seventies the Bond brothers went to Exeter Golf and Country Club so see how a club should be run. The manager was Bill Power and they were very impressed with him. They whispered to each other: "He doesn't know it yet, but he's coming to run our club." And he did!

....

St Mellion's first professional John Yeo set up a junior section for under-18s. The secretary was Graham Bond, Hermon and Rachel's son, aged 13. One of the members was Graham's brother Alan, aged 15.

....

The Bonds always insisted that senior staff wore appropriate dress – morning suites during the day and dinner suites in the evening. It was all a bit flash, but it projected the proper image to the public.

....

John Collins, when he was chief executive of Caradon District Council, attended a Benson & Hedges International Open reception wearing a pair of shorts!

....

Part of the St Mellion Timeshare Village included a synthetic bowling green. Quite often Hermon Bond would play bowls on a Saturday if he wasn't watching a Plymouth Argyle home game with Martin and his son Graham. Hermon always won.

....

The Bonds' solicitor Edward Andreae-Jones was the administrator of the timeshare village. He was also a lay preacher and in the middle of board meetings he'd announce: 'I think now it's time for a prayer'. Board members had to stand up and pray in the middle of the meeting which didn't go down very well with some of them.

....

A man staying in the hotel expressed an interest in the timeshare properties and asked to have a look. Staff member Martin Watson showed him round one of the lodges and the man bought 12 weeks! It was the biggest single sale of timeshare weeks – and Martin was very proud of that.

....

General manager Martin Watson prided himself for the construction of the Nicklaus course, well a little bit of it. Between his morning and evening shifts he used to ride on a bulldozer with one of the American drivers. "I built a couple of mounds on the 17th," he boasted.

....

The Bonds' former shepherd Charlie Batten, who built the stone wall around the lake on the 5th hole of the new course, proved to be such a hit with Nicklaus that he flew him over to America to advise Nicklaus's own men how to build Cornish stone walls on the Pinehurst National course.

....

Once the Nicklaus course was finished, Hermon Bond used to say: "My only handicap now is two bloody golf courses and a thousand acres of farmland."

....

Jack Nicklaus officially opened the first timeshare village lodge. It was called "Demelza". Each of the lodges was to be named after a character in Winston Graham's Cornish-set Poldark novels.

....

The first time MP Robert Hicks ever played golf was with Western Morning News journalist Michael Taylor and his father James at Looe Bin Down Golf Club: "I played with Michael's father on two consecutive years when he came over from Northern Ireland in the summer. He was a good lefthander. I remember him saying to me the second year: 'D'you know, you haven't improved in 12 months'. No doubt that was very true and I didn't take offence but, for someone I only saw once a year for a couple of days, I thought it was a wee bit unkind at the time."

....

Martin Bond never took his work home and seldom talked to his wife Angela about it. Hermon always took the job home and always talked to his wife Rachel about it. He would ring Martin in the middle of the night and say: "What do you think about this?" Martin's answer is unprintable!

....

Roger Bush, a business associate of the Bonds, had a working lunch with them regularly. It would be chicken nuggets, sandwiches and coffee, always the same kind of thing. But the brothers would say: "Don't want any of that grass on the sandwiches." Grass was cress and they didn't like cress.

....

Hermon Bond insisted that a carving by their lawyer Edward Andreae-Jones should top the swimming pool complex as a weather vane. Alan Leather, the Bonds' architect for many years, said: "The swan, or was it a flying goose, was totally out of scale and out of character and it was probably entirely the wrong image, but it was there for many years."

....

During the 1989 St Mellion Trophy match staff, led by Martin Watson, organised a "sandwich shop" for spectators crossing the car park from the 9th to go down to the 10th. It was estimated they sold 2,000 sandwiches in just a few minutes.

EVENTS

The Impressive Record of Major Golf Events at St Mellion: Winners and Runners Up –

1976 The PGA Cup Match: Great Britain and Ireland, USA.

1979 The B&H International Open: Maurice Bembridge, Ken Brown.

1983 The Tournament Players Championship: Bernhard Langer, Paul Way.

1984 The Tournament Players Championship: Jamie Gonzales, Mark James.

1987 The British Ladies Open: Alison Nicholas, Laura Davies & Muffin Spencer Devlin.

1988 The St Mellion Trophy: Nick Faldo & Sandy Lyle, Jack Nicklaus and Tom Watson.

1989 The St Mellion Trophy: Nick Faldo & Sandy Lyle, Jack Nicklaus and Tom Watson.

1990 The B&H International Open: Jose Marie Olazabal, Ian Woosnam.

1991 The B&H International Open: Bernhard Langer, Vijay Singh.

1992 The B&H International Open: Peter Senior, Tony Johnstone.

1993 The B&H International Open: Paul Broadhurst, Mark James & Jose Marie Olazabal.

1994 The B&H International Open: Severiano Ballesteros, Nick Faldo.

1995 The B&H International Open: Peter O'Malley, Mark James & Constantino Rocca.

1997 The St Mellion Amateur Trophy: David Turnbull, Adam Frayne.

1998 The St Mellion Amateur Trophy: Gary Wolstenholme, Chris Gill.

1999 The St Mellion Amateur Trophy: Paul Casey, Simon Dyson.

2000 The St Mellion Amateur Trophy: David Griffiths, Danny Vanstone.

2001 The St Mellion Amateur Trophy: Tom Peacock, Damion Gee.

2002 The St Mellion Amateur Trophy: Lincoln Bolsover, Sean Mason.

2003 The St Mellion Amateur Trophy: Ross McGowan, Lee Corfield.

2004 The St Mellion Amateur Trophy: Richard Ackland, Neil Walker.

2005 The St Mellion Amateur Trophy: James Ruth, Tim Dykes.

2006 The St Mellion Amateur Trophy: Gary Wolstenholme, Llewellyn Matthews.

2006 The Midas English Seniors Open: Carl Mason, Stewart Ginn.

2007 The Midas English Seniors Open: Bill Longmuir, Carl Mason.

More to Come ? !

THE BONDS, JACK NICKLAUS – AND TO CROWN IT ALL.....

Every time Jack Nicklaus visited St Mellion in South East Cornwall the Bond brothers Martin and Hermon and everyone else involved became less remote to him. He grew to love the area and its people and he remained proud of what he achieved on this hilly farmland, once inhabited by cows and pigs and where crops grew. It had been an immense challenge, but one which he revelled in.

And, in the 21st century, Crown Golf has realised that there is potential to take St Mellion beyond what the Bonds and Jack Nicklaus achieved over 20 years from the mid-seventies to the mid-nineties. Europe's largest owned and operated golf group has created its flagship club by investing £20 million to keep St Mellion firmly on the golf map of the world.

All this is possible because of the vision, the dream, the focus and the determination of the Bond Brothers. Firstly to be brave enough to diversify away from farming. Secondly to have the courage to go for the best in the world to create a course, that once played, by the most timid amateur or the most polished professional, is never forgotten.

EPILOGUE

The Bond brothers had a shepherd called Derek Moore. He was yet another character of the Bond era. Sadly, he died in an accident. But Derek will, for ever, be remembered for this.

Over the years there was a lot of development going on at St Mellion and, on one occasion, some of the workers were complaining about how much they had to do. Derek, who was known for being blunt and straight-forward, posed this question to the group: "Lads, do you know why Rome wasn't built in a day?" "Why was that then Derek?" they asked.

Derek retorted with lightning speed: "Because the Bonds weren't in charge of that operation. So shut up and get on with it." The message got through!

It's a terrible shame Martin and Hermon weren't around roughly 750 Years BC, when Rome was being built. Perhaps if they had been, history would have shifted along much quicker and goodness knows what their impact would have been back then.

But, you can't change history and here we are, and they're both gone, having left their very individual and impressive mark – their legacy.

When they started out on the long road to create a golfers' paradise in Cornwall, they admit that in the very early days more than 45 years ago, as you have read, they didn't have a proper business plan.

Isn't it just incredible that, one day, the brothers stood in the middle of a field at St Mellion, cast their eyes over the surrounding acres and said to each other: "This will work." But Martin and Hermon can never have envisaged the impact and influence they would have, literally, on the world of golf in the professional and amateur games.

Mention St Mellion virtually anywhere on the globe and the name is instantly recognised. And that is simply because the Bonds had the "balls" to approach the iconic golfer of an era, Jack Nicklaus, to come to the extremities of England and be enthused to design such a frustratingly difficult course.

The brothers live on forever because of what they have achieved. Anybody who ever knew Martin and Hermon will always remember knowing them and will never forget the time they were lucky and privileged to spend with them. Countless legendary stories abound of their years at St Mellion, many more than can be accommodated in one book.

But here's one more tale, which can't be authenticated, for reasons which will be obvious, but which will prompt the reaction: "That's typical of the Bonds!" -

Hermon Bond dies and is spirited up to the Pearly Gates. Even he is surprised to get this far. Hermon's immediately involved in a confrontation with Saint Peter. The saint on the gate asks him what he has done to warrant entry to Heaven. Hermon, loud and large, towering over Saint Peter, talks enthusiastically about what he and his brother Martin did at St Mellion.

Hermon doesn't do his case for passing through the gates much good by suggesting that he and Martin had "created Heaven on Earth" in South East Cornwall. Saint Peter is not impressed. He had heard of St Mellion because of his fellow saint and "colleague" Saint Melaine. Also known as the Cornish Saint Melan, he was the 6th century Bishop of Rennes in Brittany. Legend has it he performed many miracles and put an end to heathen practices. In Cornwall he is the patron saint of the villages of St Mellion and Mullion and is said to have visited both villages.

That may be, but Saint Peter has never heard of golf. As the queue behind Hermon begins to grow, he thinks if he explains the history and rules of golf Saint Peter will allow him in. Hermon's reference to another saint, Saint Andrew's as the home of golf, is also wasted on Saint Peter who, overall, is unconvinced - and growing extremely confused.

Then Hermon has a brainwave. "Tell you what boy," he says, "if you let me in, I'll build you a golf course and teach you how to play." Saint Peter, whose patience and frustration has been stretched to their limit (as the queue behind Hermon stretches to infinity and, in heavenly terms, beyond it) finally relents and steps aside to open the gates and let the one-time Cornish pig farmer in.

But Hermon hesitates. He tells St Peter: "There's only one snag boy."

St Peter asks: "What's that?"

Hermon: "I can't start on the golf course until my brother Martin turns up. You see boy, we's a team, Martin and me, and always will be." St Peter says: "Whatever. We'll talk about that later. Just get on in there. Look at the queue behind you."

So Hermon enters heaven and impatiently waits for Martin to arrive. Back on earth, the years go by. Eventually, the passage of time sees Martin on his way to the Pearly Gates. The "team" is about to be re-united.

Saint Peter is there with these words for Martin: "Ah Martin, glad you're here, at last. Come on in. Now I can get my golf course built."

Martin replies, polite as ever: "I'll be delighted."

Saint Peter says: "There's just one thing."

Martin asks: "What's that?"

Saint Peter: "No need for an elaborate business plan. Why don't you and Hermon have a look round, pick a particular area and say to each other 'This will work'."

Martin: "Oh, don't you worry about that!"

So Martin and Hermon meet again and, although there's plenty of time to get going when you're in eternity, in typical Bond fashion they don't hang about. They get very busy moving heaven - and lots of earth - to create their own miracle, heaven's first golf course.

The fairways are paved with gold, the bunkers are full of diamonds crushed down to a fine, glittering, sparkling sand - and there are ducks everlastingly struggling out of the pond at the 18th and waddling across the green, just as the golfers fire their final shots into the pin to putt out.

The players in the latest three-ball are walking off the 18th and checking their score cards. Of course Hermon had kept his golfing lessons with Saint Peter as vague as possible and probably taught him all the wrong things because Hermon, being in heaven, was thinking long term and didn't want to face the humiliation of being beaten on a regular basis.

Saint Peter comes in well over par. Hermon Bond finishes on level par, but St Peter has accused him of cheating. Martin Bond has had a steady, solid, safe, secure round, finishing one under par. But he isn't that bothered about his score. He's just glad to have played the course he built with his brother.

Down here on earth, Martin and Hermon were, as Hermon told Saint Peter, a team - a classic double act, Little and Large, Morecombe and Wise, the Two Ronnies. Bouncing off each other, playing off each other. Their timing was impeccable, sometimes way beyond that of the afore-mentioned highly professional duos. They were cunning, clever, conniving, shrewd, subtle, also sincere, sometimes soft, but sure and dogged and determined that nothing would stop them in reaching their goal.

Meanwhile, back "upstairs" Martin and Hermon are in the 19th, which St Peter has christened the "SMASH" bar (Saint Martin and Saint Hermon) in recognition of the brothers' achievements - on earth and in heaven.

They're reflecting on how far they've come since more than 45 years ago the seed was sown of a dream which they had the vision and courage to bring to reality. And they're sharing stories of the golden days of the Benson and Hedges at St Mellion.

Saint Peter isn't in the bar. He's been on the practice green, trying to perfect his putting. He's also been taking a very close look at Hermon's score card to try to work out how "in heaven's name" Hermon managed to finish his round on level par. St Peter concluded it must have been a miracle.

Apologies to anyone of any faith who may be offended in any way by this rather irreverent and frivolous take on the "hereafter" and the vastness and uncertainty of eternity. But, the moral of the story is, if you have faith in what you believe - and Martin and Hermon Bond had that in abundance - you can achieve anything.

Alas, Hermon left us before the idea of this book was born. Fortunately, over the years, we spent a lot of time with him and Martin, many members of the Bond family, especially Hermon and Martin's wives Rachel and Angela and their children, and many other people associated in lots of different ways with the brothers and golf at St Mellion.

The book you have just read is their story. We hope you have found it to be a fitting celebration of, and tribute to, the remarkable Bond Brothers Martin and Hermon – St Mellion – The Bond Legacy.

OUR AIM

"We're just two ordinary chaps, ordinary farmers, but our aim was to bring first class sport to Cornwall and the Westcountry, because we were starved of it. We wanted quality golf to come here, and we achieved it. We wanted Jack Nicklaus, and we got him. But we never forgot how good we were at breeding pigs and growing tatties and grass" - Martin and Hermon Bond.

26909230R00201

Printed in Poland
by Amazon Fulfillment
Poland Sp. z o.o., Wrocław